WARNING!

If you are afraid of God's truth,
if you don't want to know who you are,
truthfully, in God's sight,

STOP!

Do not read this book!

Otherwise, proceed at your own risk!

BORN DEAD

BORN DEAD

GENESIS 2:16-17

BIBLE THREADS
VOLUME 2

ARLINGTON MCRAE

EMBASSY ONE PUBLISHERS • HOUSTON TEXAS

Born Dead: Genesis 2:16-17 by Arlington McRae
From the series, *BIBLE THREADS: Keys to Understanding the Bible, Volume 2*
Publisher: Embassy One Publishers, Houston Texas.

Your comments about this book are encouraged and welcomed. Please post online at your favorite book retailer and on book review and social media sites. You may also post comments on our website below or write to us at the email address. Thank you for your love.

Copyright ©2021, 2022 by Arlington McRae

ISBN 978-1-944539-06-1 (Paperback)
ISBN 978-1-944539-07-8 (Hardcover)
ISBN 978-1-944539-04-7 (EPUB)
ISBN 978-1-944539-08-5 (Kindle)

Library of Congress Control Number: 2022914533

All rights reserved. No part of this book may be reproduced, distributed or transmitted in any form or by any means without prior permission in writing from the publisher, except in the case of brief quotations embodied in critical articles or reviews and certain other noncommercial uses permitted by copyright law. For permission requests, email the publisher at info@BibleThreads.net.

Unless otherwise indicated, Scripture quotations are taken from the New American Standard Bible®, Copyright © 1960, 1962, 1963, 1968, 1971, 1972, 1973, 1975, 1977 and the New American Standard Bible-NASB 1977 Modernized, Copyright © 1960, 1962, 1963, 1968, 1971, 1972, 1973, 1975, 1977, 2013 by The Lockman Foundation. Used by permission. (www.Lockman.org)

Scripture marked EXB is taken from The Expanded Bible. Copyright © 2009 by Thomas Nelson, Inc. Used by permission. All rights reserved.

Referenced Internet articles are the property of the respective author(s) or website. Their inclusion is not an overall endorsement of the author(s)' theological position or other site content. Web links were verified in 2024 but are not guaranteed to work now.

Publisher's website: www.BibleThreads.net

TARES AMONG WHEAT

[Jesus] presented another parable to them, saying, "The kingdom of heaven may be compared to a man who sowed good seed in his field. 25"But while men were sleeping, his enemy came and sowed ᵇtares also among the wheat, and went away. 26"But when the wheat sprang up and bore grain, then the tares became evident also. 27"And the slaves of the landowner came and said to him, 'Sir, did you not sow good seed in your field? How then does it have tares?' 28"And he said to them, 'An enemy has done this!' And the slaves said to him, 'Do you want us, then, to go and gather them up?' 29"But he said, 'No; lest while you are gathering up the tares, you may root up the wheat with them. 30'Allow both to grow together until the harvest; and in the time of the harvest I will say to the reapers, "First gather up the tares and bind them in bundles to burn them up; but gather the wheat into my barn." ' " [25 ᵇOr, darnel, a weed resembling wheat] (Matthew 13:24-30).

CONTENTS

BIBLE THREADS

Series Preface	3
Series Introduction	7

BORN DEAD

Volume Introduction	25
Preparation for the Journey	31
Orientation	43

PART 1—THE NATURE OF HUMANKIND

1. Dying You Shall Die	53
2. Whom Will You Believe?	73
3. The Great Sin	95
4. Cain And Abel	111
5. Walking With God	119
6. Meaning of Death	131
7. Born Dead I	153
8. Born Dead II	171
9. Two Types of Peoples	191
10. Humans: The Image of God?	209

PART 2—THE PERSON OF GOD

11. God's Nature And Character	229
12. Jesus: The Image of God!	241
13. Thoroughly Helpless!	259

PART 3—MAKE DISCIPLES

14. Are You Willing?	279
15. Children of God!	289
16. Walk In His Image	313
17. Ministry of Reconciliation	333
Tares Explained	365
Final Prayer	367
Suggested Resources	369
Bulk Purchases	371
About the Author	373
Also by Arlington McRae	375

BIBLE THREADS

KEYS TO UNDERSTANDING THE BIBLE

VOLUME 2

SERIES PREFACE

SEVERAL YEARS AGO, I went to a national Christian bookstore just to browse. I stepped in, and immediately the Holy Spirit took charge and overwhelmed me with what at the time looked like thousands upon thousands of books that filled shelf after shelf after eight-foot shelf. Then He asked me, "Why all these books?" "Why?" I was silent. Then He said, "People spend much time reading books about the Bible, little time actually reading the Bible itself". But why? I pondered. Gradually sadness permeated my emotions. My heart was broken for I know the longings of the heart and the *urgent message* all peoples need to hear. I became even sadder because I understood their struggle.

There was a time, in my own life, when I would sit down to read the Bible; I would read for ten to fifteen minutes and realize I had no idea or remembrance of what I had just read. I understood it as I was reading, but now, no recollection. I was an avid reader. I would read at least ten magazines per month from cover to cover and remember. But when I read the Bible, I was left with no understanding or penetration to my memory. What was the problem? Was this real? So I tested myself to see if I had lost my reading comprehension. I took out a magazine and read a paragraph. I had no problem. Then I took the Bible and read a paragraph. Nothing! It was as if I had not read one phrase. I wanted to read and understand the Bible. My parents raised me in church. I was a Christian. I had accepted Jesus as my Savior. Why could I not understand and retain what I was reading in the Bible? I finally figured out that the only thing that made some sense to me, that I could retain, was the words of Jesus. So I concentrated my reading on the red print of the New Testament. I have met other persons who say they have had similar experiences.

I realize my experience may be an extreme case. Perhaps you are not acquainted with what I experienced. But how many persons are there who are having trouble reading the Bible with understanding? We read book after book about the Bible but not the Bible itself. Perhaps you are one of those persons who is trying to read the Bible but you cannot make sense of it. Or it just does not seem to sink in. Why is that? Yes, "The god of this world has blinded the minds of the unbelieving, that they might not see the light of the gospel of the glory of Christ" (2 Corinthians 4:4).

But what about the many believers? Why don't we understand the Bible in a truly life-changing way? I am convinced it is primarily because we lack the keys to unlock its powerful, life-changing message.

This series provides the *actual keys* to truly understand God's revelation of Himself and the actual nature of all humankind.

SERIES INTRODUCTION

IN THE MID 1990'S, God spoke audibly to me and instructed me saying, "Feed My sheep". After a couple of weeks of pondering what God had spoken, I accepted His appointment to ministry. I began to enhance my biblical knowledge by taking courses offered by my church. Upon completion of those courses, I enrolled in a Bible college and completed seventeen credit hours. God again spoke audibly to me and instructed me to go to a specific seminary and get a master's degree, which I was awarded in December 2006.

In September 2000, while in seminary, I suffered what has been called a massive heart attack. During that heart attack, I died. The medics worked extremely hard for a long time to bring me back to life. When they brought me back, I remained in a coma for three days. All my major organs were losing their function as I lay in a coma and afterward. Doctors told my wife, Pauline, to expect the worst. But her faith in Jesus, the Christ, saw a different outcome. She believed in her heart of hearts that God loved her husband as I had told her so many times in the past. Despite the doctors' hopeless prognosis, she was convinced I would recover. In the hospital, the medical staff called me "the miracle man".

During the onset of the heart attack, God came to visit me in my home. Unlike any other experience with God in the past, God's all-encompassing presence came to my house to visit me! His presence filled the room. It permeated my whole being. I can tell you with certainty that when you are saturated with the presence of the Almighty, loving God, when you are one with Him, the only thing that matters is God. That experience and the grace of God, along with much prayer and supplications, have given me a much deeper appreciation for the reality and the person of God.

Whatever He Wants

God, our heavenly Father, has shown me that most of us have our lives filled with so much "clutter" we do not have time for His presence. We are running around here "busy as a beaver". When we can, we allocate a little time to fit God into our busy schedules. A life of "clutter" ought not be our normal. When the presence of the living God has fully engulfed you, you do not worry about fitting anything in but God. You do not want anything else but God. My prayer is that you too will come to experience God's presence and His all-encompassing love as I have. That is likely to happen only when He is the foremost priority in your life.

I have told you all these things as a backdrop to tell you this: Because of the heart attack experience, I examined my life before the heart attack. I am two months beyond the heart attack now and I am looking at my life. I am talking with God and spending all my time with Him. I really could not do much else because I am very weak. I am recuperating very slowly with the aid of my wife, Pauline. I am learning that up until about three years before the heart attack, I did what I wanted to do with my life. Oh, I had a little "God time" here and there. I read the Bible from time to time. I went to church on Sundays. I was on the trustee board of my church and in the men's choir. I even led a couple of songs. But other than Sunday and a few meetings from time to time during the week, I did what I wanted to do with my life. Primarily, I lived my life my way, not God's way. *I was self-focused rather than being God-focused.* What I came to realize from the heart attack experience is that God is the One who came running after me to bring me back to life.

The only reason I live today is because God did not want me dead. He wanted me alive for Him, for His purpose (Ref. 1 Peter 4:1-3). That is what He always had in mind for me. But I wasted much of my past. When He pursued me, I did not listen. Not intentionally, but I ignored His soft tender voice and His frequent urges too many times because I had not been instructed on hearing His voice, on knowing His beckoning call (Ref. 1 Samuel 3:1-9). Therefore, following the heart attack, I committed to Jesus that I would live the rest of my new life for Him, for His purpose. I would give up what I want. Whatever He wants, that is what I want. Therefore, as I write these words, that is my motivation, to do what Jesus wants done. And hopefully, to help you move to that same place where you will want to do with your life only what Jesus wants done, and to encourage you to seek an intimate relationship with Him where you will want to spend hours each day with Jesus instead of electronic games, gadgets and television. For example, listen to the Bible, converse with Jesus and meditate on His Word during your daily commute. It can be done and you can do it!

They Are Only Toys

What is your idea of success? What is your vision of the good life? Not too long ago, I thought success was having large bank accounts, fine cars in my driveway, and a huge house. To be frank, these things are wonderful to have. Viewed appropriately, they can greatly enhance one's life. But God has shown me that there is a higher life.

One of the things God has taught me is a new perspective on the world's "things" from iPods to giant skyscrapers. He told me they have no value. They are "vanity". "How can that be, God, when we place so much value in them, from a few dollars to hundreds of millions?" "If they have no value, then, what are they?" He said, "Toys". Now I am bewildered. After much prayer and meditation, I have come to appreciate God's perspective.

Children love their toys. They are extremely possessive when it comes to their toys. They will even hurt another child, severely, for their toys. We are just like our children and grandchildren, nieces and nephews with their toys. We adults love our toys—cars, houses, smart phones, iPads, iPods, tablets, flat screen TV's, electronic games and gadgets, sports, money, buildings, etc., etc. And we will hurt someone, even kill, because of our toys. But all these toys that Satan has built up to look and feel so good are being used to keep us from spending time with our God and Father. We are not the only generation to have this problem.

The Israelites had this problem when they settled in the land of Canaan, "a land flowing with milk and honey"; containing houses they did not build and vineyards they did not plant. When they prospered, they turned more and more to their "things" and away from their God. In time, they became envious of their neighbors who had idol gods they could see. That was Satan's big play, to create envy in them for vain things. He has not changed. And why should he? His play works so well. Therefore, today, we must be aware, at all times, that Satan is working diligently to divert our attention away from our God and Father, and from our Savior and Lord, Jesus, the Christ. And for what reason does he do this? You do know that God desires all your time? He is a jealous God. He loves spending time with you. Therefore, Scripture has commanded us to "pray without ceasing", i.e., converse with Him. Satan's goal is to derail or prevent any such relationship from ever forming.

God Wants To Be In Your Life

Prayer is talking to God and interacting with Him in a two-way conversation. In case you do not know it, let me state it emphatically, **God loves you!!** Yes you! And He actually wants you to spend all your time with Him. I like to think of it this way: Scripture says, "pray without ceasing". And I used to wrestle with that concept. I have other things I must do. How can I pray without ceasing? How can I spend all my time conversing with God? How can I pray all the time? Well I tell you, I look at it like this. Let's say the two of us are enjoying one another's company having a wonderful conversation on a long leisurely walk in the country. We are walking and talking and we run into someone else. So we might stop and spend some time talking to that other person. After we have talked to that other person for a while, we continue our walking and talking. As we are walking, something else catches my attention some distance out. I begin to focus on that thing that is out there in the distance. Because my attention is diverted, you may not say anything to me for a while. And I may not say anything to you. As we continue walking, we start talking again, perhaps about my distraction or on a brand new subject, maybe on some of my innermost thoughts. As our trip continues, other matters and events may punctuate our conversation.

Well, you can see in this example that it really was an unceasing conversation with each other broken up by events here and there like when the third person came in and we dealt with that interruption. But basically, we communicated all during the trip. That is the position

God wants in our day-to-day lives. He wants us to include Him, to walk and talk with Him.

He knows we have other things to do. But He really would like to be involved in everything we do. If He is, He can smooth out the rough places and the steep hills in our lives. Like your sitting here reading this book, you could invite God's participation. You could say to God, "Lord, this man, I hope he has something to tell me that is worth hearing. Open my mind to hear him. Open my heart to receive his message." And when I have said something that does not make good sense, you might say, "God, I do not understand what he is talking about. Please, Lord, help me to see it clearly?"

Please take me seriously because the devil (deceiver) does his job very well. You may receive what I am saying initially, but the devil is going to try to make sure you do not remember it or value it after today or in a week, or maybe in a month. Or, he may distort it to confuse you to keep you from seeing the true picture. So get God involved in helping you to understand, accept, value, and remember what you read from this point on. Learn to "pray without ceasing" ([1 Thessalonians 5:16-18](#)). Even if you are not a believer, pray anyway. Begin by asking Jesus to make you a believer. What harm can it do?

He Deserves Our Best

God's business deserves our very best effort. Therefore, I encourage you to study diligently and make notes. And make sufficient notes so you can go back and read them again and again, to absorb fully the concepts we are presenting so you can then teach others. That is a primary characteristic of a true disciple, as well as one who is seeking God but has yet to find Him. As you teach, do not teach solely from what your memory says but from your copious notes. You may not realize it but repetition is the best learning method for the human mind. I can say that without fear of contradiction. So you say, "How can you be so confident?" Because my Father in heaven uses that same method in His Bible. If He thinks I need repetition, then I know I need it. How does He use the same method? Look at your Bible. It contains a lot of repetition. The message of the Bible is simple. But He keeps telling it to us over and over. From different perspectives, He goes a little deeper, and a little wider, to help us grasp the broader message of the central story. But it's the same message over and over again. So, by writing it, reviewing it, and meditating on it, the message is reinforced in your memory and eventually it penetrates to your heart. From there, it is manifested in your thought process, and in the way you live your life as a disciple, witness, and teacher for Jesus, the Christ.

Let me give you another reason why I am asking you to make notes. Some of us have bad memories. So what we hear today we may not remember half of it by tomorrow or in a week. I am not asking you to rewrite this book series. But I am asking you to make copious notes on those items that speak to your heart and/or to your spirit. Definitely document what your spirit hears from God exactly as you hear it. Add your editorial comments to it if you must. But first write exactly what God speaks to your spirit. When we write it down, that will help us to remember. Second, if we need to go back to refresh our recollection, we have precise documentation to do that. Third, if we want to share our thoughts and insights with others, we have an exact rendering of them written at the time we received them. This is important! Very important!

During my first couple of years at my university, my professors regularly stressed the point that, "if you are not writing, you are not studying". Therefore, let me give you this perspective on notes. The Bible teaches us that, as Christians, we are all priests for the Most High God. The Israelites, the entire nation, were priests for the Most High God. They were to become more like God and less like the society around them. They were to live the life that God laid out for them. By their example, they were to be teachers for God. Their lives, their culture and their testimonies were to teach others about their Creator. God has put that same responsibility on those of us who are Christians (1 Peter 2:9-12). Therefore, I strongly recommend that you obtain a spiral notebook (perhaps two) with sufficient pages for maintaining all your thoughts, questions, answers and notes on what you learn throughout the rest of our sessions together. A spiral notebook is bound securely so you do not lose sheets, thereby making it excellent for maintaining permanent notes. Or, consider making digitized notes on your laptop, tablet or smart phone. If you digitize your notes, be sure to make frequent redundant backups that you keep in multiple, very safe places. This too is extremely important.

You will obtain far more return from the investment of your time and money if you commit yourself to making notes as the Holy Spirit gives you insight with understanding. Your notes could very well transform your own life or the lives of your family members, friends, neighbors and co-workers. So please, make copious notes and share them. Else, the devil may snatch your newly acquired biblical understanding and perspective from you thereby reducing your effectiveness on the earth and your eternal rewards in the everlasting kingdom of Jesus Christ.

A final comment on notes—hold on to your unresolved issues. As you journey deeper into the series, let's see if you and I can come to some kind of reasonable accommodation for each of us by the time you complete the first two books in this series, certainly by the time you reach the end of this series. You may have questions anywhere along the way. So write them down and look for the answers as you dig deeper. The series will not answer all your questions. It is meant to be a powerful guide to aid your personal Bible study. Hopefully, it will put you on a path to discovering answers for yourself. And when your questions are answered, at a minimum, make a note of the answer along with an indication of the location—volume and page number, or internet article title or URL—where the answer is found. Keep your notes well organized and leave sufficient space on each issue for future additions. Preplan the structure of your notes. Organize your notes well so you can locate your answers at will as you meditate on the biblical concepts and as you share your new insights with family, friends, neighbors, and co-workers. May God reward your diligence by sending others to you for you to educate and provide answers to their questions.

A primary objective of this series is for us to get all its concepts etched into our brains, and eventually into our heart through repetition and meditation. Then incorporate them into our daily Bible study, from which we learn the way we ought to live our lives for Jesus Christ. So, give Him your very best and He will reward you accordingly.

Bible Threads

I grew up on a farm in North Carolina. From time to time, we would have quilting parties. Neighbors would come to our home to help us make quilts. I enjoyed these times playing with their children and helping with the quilting. I especially enjoyed the quilting. A quilt is made using multiple layers of materials that are sown together to hold the layers in place. One of the things I would do is thread my needle with as long a line of thread as I could handle. I was attempting to use a single piece of thread from one end of the quilt to the other. Often I would stitch a design in the quilt as I worked. But more times than I can count, my thread ran out long before I reached the other end. So I would tie another very long thread to the first one in such a way that one could not see the knot. To the casual eye, the stitch looked like one continuous thread. We made our quilts from multi-colored scraps of cloth my mother would save from her sewing projects. Sometimes, I would use colored thread that matched the dominant patches of cloth in the quilt. Therefore, one would notice that at times, the contrasting threads would be quite visible. But in other patches, the thread would barely be noticed because the thread and the patches were so similar in color. God has done the same thing in His Bible.

God has woven overarching unifying themes (i.e., threads) into the pages of the biblical text to unify (keep together, hold together or link together) the various narratives and stories which on the surface may seem to have nothing in common with one another. Alternatively, one could say that God has wrapped the narratives and stories around overarching themes or threads. The biblical authors have written from the perspective that the reader already knows these threads. Sometimes these threads are conspicuous and obvious. At other times, the reader must search for them. Identify these threads and you have the keys to interpreting and understanding the characters, their acts and their motivation from God's perspective. These threads not only provide God's perspective but they also illumine the broader context for everything written in the biblical text. Look for and observe these threads as you study, and the Bible will begin to make perfectly good sense to you.

Keys To Understanding The Bible

One intent of this series—*BIBLE THREADS: Keys To Understanding The Bible*—is to provide not only new and significant information simply and clearly, but also to be motivational and life changing for both believers and non-believers as you learn to study the Bible more intelligently. My prayer is that you will not only read all the books in this series but also diligently study them and the referenced Internet articles. Then use what you have learned to read and study your Bible, enlisting the aid of the Holy Spirit who will teach us if we ask. Scripture, speaking of the things important to God, encourages you to "Ask, and it shall be given to you;

seek, and you shall find; knock, and it shall be opened to you" (Matthew 7:7-8). Then, take what you receive, no matter how little or how great, and teach others. Your efforts are sure to yield great rewards not only for your own life here on earth and in eternity, but also for the lives of all those you touch.

Keep in mind that today, using the Internet from your home, you have the ability to touch lives all over the world.

At this writing, my goal is to provide the primary keys (i.e., threads) to understanding the Bible in five volumes:

Volume 1—*The Bible for Beginners And The Rest of Us: A Guide to Making Basic Bible Sense*—introduces you to the Bible and provides an eagle-eye view of the Bible and its essential message. I have attempted to provide significant information in a compact volume that is brief and to the point. A major part of its core content is contained in chart form with the understanding that "a picture is worth a thousand words". In addition to the text, expanded discussion and/or additional content by other more reputable authors is available in the Expanded Version via web links (live web links in the digital versions) to insightful Internet resources.

Volume 2—*Born Dead: Genesis 2:16-17*—presents the dominant thread for understanding the Bible. Its design is to present a biblical perspective of humans, God and the problem between them through God's eyes. It also provides a Bible centered context for the church—"the called out ones".

Volume 3—*A Hostile Environment: A World of Lies, Conflict and Deception*—presents an enlightened picture of the hostility (the enmity) in the world between the "seed" of the serpent and the "seed" of the woman by exploring its cause and the resulting turmoil and violence from Genesis through Revelation and to include even the present day.

Volume 4—*The Bible in 3D*—argues that, while the primary focus of the Bible in this present age is making "disciples of all the nations," the program of God also includes "the rulers and the authorities in the heavenly places".

Volume 5—*Why Do You HATE Me?*

Throughout this series, you will encounter references and bridges to valuable resources by other faithful servants of God. At the outset, I determined not to rewrite what other servants have spent years developing. That would not be a good use of my time and gifts. Rather, I would make a concentrated effort to teach all others what my heavenly Father has taught me. This approach allows me to stay in the big picture or at the summary level and let others provide the details. Combined, our resources should provide sufficient coverage of the Bible to satisfy your quest to know the person of God, the Bible's message and its importance to your life.

Bible Believing Jesus Disciples

The stated goal of my seminary degree program was to teach us how to study the Bible. My goal in this series is not to teach you how to study the Bible. There are many well-written resources for that. Rather, my goal is to provide you the keys to unlock its treasure chest. If I do my job well, you will be able to extract and understand the Bible's essential message in a way that will allow you to accept it and live it; then, teach others who in turn will do the same. *My prayer is that this will become an unbroken chain eventually touching the lives of hundreds of millions of lost souls all around the globe.* I invite you to join others who are already active participants in this process. Begin by starting your own link in this chain by gathering study partners and by regularly sharing this book series with as many people as you can. Give it as birthday, graduation, wedding and Christmas gifts. Inspire and implore them to commit to reading and meditating on the Bible daily.

The ultimate goal of this series is to create a worldwide host of Bible believing Jesus disciples by providing you the enlightenment, the encouragement and the enthusiasm to joyfully read and diligently study the Bible each and every day, with deep understanding and with *insight*, i.e., your ability to accurately perceive and clearly articulate the Bible's illuminating truth. Then allow the Bible to dictate how you prioritize and live your life. Please come join us on this exciting and adventurous journey!

When you have completed your study of each book in this series, and when you have completed this entire series, perhaps a systematic review of its concepts, assertions and the implications for your life and the lives of your family, friends, neighbors, and associates might be in order.

Let us pray: May Jesus, the Christ, God's Messiah, reward your reading, study efforts, meditations, and ruminations with great insight and deep understanding beyond your wildest expectations. I pray that one outcome of your reading and study efforts is that you come to know Jesus intimately and that you experience the blessed life of Deuteronomy 30 "by loving the Lord your God, by obeying His voice, and by holding fast [clinging] to Him; for this is your life and the length of your days" (v 20). This we ask in Jesus name, amen!

BORN DEAD

VOLUME 2

From the series

BIBLE THREADS: Keys to Understanding the Bible

VOLUME INTRODUCTION

WHY WAS I born and what eternal purpose do I serve?

Is there, in fact, a righteous God who created the heavens and the earth?

If there is a righteous God, the Creator, then how does one explain the evil and calamities in the earth?

If humankind is created in the image and likeness of God, why are we so ungodlike?

If Jesus is God's righteous Son who has been raised from the dead, why is there so much sin and wickedness in His church, those whom He has called out of the world?

If the Bible is in fact the revelation of God, why is it so difficult to truly understand, accept and adhere to its precepts and commandments? It would seem that God would have written it in such a manner that the common person could read, understand and believe.

What about this: How is one to understand the world and the people in it? Better yet, why does the world even exist?

Where does one find the answers to these and other "why" questions?

Many have searched far and wide (some for a lifetime) attempting to find the answers to these and similar questions. Yet all they found was disappointments.

Many are hoping to find the answers in God's Bible. Surely, if the Bible is God's revelation and He is the Creator, the answers are in His Bible. Yet for so many of us, we have yet to find what we seek. One reason why is we read books and books about the Bible rather than read the Bible itself. We accumulate lots and lots of facts and observations about the Bible and its message. Yet we are not satisfied with what we know. We are still not able to coordinate and harmonize it all in a way that satisfies the soul. So what is one to do?

There was a time in my own life when I had a slew of "why" questions. Because I had no answers, I could find no peace. But God has answered my prayers. He has taught me what His Bible is about. Now my "why" questions are few. And those that remain no longer disturb my spirit.

What am I saying? I have found peace within and peace with God by studying the Bible, praying daily, obeying His Word and meditating daily on what God reveals to me.

Since God is no respecter of persons, you too can have the satisfaction and peace that I have found. All it takes is a willingness to commit your life to God, our heavenly Father, and to His Son, Jesus the Christ. Then diligently read and study His Bible every day, even multiple times per day. And seek His face through prayer and meditation.

Beginning with the guidance in this series, study each volume diligently. Then use the techniques and knowledge you gain to study your Bible daily with true understanding. Pray often in the faith that Jesus still answers prayer. He certainly will reward you with many of the answers you seek and some you do not know you want to ask.

In this volume, we explore the Bible as one would venture into a wilderness containing various types of terrain, thick trees and shrubs and other obstacles such as steep hills and cliffs, rivers and streams. Beginning with select key passages, we shall walk together through specific verses identifying their truths along with their implications and significance. Every aspect of our logical flow will be covered in detail. Using repetition and other techniques, we shall revisit our selected text from different perspectives and vantage points to fully illuminate our passage. Our presentation is basic and step by step so that you are able to appreciate all logic. Along with your grasp of this foundational thread, you will learn how to apply the same logical approach to the Bible as a whole and to specific passages you choose to explore.

Why should you trust what I say? Because God actually called me with an audible voice and anointed me for this very purpose.

Let me tell you. My call to minister before the Lord was profound! Years before, I had prayed daily for nearly three years asking God to speak to me like He was speaking to other servants of His. There was this one particular lady whom I would see several times in a year. And each time I saw her she would say, rather matter of factly, God told her this and that. So I wanted God to speak to me like He was speaking to her. Therefore, I asked her why would God speak to her and not speak to me. She said pray and ask Him to and He will. But pray as I might, He did not speak to me. Along the way, I prayed, if God ever wanted me to do His work, I promised Him that I would be willing. And I would commit wholeheartedly as long as I knew for certain it was He calling me. I let Him know I did not want to simply think He was calling or feel an unction. If I could be absolutely certain, I would commit totally to His desire to use me.

In those prayers, I was asking God to speak to me. I wanted to hear His voice or have Him let me know in some undeniable way that God, our Creator, was calling me to work for Him. But after three or more years of asking, I concluded that God obviously did not care to speak to me. So when I gave up that prayer, I let God know that I would still be available if and when He called.

Several months, or more, after I gave up my expectation to hear from Him, God astonished me in the most profound way. While sitting alone in the sanctuary praying and waiting for church services to begin, God spoke audibly to me saying, "Feed My Sheep".

If you have ever heard crystal clear stereo headphones, then you know what it sounds like. I will not go into detail about that experience except to say He spoke those same words to me three times, probably because I could not believe or accept what was happening to me at the time.

Think about it! I was hearing a voice without a visible source. Are you hearing me? So I thought I might be losing my mind because I was hearing a voice in my head and there was no one near me to speak those words.

As a result of that *epiphany* and the experience of His loving presence during the heart attack, I have fully committed my life to serve Him. I still fall short often, but I continue to "press on toward the goal for the prize of the upward call of God in Christ Jesus".

Since graduating from a prestigious seminary, God has continued to educate me with (what I believe to be) great insights into His Word. What you will learn in this entire series is what He has given me to pass on to you. So please, diligently study and meditate on every word.

This book, however, is not a presentation on how to study the Bible. Instead, it presents the *overarching Bible thread (or key)* necessary for a true understanding of the biblical text. It is also a study guide to demonstrate our approach to identifying major Bible threads. Finally, it presents a concrete analysis of related scriptural concepts to fully illumine this foundational thread. With this knowledge and the other books in this series, you will be enlightened and equipped to perform your own valid analysis of the Scriptures and reach reliable biblically based conclusions.

To assist you in this objective, the next two sections—Preparation for the Journey and Orientation—are designed to create in you the appropriate mindset for what will follow.

May Jesus Christ richly prosper you in His Word and in all you undertake on behalf of His Kingdom.

PREPARATION FOR THE JOURNEY

Scripture: <u>Acts 2:1-21</u>

Prayer: Heavenly Father, hallowed be Your name. Your kingdom come. Your will be done on earth and in our hearts, just as it is done in Heaven. Teach us Your Word so that we may truly understand Your Bible. Open our eyes. Remove the blinders.

We want to know Your Word, not to walk around with our heads puffed up because we can quote the Scriptures. But because in knowing Your Word, my Father, we would come to know You and desire communion with You and You with us. O' God, hear our prayer today as a few of Your servants have gathered here to learn who You are and who we truly are in Your sight. Stay in our midst. Pierce our hearts. Saturate our whole being.

In the name of Jesus, we ask that You give us wisdom, give us knowledge, give us Your perspective. And give us compassion for Your people, especially those who have yet to believe in Your Son, Jesus. Give us a passion for Your Word so that Your people may truly understand and know, and be able to teach others that they too may come to understand and know, who in turn will teach others as well, thereby, spreading the knowledge of You all over the earth as You originally prescribed to Adam. This is our supplication, O' God. Hear our prayer in the name of Jesus, the Christ, we pray, amen!

∼

We invite you to come along with us on an exciting adventure to explore the deep mysteries of the book known all over the world as the Holy Bible. In preparation for our journey, please pull out your Bible or borrow one from your parents, siblings or friends, even from a neighbor if necessary. Holding it in your hands while flipping it over and around, take a good look at all sides and ends of this book. It is unlike any other book on earth. It contains the living Word—revelations and instructions—of the only true and living God who created the heavens and the earth and all that is contained therein, including "you". *In this book, the Holy God makes Himself known to His creation that otherwise would not have come to know Him* (John 1:1-10). Even now, most still do not know nor do they desire to truly know Him. Even so, this Bible has been handed down to us over many, many centuries, being preserved and promoted by God's Holy Spirit. It has saved lives, protected lives, and, it has changed lives.

So, let me ask you a question about this Bible. Do you believe the book you are holding in your hand (the Holy Bible) contains the authentic Word (revelations and instructions) of God, our Creator? Think about that for a moment. Do not give me the churchy or religious answer. Or, if you are atheist, do not simply speak the so called obvious. Search your own heart. Search everything within you and answer honestly for yourself, not for me, but for you and for your Creator.

For those of us who are Christians, we know God already knows our heart. He knows our thoughts. Psalm 139 says God knows our words before they are even formed on our tongue. He is observing you now as you read these words. So the first question is, do **you** believe that this Bible contains the Word (revelations and instructions) of the only living and the only true God?

The next question I have for you to explore before you answer is this: Do you believe that this book (the Holy Bible) is inerrant, that is without error, in its original manuscripts? Now, we put the original manuscripts in there because we know that humans, even though they have generally done it with the guidance and grace of God, have made translations from one language to another. There are many ways to translate a given word or idea. So they have made their well-considered choices, hopefully with prayer and meditation. Yet there could be a few poor choices here and there, i.e., not the best choice.

However, there are scholars, many scholars, who have looked at the various translations and concluded that they cannot find anything wrong with prominent translations of any major significance. Now, are we going to argue about a few insignificant matters and lose sight of the main thing—your life here and now and throughout eternity? You do know that you are going to exist forever? Do not be deceived! The only question is the quality of that existence, forever. Please consider these questions wisely.

So, the questions are, "Do **you** believe that the Bible is the Word of God?" "Do **you** believe that it is inerrant in its original manuscripts?"

Now then, if you say, "Yes, I believe the Bible is the Word of God." "Yes, I believe that it is inerrant in its original manuscripts." Then I have this question for you: What role does this Bible have in **your** life? What **role** does it play in how you live and prioritize **your** life? As you ruminate on your answer to these questions, do not look at yourself and say, "Oh, I'm doing what it says here. I am doing God's Word here, too. Yes, I am striving to become what Jesus wants me to become." Do not look at it through your eyes. I am asking you to look at it through your family's or your neighbors' eyes. Would your family members and your neighbors say that this Bible has the foremost role in guiding your life? Would they say that? Would your friends say it? Would your fellow church members say that this Bible is the guide for the way you actually live and conduct yourself?

On the other hand, you may tell me, "Well yes, I believe this book is the Word of God. I believe it is inerrant. But it **does not** have a major role in my life." Or, "It has a role, but it is not as significant as I think it ought to be". Or, maybe you might say, "It is significant but not what God desires it to be". Then my final question to you is this: What do you plan to do about it? That is the question for you. What do **you** plan to do about **your** relationship with Jesus, God's Christ, the Son of the Almighty, all-knowing, Creator God who loves you beyond your ability to comprehend? And He wants nothing but the very best for you!

What if you were to die tonight and open your eyes with Jesus standing over you? Imagine that for a moment. You die tonight and when you open your eyes, Jesus is standing over you. And you see your life streaming before you. Would you be pleased? But more importantly, would Jesus be pleased? For you do know that one day you shall stand before Him and He has an excellent memory?

The Scriptures say each of us will give an account of his or her life (Romans 14:12). So as we proceed on our journey to explore the mystery that is the Bible, keep all these questions in mind. Is the Bible the Word of God? Is it inerrant in its original manuscripts? What role does it have in my life? And if it does not have the role it should have, given that it is your Creator God's revelation of Himself for **your** benefit now and in eternity, what are you going to do about it?

What is your response? Please write your answers down in your notes and include appropriate context for future reference.

If your answers to these questions are a resounding, "NO! I don't believe any of it!", please do not stop now! Come along with us on our journey into the mystery of God's revelations and instructions. We are especially grateful that you are joining us! God had you in mind when He commissioned me to write this book. So please come with an open, curious, thoughtful and inquiring mind. *Keep your doubts!* But rid yourself of any preconceived notions. And please try to be objective in your evaluation of the concepts we present. I seriously doubt you will be disappointed. For you are sure to learn something that you do not know presently, yet is so vital to your life and your wellbeing.

Our adventure awaits. So please, come on along with us. We are truly excited to have you!

Knowledge And Wisdom

God has told us, "My people are destroyed for lack of knowledge. Because you have rejected knowledge, I also will reject you from being My priest. Since you have forgotten the law of your God, I also will forget your children" (Hosea 4:6). So acquire knowledge. Acquire wisdom. "And with all your acquiring, get understanding" (Proverbs 4:1-7).

There is great knowledge in the world, especially today. Currently, those who say they know tell us that knowledge doubles every twelve months or less. We have tremendous knowledge available at our finger tips. One can go on the Internet and get any kind of worldly and spiritual knowledge one desires. But in general, that is not the knowledge God has in mind. God is concerned about your knowledge of Him and the culture of His kingdom (Matthew 6:31-33).

"My people are destroyed for lack of knowledge" (Hosea 4:6). How are we going to get this knowledge? We spend hours and hours, just like children, learning all sorts of things. Compare that to how much time you actually spend seeking and gaining knowledge of God through His Bible (and from His servants) accompanied by much prayer and meditation? How much time do you actually spend exploring the full content of the Bible? How much time do you actually spend preparing for life after this life, for all eternity?

Eternity does exist for us Christians and for the disbelievers too whether you choose to believe it or not. *Your belief in a falsehood does not negate a true reality.* Hell is a real place, too, with real suffering (Luke 16:19-31). And people who go there do not want to stay there. But, unfortunately, there are no exit doors in hell.

Know this: you are going to exist forever! The only question is the quality of existence waiting for you in eternity.

Jesus is the way to the highest quality of life for all eternity (John 14:1-7). So what are you going to do about Jesus Christ, the Son of God, the future ruler of heaven and earth? He loves you so very, very much. He persists in waiting for you to invite Him in and surrender your life to Him (Revelation 3:19:20), if you have yet to do so.

Special Features

Some biblical concepts can be difficult to fathom and accept. Therefore, as we proceed on our adventure, we are going to encounter some perplexing and puzzling concepts and obstacles. So we employ various techniques to simplify your comprehension.

One prominent technique we employ is *dialogue* similar to a classroom setting. You can identify the dialogue by the block quotations. You should assume that there are multiple speakers interacting with the author. The words of each participant are presented in quotation marks. The change in speaker is identified by a blank line. The author's participation in the dialogue is presented without quotation marks so you will know when the author speaks.

Consider yourself a participant in the dialogue. Therefore, give careful thought to how you would respond in the situation and discussion. We encourage you to ponder and ruminate on the significance of each aspect of the dialogue to enhance your knowledge and understanding. Please note, you will find dialogue interspersed throughout our presentation to keep you engaged in this challenging portion of the Scriptures.

Repetition is another learning enhancement technique we prominently employ. Each encounter with repetition goes deeper, broadens your understanding and increases retention. So instead of considering it annoying, eagerly embrace it.

We adopt appropriate techniques to fit each challenging encounter to help you negotiate through it with minimal frustration. For your part, frequent prayers, constant meditation and attention to detail are the keys to illuminating each challenging encounter.

A Spiritual Adventure

We are going on a spiritual adventure. And there is sure to be spiritual resistance from demonic forces (2

Corinthians 1:8-11, 2 Corinthians 4:3-10). Therefore, each lesson begins with Scripture and prayer. Consuming Scripture before prayer tends to open a pathway for the Holy Spirit.

If you desire to be an overcomer in these circumstances and beyond, apply the following wisdom daily throughout the remainder of your life:

> No prayer, no power. Little prayer, little power. Much prayer, much power.

Each lesson will also end with prayer. After you have read the prayers, let God know whether you agree with the prayer by your own personal "amen". Additionally, please feel free to craft your own heart-felt prayers especially should evil forces persist.

Our Roadmap

This book is presented in two parallel tracks—The Nature of Humankind track and The Person of God track—both leading to a single objective.

The Nature of Humans track reveals the reality of humankind according to the Scriptures. This is the fix humans have gotten themselves into for all eternity, seemingly with no way out.

The Person of God track reveals the Creator God high above His creation in splendor and wisdom in all His magnificent glory, according to the Scriptures. Yet He is a God who involves Himself in earthly affairs.

Following the track presentations, in Part Three, we shall discuss the program God created to address these biblical realities and their consequences. This includes an exploration of the church's primary role and obligation to participate in and further the program of God. Whose mercy and grace exceedingly abounds over iniquity, transgression and sin. And whose lovingkindness is forever faithful.

Please take a moment now to review the structure of the table of Contents to formulate a clear picture of our pathway for this journey.

As we move forward, we shall explore our two tracks, concurrently, in parallel. On the one hand, we have the book of Genesis, primarily chapters one through six. On the other hand, we have Exodus 34:5-9. Our paths are separate but in parallel. We shall examine each path in a separate but alternating stream. Eventually the paths will converge and merge. Hopefully, when they do, your eyes will truly be open. And you will see clearly your roll in God's program.

Final Preparations

To help you maximize the return on the time you invest in this volume, I urge you to read carefully (seven or more times) and meditate on the first six chapters in your Bible—Genesis chapters 1 through 6—to prepare your heart before beginning your journey. Complete your reading assignment with John chapter 1. Then meditate on all that you have read by seeking its point and purpose through harmonious appreciation of the significance of it all.

If you are an inquiring and curious spirit, please read through Genesis chapter 12 several times.

Our recommended translation is the New American Standard Bible (NASB 1977 or 1995). Additional recommended popular modern-day translations include the New English Translation (NET) with or without full notes or the New King James Version (NKJV).

We do not recommend the King James Version (KJV). It requires entirely too much effort for one to comprehend it. If you have a great attachment to the KJV, I urge you to reconsider your position and replace your Bible with the NKJV or one of the other recommended translations.

For those who desire to reach deeper into God's Word, we have included references to pertinent internet articles. As you encounter them, make careful study of each article to expand your biblical knowledge and increase your comprehension.

For ebook readers, simply click the highlighted article title.

For print book readers, article titles are underlined for easy identification. Scan the QR code for quick access to the online list of articles at

www.biblethreads.net or enter the URL into your browser. Click Articles in the menu and choose your book title.

Using each article's internal hyperlinks (if available) with your own Bible or an online Bible study tool such as www.biblegateway.com or https://netbible.org, incorporate the article's referenced Scriptures into your study. This time,

Access Web Articles

multiple study partners would be especially beneficial in helping you explore the deep recesses of God's Word.

Along the way, use what you have learned to practice applying your new knowledge to your daily Bible study. When you have completed this volume, make it a habit to apply all you have learned to enjoy your study and examination of God's Word. It truly is food for the soul (Matthew 4:1-4).

One final thing: The following chapters include various illustrations and charts. If you would prefer letter size copies of those illustrations and charts, you may download color (if available) PDF versions FREE of charge using this web link: https://books.bookfunnel.com/bundle-944-539-06-1.

Well, there you have it, a glimpse into our journey from this point forward.

May Jesus Christ bless you abundantly each and every day as we undertake this journey of the wise.

ORIENTATION

Scripture: Acts 3:1-10

Prayer: Be gracious to me, O God, according to Your faithfulness. According to the greatness of Your compassion, wipe out my wrongdoings. Wash me thoroughly from my guilt And cleanse me from my sin. For I know my wrongdoings, And my sin is constantly before me. Against You, You only, I have sinned And done what is evil in Your sight, So that You are justified when You speak And blameless when You judge. Behold, I was brought forth in guilt, And in sin my mother conceived me.

Behold, You desire truth in the innermost being, And in secret You will make wisdom known to me. Purify me with hyssop, and I will be clean; Cleanse me, and I will be whiter than snow. Let me hear joy and gladness, Let the bones You have broken rejoice. Hide Your face from my sins And wipe out all my guilty deeds. Create in me a clean heart, God, And renew a steadfast spirit within me. Do not cast me away from Your presence, And do not take Your Holy Spirit from me.

Restore to me the joy of Your salvation, And sustain me with a willing spirit. *Then* I will teach wrongdoers Your ways, And sinners will be converted to You (Psalm 51:1-13). In Jesus name we pray, amen and amen.

~

In the May 1919 foreword to the revised edition of Lewis Sperry Chafer's insightful and anointed book, *True Evangelism*, A. B. Winchester quotes the fourth century writer, Jerome, who declared that, "light views of sin induced false views of God". Unfortunately, that light view of sin continues to grow stronger even through today, impacting humankind's view of who we think God should be versus who God actually is. We want to define God rather than allow God to define Himself.

Here in the twenty-first century, our light view of sin may be caused, in part, by the fact that a realistic view of sin would demand a realistic view of self. And a realistic view of self may reveal the incredible and the unacceptable wickedness of humankind.

A realistic view of self would also shatter the worldview that claims humankind is good and getting better through the ages. God's view, however, is contrary but accurate in its depiction of humankind.

When we observe humankind through God's eyes, from a solidly biblical viewpoint, we will agree with God. Humankind without Jesus Christ is devilish—"being filled with all unrighteousness, wickedness, greed, evil;

full of envy, murder, strife, deceit, malice; they are gossips, 30 slanderers, haters of God, insolent, arrogant, boastful, inventors of evil, disobedient to parents, 31 without understanding, untrustworthy, unloving, unmerciful; 32 and, although they know the ordinance of God, that those who practice such things are worthy of death, they not only do the same, but also give hearty approval to those who practice them" (Romans 1:29-32).

The only remedy for our deplorable and wretched condition is found exclusively in Jesus Christ, the Son of the only true and living God.

This book is written from the perspective and conviction that the Bible is the authentic revelation of the God, Yahweh. It is inerrant in its original manuscripts. And the first profound truth that the Bible teaches us is found in its first sentence, "In the beginning God created the heavens and the earth" (Genesis 1:1). Its message is clear and simple, "The earth is the Lord's and all it contains, the world, and those who dwell in it. For He has founded it upon the seas and established it upon the rivers" (Psalm 24:1-2). "For every beast of the forest is Mine, the cattle on a thousand hills" (Psalm 50:10).

And since God is the Creator and Owner of all that we see and cannot see, He obviously knows more about His creation than anyone else, even you, even me, and even the greatest minds, living or dead. What God says about humans is true. What God says about Himself is also true. And this writer (the author) takes as absolute truth, without reservation or apology, everything written in the original manuscripts of God's revelation of Himself, the seen and unseen world and the state of the human heart as revealed in God's Holy Bible, His magnificent portrait of Himself, of humans, of sin and sin's consequences.

Appreciate The Art of It All

A genuine appreciation for fine art, I believe, is a great asset. And here I speak primarily of artful paintings and other forms of art such as books. As will soon become apparent, when it comes to art, I am a true novice. My alma mater struggled to instill some degree of sophistication in me as they chiseled away at the rough edges of my rural upbringing. In the course of their work, I seem to recall taking a class that included some aspect of art appreciation. By this comment you can tell that I did not gain a great deal from the class. My minimal growth, however, in appreciating fine art rests squarely on my shoulders alone. Yet I am still fascinated by art in its various forms and the artists who create them.

My wife, Pauline, probably would not think so, but from time to time, I could enjoy spending a leisurely day (well, maybe a half day) in an art museum casually enjoying the fruit of some dedicated, talented and provocative artists. Those who poured his or her heart and soul into their work to give us a taste of what he or she saw or understood through the lens that God gave them.

As I would stare at these works of art, I would try to imagine the story that the artist would tell me if he or she were standing next to me. I would be mesmerized by their attempts to satisfy my passionate desire to see the painting, book or other work through their eyes. It would truly be gratifying to gain the insight, from the perspective of the artist, of the meaning behind and the message in a well-done painting or book.

Why has he/she chosen to include the pieces or persons that they have? Why did she/he choose to leave out other objects, pertinent pieces or points of view? What was she/he trying to say with the color choices, the setting and the distant background? How did she decide on the size of the canvas for her particular painting or drawing?

What audience did he have in mind as he labored week after week after week? Was she concerned that the real message could be lost due to the perspective or the inattention of the observer? Or did she hope (or intend) that I would look upon her work and simply form my own opinion? Maybe that could be the point, to make me think!

Admittedly, my knowledge of art is meager. Yet I am led, as you are, to wonder and be in awe at the artful works of our Creator, e.g., Genesis chapters 1 through 18, Romans chapters 1 through 8, Ephesians chapters 1 through 6, Psalms 1, 23, 39, 98, 103 and 139, John chapter 14, even the entire Bible, the stars, mountains, rivers, oceans, life, death, animals, birds, fish, insects, the ant, the butterfly, microscopic life, the myriad varieties of flowers, plants, mushrooms, trees and fruit, the sky, clouds, rain, hurricanes, tornadoes, humankind, reproduction, skin color, hair texture, children, friendship, imagination, aspiration, sadness, grief, joy, love, hope and faith.

Furthermore, I am invited, as you are, to discover and appreciate, value and treasure the masterful story (word painting) our Creator has woven into and throughout all the fascinating pages of His Holy Bible. His purpose being that we might come to know Him as He truly is, love Him for Who He actually is, then submit and commit ourselves totally to His will and to His way.

Unfortunately, for so many of us, we never gain the insight or understanding necessary to give God's story (His painting and portrait) clarity and real meaning. The message of the Bible is profound and vitally critical to each and every human soul. We (Christians) are obliged to do all we can (with a sense of urgency) to help all others appreciate the Bible's message and warnings through Jesus' ministry of reconciliation (2 Corinthians 5:18-21).

This book, along with much prayer and meditation on your part and mine, is part of our obligation to help all others gain the understanding and insight necessary to truly appreciate the powerful and crucial message of the Holy Scriptures through the eyes of the God of the Bible (Yahweh).

We present this entire series in the hope that the world would or might be reconciled to God through faith in Jesus Christ. We pray therefore, when you have completed it, that you would use all the books in this series to train many, many (even thousands of) others to reach out and do the same for those who are perishing right before our eyes.

May God richly bless all that you put your mind, heart and soul to in order to advance and enlarge the

Kingdom of our Savior and Lord, Jesus Christ, through His ministry of reconciliation.

I urge you, therefore, to invite friends and loved ones to come along side you. United in one hope, explore these truths together beginning with chapter one.

Are You Ready?

If you are ready, having considered the full content of this front matter, including the Bible reading assignment, diligently read and consume every thought, concept, idea, assertion and precept. There are no wasted words. Therefore, every word is important if you are to learn to view and interpret the Scriptures for yourself, through the eyes of God, our Creator and Father, and not through the eyes of men and women.

As we proceed, make every effort to share your adventure experience with others as we venture deeper and deeper into God's Word. Encourage them to join with us as well by becoming members of your personal Bible study group or by beginning their own group study.

All right then! Let's jump right in to our exciting journey and mystery that is the Bible.

PART 1—THE NATURE OF HUMANKIND

Then the LORD saw that the wickedness of man was great on the earth, and that every intent of the thoughts of his heart was only evil continually (Genesis 6:5).

Now the earth was corrupt in the sight of God, and the earth was filled with violence. 12And God looked on the earth, and behold, it was corrupt; for all flesh had corrupted their way upon the earth (Genesis 6:11-12).

1

DYING YOU SHALL DIE

SCRIPTURE: <u>Genesis 1:1-25</u>, <u>Exodus 34:1-9</u>

Prayer: Our Father, which art in heaven, hallowed be Your Name. Your kingdom come. Your will be done on earth, and in our lives, just as it is done in heaven.

Most Holy Father, in the name of Jesus, we come before You as children and seekers, beloved of You. We stand before You in the confidence that You love us, knowing that You want what is best for us, knowing that Your desire is that we would become more like You, more like what Your Son, Jesus, has taught us, knowing that nothing would make Your heart happier. Nothing would comfort You more than to have Your children love and behave like You—think like You, do as You do, say what You say! Therefore, we confess to You, Father, that we do not look as much like You as we should.

We do not love You as You have commanded us, nor have we given You first place in our lives. We do not love our fellow humans as Jesus has loved us. We do not speak the words You have given us to speak. Nor have we taught one another as Jesus has commanded us. Forgive us, Father. Forgive us and cleanse us. Cleanse us and renew in us the right spirit, the spirit that desires to follow after You, that yearns for Your presence and Your righteousness, that desires what You desire. Oh God, we know that if You do not do it in us, it will not be done. We cannot do it in our own strength. Try as we might. Commit ourselves as we might. Dedicate ourselves as we might. We cannot do it without You! So, Father, we are asking You to do a wonderful work in us. Open our eyes that we may see and see clearly. And if there be anything in us that is preventing You, we give You permission to remove it. We give You permission to pierce the veil of free will and do whatever You will in us, to us and through us. In Jesus name we pray, amen.

In the second book of your Bible, you will find these words in Exodus 34:1-9:

> Now the LORD said to Moses [the obedient servant of the Lord], "Cut out for yourself two stone tablets like the former ones, and I will write on the tablets the words that were on the former tablets which you shattered. 2"So be ready by morning, and come up in the morning to Mount Sinai, and present yourself there to Me on the top of the mountain. 3 "And no man is to come up with you, nor let any man be seen anywhere on the mountain; even the flocks and the herds may not graze in front of that mountain." 4So he cut out two stone tablets like the former ones, and Moses rose up early in the morning and went up to Mount Sinai, as

the LORD had commanded him, and he took two stone tablets in his hand. 5And the LORD descended in the cloud and stood there with him as he called upon the name of the LORD. 6Then the LORD passed by in front of him and proclaimed, "The LORD, the LORD God, compassionate and gracious, slow to anger, and abounding in lovingkindness and truth; 7who keeps lovingkindness for thousands, who forgives iniquity, transgression and sin; yet He will by no means leave the guilty unpunished, visiting the iniquity of fathers on the children and on the grandchildren to the third and fourth generations." 8And Moses made haste to bow low toward the earth and worship. 9And he said, "If now I have found favor in Your sight, O' Lord, I pray, let the Lord go along in our midst, even though the people are so obstinate; and do You pardon our iniquity and our sin, and take us as Your own possession."

Now take some time to think about, meditate on and consider what you just read in order to form a clear picture in your mind. Focus primarily on verses 5-9.

This passage describes the person of God, His nature and character, from the mouth of God Himself and how Moses, the obedient servant of God, reacted to that knowledge. Ruminate on it each day until its reality is etched in your brain.

∽

In the beginning God created the heavens and the earth (Genesis 1:1). Genesis chapter 1 contains the creation narrative. Verses 1-25 describe the creation of all things except humans, over a period of five days. And God saw that it was good.

God Creates Humankind

God set aside an exclusive day to skillfully and artfully fashion with His own hands the crown jewel of His creation—humankind. On the sixth day, God creates humankind "in Our image according to Our likeness". After creating humankind, "God saw all that He had made, and behold, it was very good".

Let us look closely at Genesis 1:26-28:

> Then God said, "Let Us make man in Our image, according to Our likeness; and let them rule over the fish of the sea and over the birds of the sky and over the cattle and over all the earth, and over every creeping thing that creeps on the earth." 27God created man in His own image, in the image of God He created him; male and female He created them. 28God blessed them; and God said to them, "Be fruitful and multiply, and fill the earth, and subdue it; and rule over the fish of the sea and over the birds of the sky and over every living thing that moves on the earth."

Most likely you are familiar with this passage, right? In general, this passage is saying the originally created human ("Adam") was made in the character and righteousness of God but with the free will to choose his own way just as God does. And he is to be God's ruling representative ("let them rule") on the earth.

Now, let us move on to Genesis 2:7-9:

Then the Lord God formed man of dust from the ground, and breathed into his nostrils the breath of life; and man became a living being. 8The Lord God planted a garden toward the east, in Eden; and there He placed the man whom He had formed. 9Out of the ground the Lord God caused to grow every tree that is pleasing to the sight and good for food; the tree of life also in the midst of the garden, and the tree of the knowledge of good and evil.

So, in Genesis chapter 1, God said let Us make humankind and We are going to make them exceptionally special. We are going to make them "in Our image, according to Our likeness" (v26). We want them to be like us. Now, if you think about that, if you are a woman, let's say you're pregnant. If you are a husband, let's say your wife is pregnant. This is your first child. You are about to have your very first offspring. What is your heart's desire? What would your thoughts be? "Oh that this boy would look like me!" "Oh that this daughter would be like me!" So God is looking at humankind in much the same way. God is saying, I am going to make this human. I am going to make him like Me, in My image, My icon, My likeness. We are going to let them rule over all the creation that We have made. So, how are humans supposed to rule? In what way are they supposed to rule? What should humankind's rule look like? God has said the human was made in His image, according to His likeness. Therefore, the human should rule the earth just like God would, i.e., with God's values, mores, culture, nature and character.

The First Covenant

God created the humans with absolute freedom to do as they pleased but with a single exception. Look now at Genesis 2:16-17:

> And the LORD God commanded the man, saying, "From any tree of the garden you may eat freely; 17 but from the tree of the knowledge of good and evil you shall not eat, for in the day that you eat from it you shall surely die.

Now, take a moment and explain this first covenant to an imaginary me in plain English. Explain it to me just like you would to ten year old children. Please do that now before continuing. Write your response in your notes.

OK, let me paraphrase what you may be saying to imaginary me. You may eat of every tree in the garden but one. And if you eat of that one, you are going to suffer severe consequences. You are going to die or cease to exist!

> Does that come close to agreeing with your interpretation of what's being said there? What did I omit?
>
> "You will spiritually die."
>
> Did it say that?
>
> "No! That's what I say. That's what I'm saying. That's my interpretation."

That is your interpretation? From where did you get that?

"Our teacher."

So, according to what your teacher says, they will die spiritually. What do the Scriptures say right here in these verses?

"Just that they would die."

Now, I am not saying anything against what your teacher says. Very likely we are on the same page. But here is the thing. What we are dealing with here is what does the Bible say right here, in these verses. In the verses we read, what does it say?

"They will surely die."

The Scriptures have not told us yet what death is. So for the purpose of our discussion here and for the remaining times you spend reading, studying, meditating on and interacting with this volume, I would like you to forget about your definition of what that death is. I am asking you to set it aside and look solely at what the passage says. And what does it say?

What is going to happen if they eat?

"In the day that you eat of it, you shall surely die."

Thank you!

Now, do you believe that God speaks the truth? That is the thing you have to settle in your mind. As you read these Scriptures, look at what your God is saying right then and there. When will they die? The day, the same day that you eat you shall surely die. The very day that you eat of it you shall surely die.

"Well, does that mean right then?"

First of all, we do not want to say anything that the Scriptures do not say or imply. Second, we want to say everything the Scriptures do say or we can infer.

The passage does not say at the exact moment or exact second that you eat of it you shall die. It does not say that. But it does say what?

"In the day..."

"May I say something?"

Yes, please say what you will.

"OK. In the day that thou eat of it, that very day, thou shall surely die?"

Yes!

"They are not saying that they are going to physically die; that their bodies are just going to drop dead? But all this 'good' that you currently have is going to leave you."

Do you see that in this passage that you are reading?

"Yeah!"

You do?

"That's what I'm interpreting!"

But do you see that in the verses that you are reading?

"Yeah!"

Dying You Shall Die | 61

You do?

Somebody please help her. I want someone to tell me, do you see in that passage what she is saying?

"Let me explain to you what they are saying because they are speaking from my teaching."

Yes. I understand that. But, I asked everyone to do what? Set aside what you know or what you think you know. And let us look solely at what the passage is telling us. It says, "in the day that you eat from it, you shall surely die".

It is important for you to get this now. You may think that this is just an insignificant little challenge on words, i.e., not very important, minor, or whatever. However, it is extremely important that you see the passage exactly like it is presented to you. Do not add anything to it. It does not matter how much you know. That is not suggesting that what you know is wrong.

What I am asking you to do is focus on what the verse actually says and nothing else. Otherwise, you may be deceived like Eve.

"OK. You got us now!"

Very good!

Now, God says, "you shall surely die". He does not tell us the nature of that death. He simply says, "in the day you eat of it you shall surely die". So, do not look at your picture of what you think death is. He simply says you shall die. And He says you shall die when?

"The same day you eat."

That is the day they shall die. He does not tell us what time of day they will die nor how many minutes after they eat.

Did you read Genesis chapter five in your pre-assignment reading? What do we see happening in Genesis chapter five?

"These are the generations of Adam."

And what is the major thing that is happening to all the generations?

"They lived a long time."

And then?

"They died."

That is right. They lived a long time and then they died. Many persons, when they read Genesis chapter two verses sixteen and seventeen (2:16-17), say that chapter five is the death that God promised. I am sure you have heard persons say that. They ate. God said they would die in the day they ate. In chapter five, they are dying or they died according to God's Word. Have you heard or said that yourself?

"That is where I have a problem. Let's go back to Genesis 2:16-17. They are going to eventually die. But you're saying they are already dead."

OK! Let me help you out a little bit. Now, you are saying, I, Arlington McRae, am saying they died in chapter three when they ate. But I am not saying that. Who is saying that?

"God."

Who?

"God said it."

Now, if I say it, you might have some doubt.

"Right."

But God said it. The Almighty, all-knowing God said it! He does not make mistakes. And He said that, "in the day that you shall eat from it, you shall surely die". We began our preparation for this journey by asking you what? Is this Bible the Word of God? Do you believe it is without error? Then in Genesis 2:17, God says when you eat, in the day that you eat, you shall surely die. Therefore, I implore you to take another look at your Bible. Take a good hard look. Scan a few pages in the middle and near the back. Do you believe the Bible is God's true and authentic revelation of Himself so that you could get to know Him and yourself? Finally, have you made a decision to believe God or to reject His revelation and instructions? A lack of decision is a choice to reject God and His revelation.

In Genesis chapter one, God says He is going to make humankind and so He did. In chapter two, God provides more details of the human's artful creation and guidance. Later, He majestically creates Eve, Adam's wife, to be his helper. At his creation, God tells Adam, the first human, what he is permitted to do and what he is not permitted to do; what would happen should he decide to disobey Him, i.e., eat of the tree of the knowledge of good and evil (not the apple tree)!

"Therefore, going over to chapter five, they lived a long time. They lived nine hundred years. So, they were not going to die right then. But they will die. But they have

> to suffer everything before they die. They have to do the tree of the knowledge of good and evil. I hope I am on the right point."

And your point is what?

> "They would not die right then. But they're going to die. They are going to live a long time. But they got to suffer before they die."

> "I see that God is talking about the knowledge of good and evil. It is knowledge that they don't have. It is knowledge they can obtain that is detrimental to them."

> "They lived long but as time went on their lives were cut shorter and shorter. They started out at something like nine hundred years. And as time went on, they weren't living that long."

OK. Pause and take a deep breath. What do you (the reader) say? Please make notes on your thinking at this point before continuing the dialogue.

> Now, I want you to listen to what both of you are saying. You are saying to me that chapter five of Genesis is saying they lived and then they died. They lived a long time but they died. As time went on, life got shorter and shorter. That is what you are saying. Look at chapter two, verse 17 again. Tell me what it says. What does God say is going to happen? God says, "for in the day that you shall eat of it, you shall surely die". Now you are saying, "But they did not die!". So I ask you, is God a liar?

> "No. He is not."

You might say that in the day that they ate, they actually began to die but they did not actually finish dying until sometime in chapter five.

"Right."

That would be a reasonable conclusion since many translators say the literal translation should be, "dying you shall die," implying a possible process to that death.

For a deeper understanding of possible translations of Genesis 2:17, see the article Genesis 2:17-"You Shall Surely Die" by Dr. Terry Mortenson.

The Problem

I hope you are gaining something from this dialog. One thing I hope you are gaining is this: When I say to you, do you believe this Bible is the Word of God? I assume you know something of the Bible and who God is. And you know that our God speaks truth. "I am the way, the truth, and the life" (John 14:6). I am the way. I am the truth. And I am the life. What Jesus is saying in that verse is, I am the truth so I speak what is true. The other stuff you are hearing out there from the world (society at large), that is the lie. What I (Jesus) speak is truth. Therefore, in Genesis 2:17, God spoke the truth. And what He says, you can trust completely. You eat the fruit today. You die today. But now we want to be like our children. You know how our children do? You tell your children, you do that, I am going to spank you today. You misbehave in church, I'm going to spank you in church. What does the child say in his or her mind? "She's not going to spank me in church. She's going to be too embarrassed to spank me in church. She has never done it before. Why should she do it now?" And we are acting just like our children. God said it. And we say, He didn't really mean it. Adam and Eve did not really die that day.

> "Yes, we know they are going to die, but it will be sometime later."
>
> "So death is OK because I'm not dying right then?"
>
> Exactly.
>
> "We are starting to just add and take away from God's Word even as we study it."
>
> That tells me (the author) you are a blessed man because the light has come on for you!

If you are a church member, you must realize you are at a disadvantage from a person who has never read anything in the Bible. You have read throughout the Old Testament as well as the New Testament. You have heard teachers and preachers speak on any number of subjects and passages. So you have all that stored in your brain and perhaps in your heart. And you are interpreting what you read through all those facts and thoughts planted in your head. What we were taught in seminary is, what I just described is called "pre-supposition". We come to the Scriptures with "pre-suppositions". All of us do it. In other words, we already have in our minds what we think Scripture is going to say. So when we read it, we see exactly what we are expecting. Therefore, the struggle that one has is to read the Scriptures with no pre-conceived notions. See the words. Examine what it says exactly and believe exactly what it says. That is important. That is very, very important.

Allow me to say one last thing about seeing the Scriptures as they are written and nothing more. Biblical writers often use literary techniques such as hyperboles and metaphors to emphasize, stress or clarify their points. The reader, again, must see the Scripture for what it really is in such cases, a hyperbole or a metaphor that the author is using to make his point clear to you, the reader. These must be considered for what they actually are. However, no such techniques are employed in Genesis chapters 1-3.

Questions?

"Yeah! But you still haven't solved the problem!"

What is the problem? I do not see a problem. What is the problem?

"I got a problem."

OK. Tell me your problem.

"God says that the day that you eat of it you shall surely die. And we know God's Word is true. And we look and see in Genesis 5 that they didn't die the day that He said. They died but it wasn't the day that He said."

So God lied?

"No, He didn't."

Well, explain that to me.

"That's what I want to ask you. You see, there are two types of death."

Oh really? Where does it say that?

"No, there is a spiritual death."

Yes, but where does it say that in the passage that we read?

"OK, if He didn't lie, and He said they are going to die that day."

Right.

"Adam did not die that day."

He didn't?

"No. He spiritually died."

Where does it say that?

"He died a spiritual death."

Wait a minute. I do not see in that passage or the surrounding text anything that references spiritual death. I do not see where it says anything about physical death. All I see is that it says, "you shall surely die". And we can rightly conclude that the result of dying is "death".

"So they died. Adam died?"

My God says he will die; I believe what my God says.

"He died."

"He did that. You and I are going to have to have a discussion."

That will be fine.

"Because, God does not lie. He cannot lie."

And what did He say?

"He said they are going to die."

When?

"That day."

And you say they died when?

"They died that day."

OK then! We have the same interpretation. Problem solved!

Remember, we are focused only on Genesis 2:17. We are not focused on anything else in the Bible. Because, when we are looking down the road instead of looking at what we see immediately before us, we can make the wrong turn. You have to make sure that you get exactly what the writer is saying to you, in the passage before you, prior to moving on! And if you say, "I know who God is. I know He does not lie. And God says, 'In the day that you eat of this tree that is the day you shall certainly die'". Then, you must believe that is exactly what will happen. Otherwise, you make God a liar! When Adam and Eve disobeyed God and ate, through the eyes of God, they died the very day that they ate!

Any final questions before we close our lesson?

Additionally, please document your position on this discussion now.

Looking forward to our future sessions together, make sure you understand me. I am not saying what you say or think is wrong. I am asking you to focus solely on what the

Scriptures are saying right here in these chapters. So take some time to analyze verse 17 (include the referenced articles above in your research) and see what conclusion you reach. You will find this exercise very profitable for understanding future chapters in this volume.

> "I understand, because pre-supposition is a big issue. We say we believe the Bible. And if it says something, we just need to believe it faithfully, regardless as to whether we can see it happening or not. We just have to believe what it says and go from there that God is true."

> Very good! Based on what you have said then, you might pray as follows: "Now, Lord, this man is pointing out his interpretation of what Your Word is saying there in Genesis. And it does not make sense to me. I am simply telling You God, it does not make any sense to me! Therefore, I am asking You to show me so it does make sense."

> Isn't this fun?

> "I just want to say something. It does make sense to me. But, I guess it means I have a problem trying to make something out of it that is really not there. It means what it says, when they would die."

> That is correct.

Therefore, take the rest of today to encourage your family, friends, neighbors and co-workers to get this book this week and the first volume in the series also. Invite them to become your reading and study partners. Working together may encourage each of you to learn a fresh perspective on studying the Scriptures. Working together may also encourage you to learn new concepts designed to make the Scriptures come alive and be more meaningful to your mind, heart and spirit.

Final Remarks

Allow me to provide you a caution. Before today is over, Satan is likely to tell you, "Arlington McRae does not know what he is talking about". He may have told someone that already! So, you are going to say to Satan, "McRae did not tell us what he is saying". "McRae showed us, and we now understand, what God says in His Bible." Make sure you take special note now for Satan is surely going to tell someone, "McRae does not know what he is talking about" or something similar.

When I was recuperating from a massive heart attack having suffered cardio-pulmonary arrest (i.e., I died), my memory was extremely poor. Really, I could not recall very much of anything from before the heart attack. Initially, my brain was nearly as blank as a baby's. So, I said to God, if I don't get my memory back, that is fine with me. Just make sure You put in me everything I have learned about You. That is all I want if I cannot remember anything else. Please put in my brain everything I have learned about You. Let me remember that. So until our next session together, review what the Scriptures we read say. Rehearse them. Memorize them precisely as written. Meditate on them to push them into your long-term memory so you will remember them. Ask God for assistance.

Make an effort to remember everything you learn about the Word of God. Revisit it often, asking God to help you. So you can take it with you into all future interaction with this book, in all your Bible studies and into the rest of your life and ministry.

I encourage you to read the pre-assigned Scriptures again—Genesis chapters 1-12 and John chapter 1—and meditate on them. You cannot read them too many times.

Let us pray: Most gracious Father and Lord, once again we say thank You. Thank You for Your Son, Jesus. Thank You for Your Holy Spirit who is here with us and in us who believe. Forgive us, Lord, for being in the presumptive state when hearing Your Word and trying to add to it. Your Bible clearly says do not add or take away from the Scriptures. And we thank You for bringing us back to these basics because we need the basics. We just thank You so much, Lord.

We thank You for this opportunity that we can all come together, reason and learn to study Your Word together. And we can learn to stay in Your Word and not be tossed about like the raging sea. We ask You to rebuke Satan in the mighty name of Jesus that he would not be able to hit us with these fiery darts to get our minds off the true Word. And we know Your Word is true. So we thank You for it. Continue to teach us and keep us in Your Word. In the name of Jesus we pray, amen, amen.

2

WHOM WILL YOU BELIEVE?

SCRIPTURE: Exodus 34:1-9

Prayer: Heavenly Father, in the name of Your darling Son, Jesus, we pause to acknowledge You are God alone. We acknowledge that You are a God of love and compassion, mercy and grace. We acknowledge that You desire all who call on the name of Jesus to love one another and to be obedient to Your Word. And we acknowledge that we have failed to comply with Your imperatives.

Where we lack a willingness, we pray that You would give us that willing heart. Remove the pride. Remove the self-centeredness. Remove all desire to operate independently of You. Do Your renovation work in us. Cause us to commit ourselves to You, to Your will and to Your way. Put in us this day a great desire to hear from You. Teach us what You want us to know. Teach us Father! Teach us as only You can teach us. Cause us to see Your Scriptures through Your eyes. Help us to gain Your perspective. Then, Father, cause us to live according to what we are learning. Cause us to be doers of Your Word and not simply hearers only. For we know that this is Your will for us.

To You belong our thanks. To You we give the praise. To You we shall give the honor and all the glory. In Jesus name we pray, amen.

God's Nature And Character

In this chapter, we shall first continue our examination of the initial biblical text we read at the beginning of our previous chapter and here as well: Exodus 34:1-9. However, before we give our attention to that passage, allow me to provide a little background so you will have the context for what is said in this passage.

In the Bible, let us go back a little in Exodus to chapter 32 beginning at verse 25:

> Now when Moses saw that the people were out of control— for Aaron had let them get out of control to be a derision among their enemies—26 then Moses stood in the gate of the camp, and said, "Whoever is for the LORD, come to me!" And all the sons of Levi gathered together to him. 27And he said to them, "Thus says the LORD, the God of Israel, 'Every man of you put his sword upon his thigh, and go back and forth from gate to gate in the camp, and kill every man his brother, and every man his friend, and every man his neighbor.' " 28So the sons of Levi did as Moses instructed, and about three thousand men of the people fell that day.

The golden calf incident (Exodus 32:1-24) is the setting for what is going on here. You may recall that this incident occurred on the way to Mount Sinai as Moses was leading the children of Israel out of slavery in Egypt to the Promised Land (the land God had promised to Abraham, Isaac and Jacob and their descendants). At God's request, Moses went up the mountain to meet with God. In his absence, the people built for themselves an idol god—a golden calf—and began to worship it. God saw it and He was beyond angry for the pain of it all. After all, He had just delivered them from 400 years of slavery in Egypt with miracles never before seen on the earth. So, God says to Moses, you take these people to the land that I promised them. The people you brought from Egypt, you take them. If one is careful to read the Scriptures prior to Exodus 32, one will see that God had previously said to Moses, these are the people "I" brought out of the land of Egypt. But now, He is saying these are the people "you" (Moses) brought out of Egypt. So God is beyond furious because the people are acting like God had nothing to do with their deliverance.

In Exodus 32:30-34 we read:

> And it came about on the next day that Moses said to the people, "You yourselves have committed a great sin; and now I am going up to the LORD, perhaps I can make atonement for your sin." 31Then Moses returned to the LORD, and said, "Alas, this people has committed a great sin, and they have made a god of gold for themselves. 32"But now, if You will, forgive their sin—and if not, please blot me out from Your

> book which You have written!" 33And the LORD said to Moses, "Whoever has sinned against Me, I will blot him out of My book. 34"But go now, lead the people where I told you. Behold, My angel shall go before you; nevertheless in the day when I punish, I will punish them for their sin."

Now, let us move on to Exodus 33:1-3:

> Then the LORD spoke to Moses, "Depart, go up from here, you and the people whom you have brought up from the land of Egypt, to the land of which I swore to Abraham, Isaac, and Jacob, saying, 'To your descendants I will give it.' 2"And I will send an angel before you and I will drive out the Canaanite, the Amorite, the Hittite, the Perizzite, the Hivite and the Jebusite. 3"Go up to a land flowing with milk and honey; for I will not go up in your midst, because you are an obstinate people, lest I destroy you on the way."

Here, God is saying to Israel, you are a stiff-necked, stubbornly disobedient people. You are doing what you want instead of what I have commanded you. Yet, I am still going to send you to the land I promised to your forefathers. But, I am not going with you. For, if I go with you, because of your irreverent disregard for Me, I will surely destroy you. I will be right in your midst and I will explode in My righteous anger. Therefore, I would surely destroy you! So, the best thing for you is that I not go with you. I shall send My angel with you instead. He will go before you.

Do you have the picture now? OK. Let us move on to verses 12-13 in chapter 33:

> Then Moses said to the LORD, "See, You do say to me, 'Bring up this people!' But You Yourself have not let me know whom You will send with me. Moreover, You have said, 'I have known you by name, and you have also found favor in My sight.' 13 "Now therefore, I pray You, if I have found favor in Your sight, let me know Your ways, that I may know You, so that I may find favor in Your sight. Consider too, that this nation is Your people."

In verse 13, Moses is saying to God, if I have found favor with You as You have said, show me who You are that I may truly know You. And keep in mind, God, that these people are indeed Your people.

Now move down to verses 17-20:

> And the LORD said to Moses, "I will also do this thing of which you have spoken; for you have found favor in My sight, and I have known you by name." 18Then Moses said, "I pray You, show me Your glory!" 19And He said, "I Myself will make all My goodness pass before you, and will proclaim the name of the LORD before you; and I will be gracious to whom I will be gracious, and will show compassion on whom I will show compassion." 20But He said, "You cannot see My face, for no man can see Me and live!"

So, in response, God says, I shall show You who I am. I shall pass by and My glory shall come before you. However, you cannot see My face because any human who looks Me in the face will die. God goes on to say, I am going to put you in the cleft of the rock and I shall put My hand there to cover you. Then I am going to pass by you and declare to you My glory, i.e., I am going to reveal to you who I truly am.

Now, read Exodus 34:5-9:

> And the LORD descended in the cloud and stood there with him [Moses] as he called upon the name of the LORD. 6Then the LORD passed by in front of him and proclaimed, "The LORD, the LORD God, compassionate and gracious, slow to anger, and abounding in lovingkindness and truth; 7who keeps lovingkindness for thousands, who forgives iniquity, transgression and sin; yet He will by no means leave the guilty unpunished, visiting the iniquity of fathers on the children and on the grandchildren to the third and fourth generations."8And Moses made haste to bow low toward the earth and worship. 9And he said, "If now I have found favor in Your sight, O' Lord, I pray, let the Lord go along in our midst, even though the people are so obstinate; and do You pardon our iniquity and our sin, and take us as Your own possession."

In this passage, we see God passing in front of Moses and declaring to Moses who He truly is, i.e., His values, nature and His character. It is my contention that this passage is where God says to Moses and to people today, this is who I am. Your world will see Me doing many things. Some you might not understand. Some you may question. But judge Me, judge My action or inaction by My character and My nature in order to obtain an understanding of My motives. This is who I am—"compassionate and gracious, slow to anger, and abounding in lovingkindness and truth; who keeps lovingkindness for thousands, who forgives iniquity, transgression and sin; yet He will by no means leave the guilty unpunished, visiting the iniquity of fathers on the children and on the grandchildren to the third and fourth generations."

Please solidify this picture in your mind. Meditate on it and its implications daily, even several times a day. A.S.K (Ask, Seek and Knock, Matthew 7:7-8) God for clarification and insight, with thanksgiving! Please make it your firmly committed goal to have the essence of this passage (Exodus 34:6-7) memorized in its entirety over the next two weeks. Along the way, ask God to give you His perspective of the picture this passage paints of Him. You are sure to find this to be a very productive and rewarding exercise.

Before we move deeper into our adventure for this session, let us perform a quick review. Our attention last session was in Genesis chapters 1 and 2. Specifically, our focal verses were Genesis 2:16-17:

> And the LORD God commanded the man, saying, "From any tree of the garden you may eat freely; 17 but from the tree of the knowledge of good and evil you shall not heat, for in the day that you eat from it you shall surely die."

During our last discussion, we gave much of our attention to the most significant biblical event (following creation) in the Old Testament—Adam and Eve eating the forbidden fruit—as if it had already happened there in Genesis chapter 2. However, the game-changing disobedience we talked about there in Genesis 2:16-17 did not happen yet. Instead, what we have here in actuality is God giving Adam instructions (Eve is not yet created) about what he is permitted and not permitted to do—the <u>Edenic Covenant</u>.

In this same way, you give instructions to your children regarding the limits of their boundaries and what the consequences are should they venture beyond them. God says to Adam, if you eat of this fruit, there will be a serious consequence—"you shall surely die". And we had an intense debate about that. The greatest point of contention had to do with when would Adam actually die should he disobey God. Hopefully, you have settled in your mind that in the day that Adam should eat of it, he will surely die.

Take a moment to review and expand your notes to refresh your memory and solidify your own thoughts on this matter. Also include your unanswered questions.

If you have not already done so, now would be an excellent time for you to study our first publication, *The Bible for Beginners And The Rest of Us*. That volume provides an overview of the Bible's essential message and other key insights. More specifically, it provides an enlightened perspective and context for a better understanding in your future Bible studies and in our current discussions as well.

When Will Adam Die?

We are going to begin today's adventure session pretty much were we left off in the previous chapter.

The question before us is this: When does Scripture say that Adam will die? This is not a trick question. It is right there in Genesis 2:17. If he eats, in the day that he eats, he shall surely die. God did not say following so many days, plural. He said in the day, singular.

Today as we look at it, since God did not say in one hour or at 12 noon or 6 pm, some of us think He is not being specific enough. But in those days, He was not so concerned about being that specific. He said, in the day, that very day you eat, you shall "surely die"! That was specific enough for God's purpose.

Is there any debate in your mind regarding that understanding? Do you differ with that interpretation? Be truthful to yourself. If you believe that is not what that Scripture means, solidify the logic of your thought process and document it. Be certain you can prove your position to someone else holding a different view.

> "Why didn't Adam and Eve die then?"
>
> Well, first of all, we have not gotten to the point where they actually ate. We are still discussing chapter 2. But the thing is, your question suggests that they did not die when, in chapter 3, they ate. Therefore, this is a question with which we must contend and resolve in our hearts. By the way, I love this question!
>
> Pickup your Bible and look at it. Turn it over and around. You see, this is the Bible. Do you believe this

Bible is the Word of God? You must decide for yourself whether you believe the Bible is in fact the Word of God or not. If you say, yes, I believe the Bible is in fact the Word of God. Then the next question I have for you is, do you believe that the Bible is without error in its original manuscripts? In other words, there are no mistakes. It says what God instructed the original writers to say. And of course, the final question is, if you believe that this Bible is the Word of God, if you believe the Bible is without error, then, what role does this Bible have in guiding your heart, your thinking and your relationships in this present life and for all eternity?

Now, on to the question before us, when you read Genesis 2:17, it says specifically without question when Adam would die. So there should be no difficulty understanding what it says. It clearly says, in the day, on the day, the day that you eat, you shall surely die. Your question suggests that (and we have not gotten to that point yet), if in fact Adam does eat, he is not going to die. Or, having eaten, he did not die.

Also remember at this point in chapter two, Adam is alone. There is no Eve.

It is extremely critical that we decide if we are going to believe the Bible. We say it is the Word of God and it is true. If God says to you, in the day you eat you shall surely die, and should you eat, do you believe you would die on that day? Do you believe God is truthful? Or, do you believe He is misleading you or that God is playing tricks with you? Do you believe His instructions are not specific enough? This is a matter of life or death. So it is extremely critical that your understanding be one hundred percent accurate.

Questions? Please document any of your questions or comments at this point.

> Once again, pre-supposition is raising its ugly, distorting head. It is important that you set aside what you already believe and what you think you know. I am not saying to you that what you know is wrong. What I am asking you to do, for the purpose of our current discussion, is take what you already know, set it to the side and forget it, for now. Then, focus solely on what the Bible is saying in the current passage and nothing else.

"What does it mean by 'in the day'?"

The very day! But right here, God is only giving Adam instructions about what to do or not do.

"But that's not a time though, 'in the day'."

If I say to you, if you steal my car, in the day you steal it, I am going to kill you. When am I talking about?

"The day I steal your car".

There would be no doubt in your mind, would there? In the day you steal my car, that is the day I am going to kill you! On the day you steal my car, that is the day I am going to kill you. The day you steal my car, I am going to kill you. The very day you steal my car, you shall surely die!

"How do we know what day?"

Does it matter? Just like my example above, if you steal my car, on that day you are going to die. So if you choose Thursday to die, that is fine with me. If you should choose Saturday to die, that will be fine too. I am not going to change my mind should you choose to do it on Sunday instead of Wednesday. Are you with me?

Isn't this exciting?

Let us continue our discussion now by returning to Genesis chapter 2. In the remainder of chapter 2, God creates the woman. He takes a rib from the man and shapes it into this beautiful marvelous thing and brings her to the man who calls her woman because she was taken out of man. Right?

Now, look at the very last verse there in chapter 2:

> And the man and his wife were both naked and were not ashamed (2:25).

Do you know what is the fascinating thing about that verse? Look again at verse 25 in its surrounding context. Read it for a second time, even a third time. Notice, out of the clear blue sky, with no introduction, connection or further comment, the writer (Moses) decides to say, "the man and his wife were both naked and were not ashamed". Why?

In verse 24, Moses is saying a man shall leave his father and mother and he shall cleave to his wife. Then all of a sudden, the Scriptures say, "And the man and his wife were both naked and were not ashamed". Have you ever noticed that? Have you paid any attention to that? Why, all of a sudden, did Moses happen to just throw that in there? What is it connected to? Why has the writer told us this?

So, what I am asking you to do with that observation is this: Imagine a little cork board up on your wall. And you have one of those little sticky note pads. You are going to make a note of Genesis 2:25 on a sticky note slip, put a pin in it and attach it up there on the cork board. "And the man and his wife were both naked and were not ashamed." Prayerfully, we shall come back to it at another time, perhaps in a future volume.

Any questions? Please complete your notes and list your questions and comments now.

"Did Adam have a father and mother?"

No.

"Well why does it say, 'therefore shall a man leave his father and mother and shall cleave unto his wife and they shall become one flesh'?"

Because God knew what the future of mankind would be. Adam and Eve were the only two persons He would <u>create</u>. Everyone else would be born and not created in the same sense as Adam and Eve were. Therefore, God knew that everyone else would have a father and a mother because Adam already had his wife and God gave them instructions to be fruitful and populate the earth. And He fixed it so they would enjoy doing it!

"So why wouldn't God know that Eve was going to tempt Adam with an apple?"

An apple? Let's not deal with that question for now. That is what you are dealing with. Ours is not that question. There is an issue much more important for us to consider than that question.

Now turn to Genesis 3:1-7:

> Now the serpent was more crafty than any beast of the field which the LORD God had made. And he said to the woman, "Indeed, has God said, 'You shall not eat from any tree of the garden'?" 2And the woman said to the serpent, "From the fruit of the trees of the garden we may eat; 3but from the fruit of the tree which is in the middle of the garden, God has said, 'You shall not eat from it or touch it, lest you die.' " 4And the serpent said to the woman, "You surely shall not die! 5"For God knows that in the day you eat from it your eyes will be opened, and you will be like God, knowing good and evil." 6When the woman saw that the tree was good for food, and that it was a delight to the eyes, and that the tree was desirable to make one wise, she took from its fruit and ate; and she gave also to her husband with her, and he ate. 7Then the eyes of both of them were opened, and they knew that they were naked; and they sewed fig leaves together and made themselves loin coverings.

So what has just happened?

"They disobeyed!"

And what did they do in their disobedience?

"They ate from the forbidden fruit tree."

They ate the fruit that God said you shall not eat. Look at the verse there where the serpent says, "Indeed, has God said, 'you shall not eat from any tree of the garden'?" Then the woman says, we can eat fruit from any tree in the garden. We just cannot eat of or touch the tree in the middle of the garden for God said, "lest you die". What then did the serpent say? "You surely shall not die! For God knows that in the day you eat from it your eyes will be opened, and you will be like God, knowing good and evil."

> "Did Adam know that was the forbidden fruit that Eve gave him?"

> What do the Scriptures say right there in 3:6? It says to me that Adam was standing right there with her as she conversed with the serpent.

> "I just wanted to know that he was not somewhere else in the garden and Eve brought it to him. And he said, 'Oh, thank you for the fruit'."

> I would think they were diligent enough to make certain they could recognize that particular fruit anywhere. I imagine there were quite a number of discussions about that fruit and whether they should eat the fruit or not eat the fruit, well before the serpent even came on the scene. Most likely it would not have mattered where they were when Adam received the fruit. Adam would recognize that this is the forbidden fruit.

So here is the point: When the serpent responded as he did, what was the contentious question for Adam and Eve?

"Whether or not they were going to die?"

You think that was the question? Well, that was one of the questions, but what was a more critical or significant question than that one?

"They were probably wrestling with them having knowledge and being like God."

That was one too. But there is an even more fundamentally significant question than that. Read what the serpent said again.

And the serpent said to the woman, "You surely shall not die!" (v4).

"Whom will you believe, God or the serpent?"

That is the question! Who is telling the truth?

"So they didn't believe in God?"

Well, they knew God existed. They both saw Him and had conversations with Him. It appears that Eve allowed the serpent to undermine her trust in the truthfulness of God.

In answer to the serpent, the woman says, God said we can eat of any fruit, but we cannot eat that one fruit over there, in the midst of the garden, because if we do, we are going to die. The serpent says, "You surely shall not die!" For sure, you will not die! Here is the real deal. God knows that if you eat, you are going to know something God has held back from you—the knowledge of good and evil. Not only will you know good and evil, this knowledge will make you wise like God.

So, the question Adam and Eve had to wrestle with is, "Is God telling the truth? Or, is the serpent telling the truth?"

Questions? Please take a moment now to make notes on your thoughts right now.

The Essential Question

OK! I am going to interject a special point here. The essential question for us today is, "Do you believe God (the Bible and Jesus) or do you believe Satan ('the serpent of old' or society at large)?" Adam and Eve were wrestling with that same question—do we believe God or do we believe Satan?

This question is worth writing down. Then allow it to ruminate and find rest in your soul. Oh, you do not believe in Satan? You can be certain of this one thing: He believes in you and he knows you quite well. And he makes sure to encourage you often.

> "But how would we know what Adam and Eve believed?"
>
> One's actions tell us what one believes. For example, you can tell me you love God. But you are doing everything but what God says. Do I believe what you say or do I believe what you do? (What you do speaks so loudly I can hardly hear what you say.)
>
> And the question you have to answer today for yourself is, "Do I believe God (the Bible) or do I believe Satan ('the serpent of old') (Revelation 12:9)?"

Let us take a moment to consider the message of the New Testament. What question is Jesus, the Son of God, presenting to humankind? As I meet people walking the street, I may walk up to them to ask them about Jesus. If I am speaking to someone who does not know God and I tell him or her what the Bible says about humans and about God, the question they must contend with is, "Is it the truth or is it false?" Presumably, I am speaking God's Word accurately. Each unbeliever today is wrestling with that same basic and fundamental question: do I/can I believe God? And should they choose not to believe God, then that is a choice to believe Satan's lie.

Can you see that it is the same question today as it was for Adam and Eve? And too many persons are choosing to ignore God's righteousness and truth "and they, having become callous, have given themselves over to sensuality for the practice of every kind of impurity with greediness" (Ephesians 4:19). Does that describe you?

As a youth, I remember thinking to myself that the Scriptures say, I am born a sinner doomed to hell (John 3:16-19). For further explanation, see the article, Is there original' sin, meaning men are sinners because of an inherited' sinful nature passed on by Adam? So why does God hold me responsible? Then I learned the truth.

When Jesus died on the cross, He died for all sins for all humankind, except what sin? Jesus died for the sins of the past, the sins of the present and the sins of the future. The Bible says you can blaspheme against God the Father, God the Son and be forgiven. But there is no forgiveness for blaspheming against the Holy Spirit. Jesus did not die for that one sin. What is another sin for which Jesus did not die? *The sin of unbelief.* Jesus did not die for your act of disbelieving God or God's Bible. Would you care to argue with me about that?

> "So are you saying that Jesus didn't die for unbelievers?"

No? Absolutely not! All of us were unbelievers. Jesus did not die for the sin of unbelief. That is, His death, His sacrifice did not cover those who die in unbelief, those who continue to choose not to believe God. Any disbeliever, potentially, can become a believer before death. It is a choice birthed in the heart through the work of the Holy Spirit!

Every Word Is Significant

So at this point, do I have your mind totally confused? Do I have you questioning the validity of my proposition? Maybe you are correct to do so. But please continue to press on to the end. Then draw your own conclusion. We will hopefully answer many of your questions and concerns in subsequent chapters. And if we do not, shoot me an email (see copyright page) or post on my blog, www.arlingtonmcrae.org

In the meantime, let me share with you something I have learned in my study of the first six chapters in the book of Genesis, something that is true about the entire Bible. Every word, every word is significant. And the context is critical! You must not simply read the passage and conclude immediately, "this is what it is saying or this is its meaning". Every word as small as "if" or "a" is significant. A word such as "t-h-e" is significant, every word! I have spent much time meditating on one verse, spending days on that one verse, looking at each word, each thought or possible alternative thought, meaning, or idea. Therefore, I urge you to pay very close attention to each and every word you read in the Bible as well as in this series.

Finally, please take as much time as you need to carefully consider and reconsider every aspect of our proposition thus far.

Let us pray: Father, we come before You as Your little children. You want us to see ourselves as Your children and You as our Father. You have told us that You know how to give every good and perfect gift to Your children. And just like an earthly father wants to educate his children that his children may be wise, that his children may be discerning, that his children may be knowledgeable, so You also in the same way want to educate us to know what is good and what is evil, to know the rewards of good and the consequences of evil, to know who You are and who we are. You also want us to know the realities of this world and not what the evil one has put in our hearts and minds. Teach us, therefore Father, that we may truly know. Teach us as only You can teach us. Remove the blinders over our hearts and over our minds. Take away the darkness and fill us with Your marvelous light that we may see clearly. And in seeing clearly our hearts may be satisfied that we know You and that we know what You desire us to know.

As we go forth throughout the day, and as we go through the week, continue to teach us. Set us down and make us listen to You. Put the right questions in our heart and on our mind. Then let us listen to You for the answer. Teach us to be obedient like little children. Teach us, Father, that we may know Your will. Teach us, Father, how to love You the way You deserve to be loved (John 14:21). Thank You in advance for the blessings on the way. In Jesus name we pray, amen.

3

THE GREAT SIN

SCRIPTURE: Exodus 34:1-9

Prayer: Our Father which is in heaven, hallowed be Your name. Your kingdom come. Your will be done on earth just as it is done in heaven. And may Your will be done in our lives just as You desire. May our obedience rise to the level that You desire, so that we may bring joy to Your heart and put a smile on Your face. Father, forgive us our sins and our trespasses. For we confess to You that we have indeed sinned against You and against our fellow humans. We have not been obedient as Your Word has commanded us. We have treated You carelessly and disrespectfully. We have not sought Your face as You desire of us. We have walked in the way of the world and not in Your way. O' God, forgive us for You are a forgiving God, compassionate and generous in Your love. We ask You, therefore Father, to separate us from our sins. Then Father, we pray that You would give us a clean heart and a renewed spirit that is passionate for You and obedient to Your Word. Cause us to love our fellow humans just as Jesus has taught us. In Jesus name we pray, amen.

Have you given much thought to our discussion in the first two chapters, any serious thought? Have you turned it over in your mind? Have you debated it with yourself and shared it with your family and friends? If not, I encourage you to do so during the coming week.

A Quick Review

Let us do a quick review before we dig deeper into God's Word. We want to begin with your telling us about anything from our last chapter that struck you or on which you desire further clarification?

Please write your response in your notes now. If not already done, take this time also to write all your notes and thoughts on our previous sessions. To help you get started, what Scripture was the basis for our last two sessions?

We began our last session with selected Scriptures found in Exodus 32, 33 and 34. I have previously indicated that our journey would take us down two parallel paths. One path focuses on the nature of humankind, according to Genesis chapters 1 through 6. The other path focuses our attention on the person of God, according to Exodus 34:5-9. At some point, these two paths should converge and merge. And when they do, prayerfully, you will see God's Word and your life's mission clearly with much more insight (i.e., comprehension of its true nature and purpose) and discernment than when we began.

I have asked you to write copious and clear notes. You should write notes so that six months from now, when you look at your notes, they will awaken details in your memory and tell you what you need to know. So you can then teach others precisely what you have learned and what your thoughts were at that time. Your notes will also be available for your regular review and meditation as they take root deep in your longterm memory.

It is important to me and it is extremely important for you to make detail notes. We do not want to go through the exercise of reading and studying this volume just so we can say we read it. We want to come out on the other side with something truly valuable, motivational, life-changing and inspired to impact the lives of many lost or spiritually immature souls!

My experience in observing church is this: We come to the church house; we do our rituals. But for many, that experience has little impact on our lives. We are like little children following instructions from memory. But our heart is not in it. As a result, we leave church unmoved and unaffected by the experience. Therefore, as we read our Exodus passage, ask yourself: "What is this passage truly about? What is the picture I should get from this passage and for what purpose?"

This is our third chapter. And in each chapter we have read the same passage, Exodus 34:1-9 or 34:5-9. Can you tell me now, extemporaneously, what the passage says in essence?

This I would also add: What we are doing now, what I am presenting to you now, the words in these pages, what I am asking you to do, everything is designed to teach you something significant and to help you hold on to it. Then make use of it in your own life and the life of those you encounter. Every word is important. So take it all with you into subsequent chapters and into your daily devotion and daily Bible study. What we covered in the Introduction, Preparation and Orientation, make an effort to bring it along with you. What we discussed in chapters one and two, make an effort to bring it all along with you.

It is similar to teaching your own children. You tell them over and over again because you want them to take it with them and utilize it every day. In the same way, God is teaching His children to take their new knowledge and new understanding along with them. Take it into all your Bible studies and devotionals and into your life's mission, focus and personal interactions.

∼

As we continue our review, in the last chapter we focused our attention on Genesis 2:16-17. What are these verses about?

God says to Adam, you may eat anything in the garden except from that one tree. Now just think about that. There were probably hundreds if not thousands of trees in the garden. And of all those trees, God says you may eat freely from all of them, except the one.

What does God say is going to happen to Adam should he eat of that one tree?

"You shall surely die."

When is he going to die?

"The day he eats."

Correct. The very day he eats the fruit, he will certainly die.

Then we moved on to the end of Genesis chapter 2. And I brought to your attention one verse on which we asked you to make a note.

What was that verse?

"Twenty-five?"

What does that verse say?

"The man and his wife were both naked and were not ashamed."

And what did I ask you to do with that verse?

Do you remember our cork board? What were we to do with the cork board?

We were to make a note about that verse on an imaginary sticky note and pin it on the imaginary cork board to remind us to come back to it at some point in the future. I also emphasized that, if you look at the verses immediately before verse 25, the author is talking about what is going to happen between a man and a woman in the future. Then all of a sudden, he is talking about their being naked and not ashamed. The author only mentions it in that one verse. And he went on to something totally unrelated. And the question is, "Why is that verse there?" He does not say anything about it before. He does not say anything about it immediately thereafter. He just drops it in there and moves on. But why?

As we wrestle with this verse, it is important to keep in mind that chapter divisions as well as verse numbers were not included in the original manuscripts.

We moved from there to Genesis 3:1-7. We focused most of our attention, however, on the first five verses.

The serpent comes to Eve and says,

> "Has God said you shall not eat from any tree in the garden?"

And Eve responded with,

> "From the fruit of the trees in the garden we may eat; but from the fruit of the tree in the middle of the garden God has said, 'You shall not eat from it or touch it, lest you die'."

And the serpent says what?

> "You surely shall not die! For God knows that in the day you eat from it, your eyes will be opened and you will be like God, knowing good and evil."

As we step back to grab the bigger picture, we see that God says if you eat, you shall surely die. The serpent comes along and says if you eat you surely shall not die.

In our ensuing discussion, I asked you to make a note of one particular question.

> What was that question?
>
> "Whom will you believe, God or the serpent?"
>
> Right!

Adam and Eve had several related questions to deal with. But the one question, the most critical question they were wrestling with was, "Whom do we believe?" "Shall we believe God or should we believe the serpent?" That was the question.

Allow me to interject something else here. I have it on good authority that the literal translation of the original language of Genesis 2:17 and 3:4 is, "dying you shall [or "not"] die." In this context, the wording suggests an ongoing progression relative to dying. So make a note of that.

For greater insight into the translation of Genesis 2:17, study the article, <u>Dying You Shall Die: The meaning of Genesis 2:17</u> by Stephen Bauer, PhD.

God commanded Adam (and Eve through Adam) in Genesis 2:16-17 (before they ate of the tree as we see in Genesis 3:1-7) to not eat of the tree of the knowledge of good and evil because "in the day that you eat from it you shall surely die". And our extended debate centered on when it was they would die. So we are in agreement now that on the day that they should eat they will die, not tomorrow, not later, not in a few years, not in a few hundred years, but on that very day. Now I know for some your mind may be wrestling with how that can be true because you have already read Genesis chapters 4 and 5. So the fundamental question you have to wrestle with is what? Whom will you believe? Do you believe God (the Bible) or do you believe Satan (that serpent of old)?

That concludes our review.

The Great Sin

For this session, we are going to continue our discussion of Genesis 3:1-7:

> Now the serpent was more crafty than any beast of the field which the LORD God had made. And he said to the woman, "Indeed, has God said, 'You shall not eat from any tree of the garden'?" 2And the woman said to the serpent, "From the fruit of the trees of the garden we may eat; 3but from the fruit of the tree which is in the middle of the garden, God has said, 'You shall not eat from it or touch it, lest you die.' " And the serpent said to the woman, "You surely shall not die! 5"For God knows that in the day you eat from it your eyes will be opened, and you will be like God, knowing good and evil." 6When the woman saw that the tree was good for food, and that it was a delight to the eyes, and that the tree was desirable to make one wise, she took from its fruit and ate; and she gave also to her husband with her, and he ate. 7Then the eyes of both of them were opened, and they knew that they were naked; and they sewed fig leaves together and made themselves loin coverings.

So in chapter 2, God is saying, do not eat of the tree of the knowledge of good and evil because there are severe consequences. In chapter 3, we are told they did exactly what God said to not do. We are established in the fact that when they ate the fruit of the tree of the knowledge of good and evil, they died right here in chapter three on that very day. You might not be able to grasp the reality of that death. But we can be certain that (in the eyes of God) they did in fact die that very day!

Are you in agreement with that? Or, are you still saying, "I just cannot see that because they did not die until chapter 5!" If you have turmoil turning around in your head, take a moment and write detailed notes, pros and cons, of that turmoil.

If you believe the Bible is God's Word, then you must believe what it says. They ate and therefore they died on the day they ate, even though you do not now comprehend it.

What is the very first thing the Bible tells us about Adam and Eve after they ate and died?

The first thing the writer brings to our attention is their eyes were opened just as Satan had said. And the Bible goes on to tell us something Satan failed to mention: "They knew that they were naked; and they sewed fig leaves together and made themselves loin coverings." Realizing they were naked, they were ashamed. There are negative consequences to the knowledge of good and evil. There are also negative consequences in listening to the voice of Satan instead of God's voice.

It would appear that verse seven in referencing nakedness is giving us a hint, maybe even a slap in the face, about the far reaching bodily consequences of that death. We know that it impacted the loins (the region of the reproductive organs) in some way because they covered their loins and nothing else. So make a note of that. We may come back to it sometime in the future.

As we dig deeper into chapter 3, we see that after confronting their disobedience and its consequences, our compassionate God made clothes of animal skin and clothed their nakedness (v21). Then God kicked them out of the Garden:

> Then the LORD God said, "Behold, the man has become like one of Us, knowing good and evil; and now, lest he stretch out his hand, and take also from the tree of life, and eat, and live forever"— 23therefore the LORD God sent him out from the garden of Eden, to cultivate the ground from which he was taken. 24So He drove the man out; and at the east of the garden of Eden He stationed the cherubim, and the flaming sword which turned every direction, to guard the way to the tree of life (3:22-24).

So our compassionate God made certain they could not get back into the garden to eat from the tree of life and remain in death for all eternity.

Here we see that the serpent did not lie to Eve about becoming like God ("knowing good and evil") for God says it is so out of His own mouth. From that we conclude that a part of Satan's strategy is to deal in partial truths and omitted consequences mixed in with complete lies and false implications. He uses that same strategy with us today because it works. Therefore, we must be diligent and alert to catch him in the act lest we fall into his trap. So pay very close attention to your own thoughts and their source, i.e., do they originate from your intentional consciousness, or, were they planted there by Satan?

Here in Genesis chapter 3, we also see demonstrations of God's love for humankind—the covering (compassion), driving them away from the tree of life (grace), stationing the cherubim and the flaming sword to guard the way to the tree of life (mercy). If the man and his wife had been able to eat now from the tree of life, they (and all their descendants) would be doomed to live forever in death—the horrible and regrettable consequence of their sin. That was Satan's ultimate objective. But oh the love, the grace and the mercy of our compassionate God!

Now, before we talk about what is happening in Genesis chapter 4, go back and read Genesis 3:8-19 in a modern translation such as NASB 1977 or 1995, NET, or NKJV.

Not My Fault

We see in Genesis 3:8 that God comes to visit the man and they discuss what has happened to the man and why.

God comes walking in the garden but no Adam.

So God calls out to him,

> "Where are you?"

Adam responds with,

> "I heard the sound of You in the Garden, and I was afraid because I was naked; so I hid myself."

God asks,

> "Who told you that you were naked? Have you eaten from the tree of which I commanded you not to eat?"

Adam responds saying,

> "The woman whom You gave to be with me, she gave me from the tree, and I ate."

So Adam is saying, if she had not given it to me, I would not have eaten of it. Therefore, it is Eve's fault. Yes, I did wrong, but it is the fault of the woman. And not only that, it is also Your fault too, God, because You are the One who gave this woman to be with me. Therefore, it is certainly not my fault!

In that same way today, you and I refuse to accept full responsibility for our own sinful disobedient actions. It is common for us to find someone else to blame instead of acknowledging our own intentional and unintentional transgressions.

So God turns to the woman and says,

> "What is this you have done?"

And she says what?

> "The serpent deceived me, and I ate."

In other words, it is not my fault. It is the serpent's fault. I did do wrong but it is not my fault for the serpent deceived me.

So God turns to the serpent. And He does not ask the serpent what is this you have done. He tells the serpent, you are in big trouble,

> "Cursed are you more than all cattle, and more than every beast of the field."

The other thing I want you to note here is, God goes on to tell the woman she is going to have pain in childbirth. Yet, even though she is going to have great pain, she is still going to desire her husband. It is going to be a vicious cycle for her and her female descendants.

Then God turns to the man and says here is the cost of your disobedience,

> "Because you have listened to the voice of your wife, and have eaten from the tree about which I commanded you, saying, 'You shall not eat from it'; Cursed is the ground because of you; In toil you shall eat of it All the days of your life (v17).

Note that the creation was not cursed because of the woman. Creation was cursed because of Adam who is God's ruling representative. (For many years, I believed it was Eve's fault.)

Make a note that all of God's creation is now cursed (Genesis 3:17-19, Romans 8:20-23).

In other words, Adam and his descendants are going to toil the rest of their lives just to survive. The ground is not going to produce for him as before. For the rest of their lives, he and his descendants are going to work hard to survive.

So allow me to interject this thought for your consideration: This too is the grace (favor) of God on the disobedient human. Why? Because "an idle mind is the devil's workshop".

I know I have thrown a lot of challenging thoughts your way. But we will go back through this all again. I wanted to give you a broad understanding for you to ponder for a while. So take a break. Meditate on these things and give them time to ruminate.

As we prepare now to move on from Genesis chapter 3, what is going on in chapter 4? What is the big deal when viewed through God's eyes?

Let us pray: Heavenly Father, in the name of Jesus, thank You for teaching us Your Word. And we beseech You to continue to teach us that we may understand Your Bible better and better each day. Open our eyes. Remove the blinders. We want to know Your Word, not to walk around with our heads puffed up because we can quote the Scriptures. But with Your Word abiding in us, we will know You and desire daily communion with You and You with us.

O God, hear our prayer today as one or more of Your servants have gathered here to learn who You are and who we truly are in Your sight. Stay in our midst. Pierce our hearts and overtake us today.

In the name of Jesus, We ask that You give us wisdom, You give us knowledge, You give us Your perspective, and You give us compassion for Your people. And give us a passion for Your Word so that Your people may truly understand and know, and be able to teach others that they too may come to understand and know, who in turn will teach others as well. This is our supplication, O' God. Hear our prayer, in the name of Jesus, the Christ, we pray, amen!

4

CAIN AND ABEL

SCRIPTURE: Exodus 34:1-9

Prayer: Heavenly Father, in the name of Jesus, we invite You to commune with us today as we dig deeper into Your Word. Oh God, pour out Your spirit upon us anew today. Give us a fresh anointing. Give us a heart that thirsts for Your Word, that thirsts for Your righteousness, that thirsts to experience Your presence. Give us a strong desire, even a passion for Your Word. Open our hearts and minds to understand Your Word. Let today be the beginning of a new life for the rest of our natural lives that we may walk obediently before You, that we may give You the reverence and the priority You deserve. May we honor You as our Abba, Father, Daddy. In the name of Your Son, Jesus, the Christ we pray, amen.

∼

In Genesis chapter 4, Adam and Eve have already committed the great sin and now they have two children, Cain and Abel. Take a moment and read Genesis 4:1-8:

> Now the man had relations with his wife Eve, and she conceived and gave birth to Cain, and she said, "I have gotten a manchild with the help of the LORD." 2And again, she gave birth to his brother Abel. And Abel was a keeper of flocks, but Cain was a tiller of the ground. 3So it came about in the course of time that Cain brought an offering to the LORD of the fruit of the ground. 4And Abel, on his part also brought of the firstlings of his flock and of their fat portions. And the LORD had regard for Abel and for his offering; 5but for Cain and for his offering He had no regard. So Cain became very angry and his countenance fell. 6Then the LORD said to Cain, "Why are you angry? And why has your countenance fallen? 7"If you do well, will not your countenance be lifted up? And if you do not do well, sin is crouching at the door; and its desire is for you, but you must master it." 8And Cain told Abel his brother. And it came about when they were in the field, that Cain rose up against Abel his brother and killed him.

Now, look back at Genesis 3:15 where God is speaking to the serpent after Adam and Eve sinned:

> "And I will put enmity [hostility] between you and the woman, and between your seed and her seed; He shall bruise you on the head, and you shall bruise Him on the heel."

Beginning of Hostility

In Genesis 3:15, because the humans are "dead" due to Satan's cunning deception, God is declaring the hostility (enmity) that is going to proliferate between the seed (offspring) of the serpent (i.e., Satan) and the seed (offspring) of the woman. God is also indicating how He is going to resolve the conflict between them. In other words, this is God's first reference to a future redemption (from "death") in a single person whom we now know to be Jesus Christ, the only begotten Son of God.

Adam and Eve have eaten. They are dead or dying! And I know some students are still wrestling with this dead thing. But what I want you to keep in mind is that God said if you eat you are going to die that very same day. They ate. Therefore, they are dead. What we do not know is, what is this death thing? That is our problem. We think we know. But we really do not know because the Scriptures have not told us here in Genesis what this death is in God's eyes. It simply says dying you shall die. We must believe God when He says they are going to die if they eat. We must believe that when they ate, in God's eyes, they actually in fact did die that very day. We must have confidence in the veracity of God (Numbers 23:19).

Remember our goal: to see the Scriptures through God's eyes.

Genesis 3:15 says there will come One of the seed of the woman who will bruise the serpent on the head, a serious blow. The serpent will bruise the One seed of the woman on the heel, a crippling blow not leading to cessation. Genesis 3:15 is also informing us that the offspring of Adam and Eve shall be of two types, both coming from the same womb—the seed of the serpent and the seed of the woman. Genesis chapter 4 expands on that theme (as expressed in Genesis 3:15) by painting for us a picture of the enmity (hostility) God says is going to occur between them as a consequence of Adam's disobedience.

Essentially in 3:15, God is putting the serpent (Satan) on notice that from the woman there is going to come two types of seed (offspring), not just one—children of the serpent and children of the woman—two types of seed. Satan apparently thought that, as a consequence of his deception, all offspring would be his and they would spread his image over all the earth. But God says, no, there will be two contrasting and competing seed types.

As we move into Genesis chapter 4, the Bible immediately introduces us to the two types of seed—Cain and Abel. Chapter 4 presents a picture of the current and future relationship between the seed of the serpent and the seed of the woman. Cain, who was born first, is the seed of the serpent. However, you cannot know that for certain by reading Genesis alone. God has presented only the primary elements of this picture in Genesis. I am simply telling you now from whom Cain originates so you can better appreciate the essential point of chapter 4. But I can point you to New Testament passages that clearly tell us that Cain is the seed of the serpent and the serpent is a representative or tool of Satan.

Remember, the Bible explains the Bible. So trust me on that for now.

Abel is the seed of the woman. Cain was born first. Therefore, the details of Cain's contribution to the development and structure of society are given first. That suggests that the seed of the serpent is likely to be more in number and is more apt to be foremost (most prominent in rank, importance, or position) in society and most other ways as well, as the remainder of chapter 4 delineates.

The two sons grow up and develop their own way of life. At a certain point, they come to worship God with each bringing their offerings. Cain was a gardener or farmer. He brought fruit of the ground. Abel was a rancher. He brought animals. But there is a major distinction between what they brought. Cain brought "an offering" of ordinary quality of fruits and vegetables, nothing special. Abel brought the very best that he had "of the firstlings of his flock and of their fat portions". That is what God expects from His children today as well. He expects His children to give Him the very best of themselves and the "first fruits" of the increase of their wealth, i.e., their tithes and offerings.

God was satisfied with Abel and his offering. He was not satisfied with Cain and his ordinary offering. Cain concludes that God was not satisfied with his offering because of Abel (i.e., it is not my fault).

Some theologians conclude that the problem with Cain's sacrifice was that there was no shed blood. Since the passage (vv 4-5) contains no other indicators for the nature of the sacrifice demanded by God at this point in time, and since I have found no further explanation in the Scriptures directly or indirectly confirming the requirements for their offerings, this author will limit his conclusions solely to what the passage and its surrounding context provide.

Take a good look at Cain's reaction. In their dead state, Adam and Eve both said my disobedience was not my fault. Now Cain is saying, OK, God does not like my offering. It's Abel's fault. So all I need to do is what? Get rid of the problem. Then, all is well. So Cain murders his brother, the beginning of the hostility (the enmity) between the two types of seed, as declared in Genesis 3:15.

But this is not the first expression of hostility. Read Genesis 4:5 again. Do you see it? Do you see the enmity, the animosity toward God depicted in Cain's countenance and anger as God chastises him? He could not take his anger out on God, so he chose the next available thing, his righteous brother.

For a broader understanding of Cain's actions, see the article, 1. The Legacy of Cain: Departure from God (Genesis 4:3-24) by Roger Pascoe.

Make Your Assessment

I have thrown a lot of stuff at you, probably a perspective you have not heard. It may cause you to wonder and to have questions. If it does, great! I want you to have questions. And I also want you to ask your questions. So take a moment to make some notes and list your questions and concerns. Hopefully, you will come to a point where you will see the truth in this interpretation for yourself and you will not say that

Arlington McRae said it. Instead, you will be able to say confidently, it is right here in the Bible. You do not need to say it came from Arlington McRae. I want you to be able to see it with your own eyes and understand it in your own spirit. When you walk away from this volume, you should be prepared to say, I see it with my own eyes, in my own heart. Therefore, it is not just what Arlington McRae says, I know for myself it is biblical.

I realize that for some we may get to a point where you might give up because you say, "I just cannot see that." And if we do get to a point where you say, "I know you have told me all this but I just cannot see it that way," all I ask you to do is, do not throw it away! Revisit it as often as you will. Research it in respected commentaries. Talk to God about it. Ask God saying, "God we have this man telling us this stuff and I am not sure he knows what he is talking about. No one has ever told this to me before. I think he allowed someone to deceive him; if not, then You show me. If You want me to see it like he sees it, if he is speaking truth, You show me that I might comprehend it for myself."

I have a faithful God! You have a faithful God. He knows how to give good gifts to His children. And He wants you to learn His Word well for your own priestly obligations (1 Peter 2:9-12). So in your prayers, I ask you to pray that God would show you His Word that you may interpret it through His eyes. Have you ever prayed that prayer? God, show me Your Word through Your eyes. Teach me so I may see it the way You see it. I do not want to see it like ordinary humans see it. I want to see it the way God sees it.

Pray that prayer. Go ahead, ask God. He will surely answer you in His own way and in His own time.

Let us pray: Father, in the name of Jesus, we thank You. We are thankful for what our hearts have felt. We are thankful for our eyes being opened.

As the reader goes forth to the next lesson, we pray, Father, that what we have given them here will be in their heart and on their mind, and that You would cause them to meditate on it day and night. For You say in Your Word in Psalm 1, "And in His law he meditates day and night." Father, teach them to meditate on Your Word. Teach them to study it with a passion. Give them, Father, a passionate desire to understand Your Word. And then, when they ask You, I pray that You would open their eyes that they may see. Then pour out Your blessing upon them that they would rejoice in what You have shown them.

When they come to know and understand, we ask that You would give them a consuming desire to teach others so that a host of others may understand and know also. We thank You now knowing it is already done. We bless You. We honor You. And know, Father, our desire, our passion is to glorify You and to be obedient to Your Word, Your will and Your way. In Jesus name we pray, amen.

5

WALKING WITH GOD

SCRIPTURE: Psalm 86

Prayer: Allow this Psalm of Supplication and Trust to serve as our prayer and source of meditation for this session.

∼

In this session, I thought we would take a break from our arduous journey and focus solely on our relationship with our God and Father and His Son. If this does not appeal to you, please feel free to move on to the next chapter.

I would like you to take a few moments now to concentrate your attention on JESUS, the sacrificial Lamb of God, our Deliverer, Savior and Lord. For now, forget about the cares of this evil world. Forget about what you want; think about Him and what He wants. We have already spent the past several days focused on what we want. Let us spend some time right now thinking about what Jesus desires for us.

The Christian Life

When I read my Bible, it tells me that Abba (Daddy, God the Father) desires a relationship with each of His children. Not a relationship like the one that simply claims we have a relationship. But one where we do in fact have a genuine and intimate reciprocal love relationship with Him. One that looks a lot like a faithful marriage relationship, only deeper. Keep in mind that the Father and the Son are one. Therefore, a relationship with the Son, Jesus, is a relationship with the Father also (1 John 2:21-25).

In our love relationship with a natural person, we enjoy spending time with them. We talk with them. We share. We want to be with them. Jesus desires that same intimate time with you. As a matter of fact, He is a jealous God who is passionate about spending quality time with you, preferably your daily first time (your first fruit).

So what might an intimate relationship with Jesus look like? Please take some time right now to view the YouTube video presentation by John Paine (now deceased) on one of his favorite subjects. The video presentation is titled, Don't Wait Until You're Dying Before You Start Living. This video, however, may be more appropriately titled, *Walking With God*.

Did you enjoy the video? My spirit is rejuvenated each time I view it.

The purpose of showing you the John Paine video is to give you an authentic and clear portrayal of what the Christian life should actually be. Hopefully you have received the realization that your own relationship with Jesus Christ (if you have one) needs work. I know mine does.

We live in our little circle and we often are not aware of the things going on outside of it. But if one would observe the things going on around them, one may come to the realization that what I have and where I am in life is not sufficient. I could have a whole lot more. I could even be a whole lot more. So that is what the video lesson is designed to show, that there is something greater that Jesus has for you. You are settling for the things that feel good and look good to the flesh. Jesus has something for you that is much greater and much grander than what you are experiencing or aspiring to. But it means you have to relinquish your flesh. You must give up what it desires, give up what society at large is telling you that you ought to have, that you are missing out on.

You may not realize that we are in love with and enslaved to the things of this *ungodly world system*, especially in the more developed countries such as the United States. This world has structures and institutions to keep us enslaved. The world is pumping information into our heads hundreds of times per day to enslave us and keep us there. You might say well, preacher, what are you talking about. I am talking about that shiny box that's in everyone's house. Some of us have them in every room. We call it television. And that television is telling you all the time, your life is not worth two cents because you do not have this beautiful thing right here. And if you had this wonderful thing right here, buddy, you would have it going on. Everybody would be envious of you. You would be the special one! You ought to have it. You deserve it! Your life is going to be so grand. The best thing about it, it is easy for you to afford. It can be yours for as little as $99 per month, less than $25 per week.

Being deceived, we rush out (or go to the Internet) and buy that exciting new thing. And after two months (if that long), we realize we are no better off than before we got it. But now we are enslaved to the $99 monthly payments. Then, another commercial comes on, and another, and tell us the same thing. Therefore, we have houses filled with things we do not need and barely use. Or we are enticed to take grand vacations that we cannot afford. Therefore, we spend the next twelve months or more struggling to pay it off. And the cycle continues year after year. Can you relate?

What I want you to understand is this is all the skillfully deceptive plan of Satan. He is called the deceiver and for good reason. His main job, if he cannot kill you, is to derail you so you are no longer on the track God wants you on. Instead, you are on the track he put you on.

His plan is to keep you away from God, to keep you from praying, studying and meditating on God's Word. If he can just keep your mind off God, then it is on what he offers you—vanity! Yes! He has these things in the world to keep you busy so you do not have time for God. Therefore, you try to fit God in, if you can find the time.

"God, I will go to church on Sunday. I will give You a whole hour and a half. But if they go over, I have got to go. The football (or basketball) game is coming on. I can't be in church while the game is on! Why do they have to hold church services so long anyway?"

John Paine's presentation is designed to say, those things we are all involved in, we all participate in, the things of this ungodly world system are keeping us from the superior quality of life that Jesus offers us (Matthew 6:24-33). Your highest and best life is walking with God! Luke 9:23 urges you to, "Deny yourself, take up your cross and follow Me [Jesus]". That verse is urging us to give up what we want, give up what we are seeking after, give up what your flesh is craving and take up your cross—the life Jesus has commanded you to live—take that up and follow in Jesus' footsteps. That is what JESUS wants you to do.

"Draw near to God, and He will draw near to you" (James 4:8). "For in His presence there is fullness of joy. At His right hand are pleasures forevermore" (Psalm 16:11). Therefore, "Delight yourself in the Lord; And He will give you the desires of your heart" (Psalm 37:4).

Be You Holy

All right, let's go back to the beginning of what we are talking about here. One of the questions before us is, what role does the Bible have in your daily life? What influence does it have on the way you actually live and prioritize your life? When you read it, do you say it is good to know and then go off and do the things you always have? Or, do you read it and say, I have to change what I am doing because what I am doing is not pleasing to my God and my Savior and Lord. And if you do not say that, do you say in your prayer, "God, change me? Take a look at the ugliness in me; take a good hard look at the things I desire that are not of You and remove them from me." Or, do you just gather the knowledge unto yourself so that you can spout it out amongst other Christians to puff yourself up? What role does God's Word have in shaping your life's priorities? You do know that God has called those who are Christians out of the world (society at large) to be holy (unique, righteous) and blameless before Him (Ephesians 1:3-8)?

The world is all the busy unbelievers, the social, educational, economic and political systems, values and institutions that Satan has created to take advantage of our ignorance and lust. That is the world. God has called us out of that. And He has placed us in a position where we are to be unique (holy) in the world. We are to be holy, consecrated unto God to live the life God has called us to live—to be honest and truthful, to be fair, to be loving, to be kind, to be generous, to be givers not just takers, to lookout for our fellow humans just like we look out for ourselves. In other words, God has called us to be a peculiar people (1 Peter 2:9-10) in the eyes of the society at large. When the world looks at us, the world ought to say, those are some strange people. But do you know what happens? When the world says those are some strange people, what do we say? "I don't want to be strange!" So we give up what God has called us to and we go back to being our old self so the world will accept us and love us (1 John 2:15-

17). Jesus said the world will hate you because it has hated Me. So, as a Christian, you are in the world, but you are not of the world. Notice Jesus' prayer to the Father:

> "But now I come to You; and these things I speak in the world, that they may have My joy made full in themselves. 14"I have given them Your word; and the world has hated them, because they are not of the world, even as I am not of the world. 15"I do not ask You to take them out of the world, but to keep them from the evil one. 16"They are not of the world, even as I am not of the world. 17"Sanctify them in the truth; Your word is truth. 18"As You did send Me into the world, I also have sent them into the world. 19"And for their sakes I sanctify Myself, that they themselves also may be sanctified in truth. 20"I do not ask in behalf of these alone, but for those also who believe in Me through their word; 21that they may all be one; even as You, Father, are in Me, and I in You, that they also may be in Us; that the world may believe that You did send Me (John 17:13-21).

God has called us to be unique and holy, unlike the world. You shall be holy, for I am holy (1 Peter 1:13-16). Christ is calling us also to His ministry of reconciliation (2 Corinthians 5:18-21).

Think On These Things

Please set aside some time to ponder and ruminate on these things:

- The universal (or catholic) church—all

believers all over the world from all times—comprises the family of God.
- The local church body—each corporate church family in various communities throughout the world.
- Body of Christ—The apostle Paul tells us the church is the body of Christ and Jesus is its head (<u>1 Corinthians 12:12-31</u>, <u>Colossians 1:17-18</u>). Looking at a physical body, from the neck down is the body Paul is talking about. Above the neck is Jesus Christ who is the head of the body. A physical body is composed of different organs and limbs. Therefore, Paul informs us, "…But God has so composed the body, giving more abundant honor to that member which lacked, 25that there should be no division in the body, but that the members should have the same care for one another. 26And if one member suffers, all the members suffer with it; if one member is honored, all the members rejoice with it. 27Now you are Christ's body, and individually members of it" (1 Corinthians 12:24-27).
- Resolved: The church, the universal (or catholic) church (not to be confused with the Roman Catholic Church), has lost its way.
- For the Son of Man has come to seek and to save that which was lost (Luke 19:10).
- The Great Commission—And Jesus came up and spoke to them [the apostles], saying, "All authority has been given to Me in heaven and on earth. 19"Go therefore and make disciples of all the nations, baptizing them in the name of the Father and the Son and the Holy Spirit,

20teaching them to observe all that I commanded you; and lo, I am with you always, even to the end of the age" (Matthew 28:18-20) [Brackets mine].
- Considering the last two passages, what was Jesus' purpose here on earth? To reveal the Father to those given Him out of the world and to make them into true disciples who will make other true disciples as they are going through life.
- What responsibility did Jesus give to His apostles and disciples? Their responsibility is to make disciples of all nations. Jesus did not tell His followers to seek and save the lost. He told them to go make disciples. He did not say go and evangelize. Why? Because evangelism is only an event, a phase in the process of making disciples. A true disciple is one who becomes like his Master. (Matthew 10:24-25a). And our Master is one who seeks and saves the lost. But that is only a part of His objective. He then turns them into true disciples, whose goal is to evangelize the lost and train all new converts for true discipleship. Jesus called those who follow Him, His disciples. So Jesus' ministry was devoted to the disciple-making process as He revealed the Father to His creation that does not know Him or receive Him.
- When God created the world, He created biological entities with life in them. He also gave them seed. For example, the tree or plant produces fruit; the fruit has seed. The seed produces more plants and trees, which produce more fruit with seed in them. Jesus developed

His followers into mature disciples with His seed (His Word) in them. Upon leaving the earth, He instructed His disciples to go make more disciples. Therefore, a disciple of Jesus Christ matures to what his Master is and to what His Master is doing. A disciple of Jesus Christ, therefore, is one who produces other disciples (fruit) with God's seed in them. What is the seed in His disciples? The Word of God, the gospel of Jesus Christ. A mature, true disciple then, has the Word (seed) of God in herself or himself. Therefore, they are equipped to go sow that seed in like manner as Mother Nature. As with all seed, Jesus, by the Holy Spirit, will cause that seed to germinate and produce more fruit, i.e., converts who will mature to producing fruit (converts) with seed in them. That seed in turn will be planted (sown into the life of others) to produce much more fruit.

- So when Jesus says go make disciples, He is saying go produce people who are mature and obedient in Me, who have My Word in them, who will abide in Me and who will in turn witness by word and deed to the world so that all might believe and accept Jesus Christ as their Savior. Then disciple them to spiritual maturity, having the Word in themselves and who are passionate about abiding in Christ, and so on and so on until Jesus returns (John 15:5-10).
- Too many of us have a distorted view of missionary work. So often we think missionary work means going overseas somewhere. But

Jesus told His disciples in Acts 1 to begin at Jerusalem, then to Judea and on to Samaria, then to the uttermost parts of the world. Applying that concept to the present day, we could begin in our home, to our extended family, to our neighborhood and work our way outward to our city, state, nation and the whole world. Because so many of us think that missionary work is only overseas somewhere, we overlook or we fail to begin in our home, among our loved ones. As a result, family members in our own homes are on their way to hell, perishing right under our nose. And we are ignoring their woefully dreadful plight! So what if you get push-back? Isn't it worth it to keep them out of hell's eternal damnation?

Please think deeply on these things daily with thoroughness and care as you walk hand in hand with Jesus our Savior.

May Jesus Christ richly bless all that you set your mind to for the sake of His kingdom.

Let us pray: Father we give You thanks today for Your Word. We give You thanks for these Your children who are seeking to better understand Your Word. They have joined in with us today, enthusiastically and we thank You. We pray, Father, that what they have gained today will be as seed planted in rich soil and that it would take root, that You would pour Your rain upon it and let Your sun shine bright so that it may take root and grow into a strong and mighty tree that produces much fruit with seed in it. We pray, Father, that You would continue to enlighten them with Your Word throughout the weeks and the months to come. Keep their minds on what You have shown them here today. Answer their questions. Open their eyes that they may see. Remove the blinders that they may see clearly, that Your name may be glorified in them, in their hearts and in their actions. In Jesus name we pray, amen.

6

MEANING OF DEATH

SCRIPTURE: Exodus 34:5-9

Prayer: Heavenly Father, we your humble servants are seeking Your face today. We do not come before You so we can say we have fulfilled our obligation to You for today. But we come here seeking Your face, prayerfully hoping that You would visit with us so we might experience Your loving presence. Therefore we ask You, Father, to forgive us of our sins and remove from us anything that would prevent Your communing here with us today.

We confess we have indeed sinned against You. For we have not loved You like You commanded us nor have we loved one another as Your Son has loved us. We have not followed Your commandments as You have instructed us.

Forgive us, Father, and cleanse us from all unrighteousness. Give us a clean heart, a pure heart, and renew the right spirit within us, that we may indeed commune with You and You would greatly desire to commune with us. Let there be nothing to separate us. In Jesus name we pray, amen.

I want to ask you, if you would this coming week, to study our opening Scripture passage, not one time, but make it your daily time with the Lord. Spend fifteen to thirty minutes in meditation and rumination, pondering His awesome character traits (a glimpse of His person) each and every day. Consider also how one or more of these traits are quoted or referenced throughout the Bible. Ask God to show you, through His eyes, what this passage is saying to His children here in the twenty-first century. If you have a commentary (or using an online commentary such as the Free Bible Commentary), consider what the commentators have to say about this passage. Begin with a search of the word "compassion" and/or "compassionate".

I have discovered that this passage is quoted or referenced, in part, throughout the Old and New Testaments. So review in context other passages where it is quoted. And since it is quoted or referenced so much, it has to be something that God wants us to know, understand and appreciate. So I ask that you spend some quality time this week with Jesus and with this passage. Ask God to show you through His eyes the specific message in this passage for you. And please give Him thanks and praise when He does.

∽

Meaning of Death | 133

I thought we would have a relaxed discussion this session. The idea behind this relaxed discussion is to do a review to regain our perspective. We have been away from our primary focus for a little while now. So we want to get back in tune with our main objectives.

A Quick Review

A goal of our series is to prepare you to read, study and interpret the Bible for yourself. When we began our series, we asked you some very foundational questions. Can you recall the questions we asked?

> "Do you believe the Bible is in fact the Word of God?"

And?

> "Do you believe it is inerrant in its original manuscripts?"

Then, the follow-up question in our line of reasoning is,

> "What role does the Bible play in the way you actually live your life and in all your relationships?"

I am convinced that Scripture teaches that when we know, we will be judged according to what we know. So if you believe the Bible is the Word of God and you believe it is inerrant, does your life reflect that belief? We actually order our lives according to what we truly believe.

If I believe that walking across a busy street I will likely be run over, I will order my life according to that belief. I will wait for the light to turn green or when there is no traffic. I will look both ways to be certain there is no vehicle coming before I walk across that street. In the same way, does your life reflect your sincere belief in the teachings of Jesus Christ who will judge all humankind? Have you ordered your life according to that belief?

There is a famous saying that goes something like this: "What you do speaks so loudly I can hardly hear what you say." Let us apply this wisdom to the question at hand. Looking at your life, are your actions drowning out your saying to me, "I believe the Bible is the Word of God and I believe it is inerrant in its original manuscripts?" Are your contradictory actions drowning out your boisterous words? That is a question you have to answer for yourself. I invite you to spend some time this week thinking about that during your daily time with the Lord. And if you find any failings in that regard, I strongly recommend that you repent and talk to Jesus about it.

He knows we have failings. But He wants you to admit that you do. You will not surprise Him with anything you tell Him. The words coming out of your mouth are for you and not so much for Him. So if you say God, I have been saying that I believe the Bible is Your Word. I have been saying that I believe You are the Creator of the heavens and earth and You created me. I believe the Bible is Your revelation for my good. But my actions do not lineup with what I have been saying. If you will admit that, then God wants only one more thing from you and that is for you to allow the Holy Spirit to take charge of your life.

> "God I need Your grace to make my life lineup with Your Word. Therefore, I willingly surrender my life totally to You. Amen"

You see, God knows you cannot do it on your own. But He needs you to recognize that you cannot do it on your own. Know confidently that He is able to do it in you, if you are truly willing, if you truly desire it.

Then we went further by asking you to consider seriously these additional questions:

> "What are we doing as a church? And,
>
> "What should we be doing?"

Therefore, another goal of this book is to help us answer these questions in light of the nature of humans versus the person of God. So, as we proceed, think on these questions as well.

Now that we know our focus, the next step is to take a closer look at the Word of God, the Bible, to gain God's perspective of humankind. For I am one who believes that we actually do not know who we are at the core (our heart). Therefore, we do not truly appreciate what Jesus has done and continues to do on our behalf. If one believes that he or she is already good, then God's salvation has not done very much for him or her. But that person over there on drugs, doing burglaries, gang-banging, murdering, fornicating, mugging or raping and telling lies, God has to do a lot for that person. But He did not have to do very much for me. If that is your thought process, then, you tend not to reverence God very much because He has not done very much for you.

Recall the sinful woman in the Bible who shed tears on Jesus' feet and the host was wondering how Jesus could allow her to touch Him because she was an immoral woman, a known sinner? But Jesus said, if you knew how much she has been forgiven, then you would understand (Luke 7:36-50). She indeed was a sinner. But the Pharisee was not giving thanks to God or showing deference. He had little to be forgiven as far as he was concerned. He was a faithful churchgoer. He could even have thought he had no sin to be forgiven.

So take a moment and consider this: A part of what we are looking at here in this volume is who we are and what forgiveness do we (or did we) need?

Take some time right now to appreciate the message in this song, Free by Kierra Sheard, especially if you are not yet a believer.

Who Are Humans?

So that we might truly grasp this mysterious section of the Scriptures, we are going to begin again our discussion where humankind began, Genesis 1:26-27:

> Then God said, "Let Us make man in Our image, according to Our likeness; and let them rule over the fish of the sea and over the birds of the sky and over the cattle and over all the earth, and over every creeping thing that creeps on the earth." 27And God created man in His own image, in the image of God He created him; male and female He created them.

God says we are going to make humankind and we are going to make them like Us. We are going to make them in Our image, an icon of Us, according to Our likeness. And We are going to give them dominion so they might rule the earth in accordance with Our likeness.

Now, let us look at Genesis 2:16-17:

> And the LORD God commanded the man, saying, "From any tree of the garden you may eat freely; 17but from the tree of the knowledge of good and evil you shall not eat, for in the day that you eat from it you shall surely die."

The key question for us is,

> When did God say they would die?
>
> "The same day that they eat."

That is the answer I urge you to accept faithfully. You must be convinced that on the day that they should eat the forbidden fruit, on that very day, dying they shall die? Are you convinced of it? Do not simply say, "Yes, I believe it," if you are not truly convinced.

Some study partners may still be wrestling in their hearts and minds with this question:

> "How can Adam and Eve be dead and I be here? If they died, then I would not exist because all humankind came from them. We read in Genesis chapters 4 and 5 and beyond that they and their descendants are still "alive" and producing children. So how could they have died when they ate?"

Right now make sure you get this one point: Do you believe you can trust what God says? For example, have you chosen to believe Jesus the Christ for your own soul's salvation?

This passage (2:16-17) is a quote from God's own mouth. No matter how it looks, no matter what your perspective is, do you believe God when He says they will die in the day they should eat? And do you believe that they actually died when they ate? If we cannot get past that, then there is a foggy pathway ahead in our journey with extremely limited visibility. Because, if you do not believe that, then, when you read Genesis chapter 3 and following and you see that they ate and yet are still walking around, you will conclude, erroneously, that they are not dead, that God must have lied or He did not mean what He said. But the fact is, in God's eyes, after they ate in chapter 3, they were dead and dying. So the question is, then, do you believe the Bible or not?

At this point however, what we do not know is God's definition of "death" in this particular passage. If we decide that they did not die, then we have no incentive to even probe for God's unique definition of death in this passage. There would be no reason to even ask what is God's definition of death. So keep this in mind as you study various Scriptures.

We think we know the meaning of death. But do we? This is frustrating, is it not? But we are going to solve this mystery very soon. OK?

Pause now! Take a deep breath, or two if necessary. Exhale and relax your shoulder muscles to release the tension. Take another deep breath. Slowly exhale again to release the remaining tension.

Now, let us go on to Genesis 3:4-5:

> And the serpent said to the woman, "You surely shall not die! 5"For God knows that in the day you eat from it your eyes will be opened, and you will be like God, knowing good and evil."

Focus on verse 4 for a moment. God says, if you eat you shall die. The serpent says, if you eat you shall not die. The serpent is saying outright, God is lying to you. Now Adam and Eve are faced with the question at that moment, "Whom do we believe?" And that is God's same question to you today. Jesus has presented the Word of God to you in the midst of Satan's lies! "Whom do you believe?" Do you believe what you heard (or read) from Jesus? Or, do you believe only what you can see through the eyes of the world?

Now, read the next verse:

> When the woman saw that the tree was good for food, and that it was a delight to the eyes, and that the tree was desirable to make one wise, she took from its fruit and ate; and she gave also to her husband with her, and he ate (Genesis 3:6).

What do we see?

What did they decide?

"To eat from the forbidden tree."

Yes, but whom did they decide they would believe?

"The serpent."

They made it quite clear to us, in their actions, that they did not believe the omniscient (all knowing) God. Or, they decided that they did believe Him, but they preferred death over life. You see, things are never simple, are they?

Adam and Eve were faced with the question, whom should we believe? Do we believe the serpent or do we believe God? Their actions say they believed the serpent. Or, they decided they preferred death (the knowledge of good and evil) over life, one or the other.

So the woman saw that the fruit was good for food (v6). God said that it was good for food back in Genesis 2:9. The woman saw that it was a delight to the eyes (v6). God also said so in 2:9. Then, she saw that it was "desirable to make one wise". That is the problem!

She thought, if I eat of this fruit, I will be wise; it is going to make me wise like God! I will know good and evil just like God. And she probably did not think so much about knowing good and evil, rather she probably was most influenced by the thought, "I will be like God". That was also Satan's goal when he rebelled against God (Isaiah 14:12-14).

Now, the New Testament tells us that the woman was deceived. But Adam was not deceived (1 Timothy 2:12-14). You must get your head around that. The woman was deceived. But Adam was not. Therefore, Adam intentionally transgressed the commandment of God, deliberately. And I suspect he was probably fully aware of the consequences.

Returning to the Scriptures, read Genesis 3:7-13:

> Then the eyes of both of them were opened, and they knew that they were naked; and they sewed fig leaves together and made themselves loin coverings. 8 And they heard the sound of the LORD God walking in the garden in the cool of the day, and the man and his wife hid themselves from the presence of the LORD God among the trees of the garden. 9Then the LORD God called to the man, and said to him, "Where are you?" 10And he said, "I heard the sound of You in the garden, and I was afraid because I was naked; so I hid myself." 11And He said, "Who told you that you were naked? Have you eaten from the tree of which I commanded you not to eat?" 12And the man said, "The woman whom You gave to be with me, she gave me from the tree, and I ate." 13Then the LORD God said to the woman, "What is this you have done?" And the woman said, "The serpent deceived me, and I ate."

As we observe this last passage, we see the first of the serious consequences of their disobedience—shame, fear and separation.

You may want to write a particular note of this discussion. Why? Because, at some point in the future, you may ask yourself saying, we spent a lot of repetitive time on this question. Why is this man spending so much time on this single question?

It is because this portion of the Bible provides the setting or window to truly understanding the rest of the Bible. The Bible story will make a significant pivot, or not, depending on your understanding of these passages. If you cannot see clearly through this window, you are not able to see clearly the rest of the Bible.

Death Versus Life

Recall that the New Testament explains the Old Testament. So, turn to the book of John and read 17:1-3:

> These things Jesus spoke; and lifting up His eyes to heaven, He said, "Father, the hour has come; glorify Your Son, that the Son may glorify You, 2even as You gave Him authority over all mankind, that to all whom You have given Him, He may give eternal life. 3"And this is eternal life, that they may know You, the only true God, and Jesus Christ whom You have sent.

So how does God's Christ (the Son of Man) define life?

> Look at the above passage. Tell me what is life. Read verse three again. Now, what is life?
>
> "Knowing God and knowing His Son, Jesus Christ."
>
> Amen! *Life is knowing God the Father, the only true God, and Jesus the Christ, Whom the true God sent!* That is life!

As you meditate on that and consider it, you may get hung up on the word "eternal". And the devil may attempt to deceive you by telling you that passage is talking about eternal life. It is not talking about life you can have right now. Or, he is going to try to confuse you. But this right-now life that God gives to those who believe Jesus is also eternal.

So take a moment and think about this point. What is life? Get it firmly planted in your brain. If you have a red-letter Bible, know that these are the words of Jesus Christ. These are the words Jesus spoke to the Father in prayer. So the two are in agreement.

On the day Adam and Eve ate of the fruit, they died. What is life? Knowing God and knowing Jesus Christ, His Son.

What then is death? God said in the day that you eat, dying you shall die. They ate. Therefore they died. What is death? Death is the opposite of life! *Death in Genesis 2:17 is not knowing God and not knowing His Son.*

God is saying therefore, in Genesis 2:16-17, in the day you eat you shall surely begin a journey (a fall) ("dying you shall die") leading to a state where you (and your seed after you) will not know Me. *Eventually, all your descendants shall become completely and totally separated from and lose all knowledge of, awareness of and desire for Me and My ways.*

Therefore, this death is the death of separation. What we in the church refer to (but rarely explain) as *spiritual death.* Yes, it is spiritual but it is also deadly serious and must not be taken lightly. Because this perspective opens the window to your comprehension of the actions and reactions of humans and God throughout biblical history as well as here in the twenty-first century, and beyond.

While on this subject, physical or natural death also is a death of separation, the separation of the spirit and soul from the physical body (Genesis 35:16-19).

For a more scholarly analysis of Genesis 2:16-17, see the article, <u>Lessons From The Garden: "Dying You Shall Die"</u> by Mike Boling.

For a modern day understanding of the consequences of Adam and Eve's disobedience, take some time now to listen to the sermon, <u>Satan's Tricks and Traps</u> by Dr. Tony Evans on YouTube.

I contend we find a New Testament partial explanation of the dying process experienced by our foreparents in Paul's discourse to the Romans. Take a close look at Romans 1:18-32:

> For the wrath of God is revealed from heaven against all ungodliness and unrighteousness of men, who suppress the truth in unrighteousness, 19because that which is known about God is evident within them; for God made it evident to them. 20For since the creation of the world His invisible attributes, His eternal power and divine nature, have been clearly seen, being understood through what has been made, so that they are without excuse.
>
> *21For even though they knew God, they did not honor Him as God, or give thanks; but they became futile in their speculations, and their foolish heart was darkened. 22Professing to be wise, they became fools, 23and exchanged the glory of the incorruptible God for an image in the form of corruptible man and of birds and four-footed animals and crawling creatures.*
>
> *24 Therefore God gave them over in the lusts of their hearts to impurity, that their bodies might be dishonored among them. 25For they exchanged the truth of God for a lie, and worshiped*

and served the creature rather than the Creator, who is blessed forever. Amen.

26 For this reason God gave them over to *degrading passions*; for their women exchanged the natural function for that which is unnatural, 27and in the same way also the men abandoned the natural function of the woman and burned in their desire toward one another, men with men committing indecent acts and receiving in their own persons the due penalty of their error.

28 And just as they did not see fit to acknowledge God any longer, God gave them over to a *depraved mind,* to do those things which are not proper, 29being filled with all unrighteousness, wickedness, greed, evil; full of envy, murder, strife, deceit, malice; they are gossips, 30slanderers, haters of God, insolent, arrogant, boastful, inventors of evil, disobedient to parents, 31without understanding, untrustworthy, unloving, unmerciful; 32and, although they know the ordinance of God, that those who practice such things are worthy of death, they not only do the same, but also give hearty approval to those who practice them [Italics mine].

What is a depraved mind? A decaying mind with the inability to perceive wrong in what they are doing. On the day Adam and Eve ate of the fruit, they died a progressive death leading to all their later descendants eventually having a depraved mind.

In summary then, when God says Adam shall die should he eat of the forbidden fruit, He is saying you will separate, lose, and sever your relationship with

God. And eventually, all your descendants will lose all knowledge of God resulting in the commission of horrendous sinful acts. Therefore today, children are born in households with no knowledge of God and no one to teach them about God. They are dead! The household is dead!

Nowhere is this truth better substantiated than in John 1:9-11:

> There was the true light [Jesus, Son of God] which, coming into the world, enlightens every man. 10He was in the world, and the world was made through Him, and *the world did not know Him.* 11He came to His own [Israel], and those who were His own did not receive Him [Italics mine].

Dead People Dead Children

When we read Genesis chapter 4, we see there are two sons born of Adam and Eve—Cain and Abel. We know the story that Cain murdered Abel. And the New Testament Scriptures ask the question, "And for what reason did he (Cain) slay him (Abel)?"

> By this the children of God and the children of the devil are obvious: anyone who does not practice righteousness is not of God, nor the one who does not love his brother. 11For this is the message which you have heard from the beginning, that we should love one another; 12not as Cain, who was of the evil one, and slew his brother. And for what reason did he slay him? Because his deeds were evil, and his brother's was righteous (1 John 3:10-12).

Meaning of Death | 147

The primary thing you are going to notice when you read this 1 John passage is that it says, specifically, that Cain was of the evil one (i.e., the serpent of old, the devil and Satan); thereby confirming that if Cain is of the serpent, then Abel is the seed of the woman (i.e., seed or son of God). Cain's deeds were unrighteous. Cain (seed of the serpent) slew Abel (seed of the woman) because Abel's deeds were righteous.

Therefore we see in Genesis chapter 4 the beginning of the hostility (the enmity) of the serpent's seed against the woman's seed just as God declared in Genesis 3:15. We observe this hostility throughout the Old Testament, reaching an apex in the New Testament with Jesus' (the ultimate seed of the woman) death on the cross. And the hostility continues after Jesus' death as documented in the book of Acts and the epistles and throughout subsequent centuries eventually culminating in the book of Revelation. It continues here in the twenty-first century as we wait for Jesus to return to set us free, the second coming of Christ.

Now, make a note of this important fact: Dead people have dead children. Also note, the two types of seed exist today (1 John 3:10). Keep this in the forefront of your mind as you study the Scriptures with a deeper more insightful understanding.

In this state of death (Genesis 4 and following), we see two types of children coming from a single womb, e.g., Cain and Abel/Seth, Esau and Jacob. One is the seed (offspring) of the serpent. He is dead and dying. And the other is the seed (offspring) of the woman (Ref. Genesis 3:15). He is still connected to God until Genesis chapter 6. Today however, all of humankind (now well blended from the two original seed types, Cain and Seth being examples) is still one of these two types in God's eyes (Psalm 1, Matthew 13:24-30, 36-43).

Scripture Study Assignment

At the end of this chapter, please see the list of New Testament verses relating to death. I am asking you to take the list of selected Bible verses and read at least five verses before through five verses after the selected passage. I realize this is a lot of reading. However, it is better to understand what you are reading at least in its immediate context. If we simply take a single verse and focus our attention only on that one verse, and not look at anything surrounding it, what we are doing is using the Bible as a book of famous or wise sayings. Therefore, we pick and choose what appeals to us. And we interpret that verse by what we think it is saying absent a context. Yet context is extremely critical. Therefore, I have asked you to read at least five verses before through five verses after the passage so you may obtain at least a minimal context for what is being said.

For each assigned verse, pay particular attention to what is implied and what may reasonably be deduced or inferred. Then document what you learn about "death" or "dead" from each designated verse(s) so we may review your notes later.

Please complete the Scripture study assignment before proceeding to the next chapter.

Let us pray: Father, You have spoken to us in Your Word and we accept and declare that as far as we are concerned, Your Word is true. We believe Your Word. We may not fully understand Your Word. All of our questions may not be answered. But we know, and we are convinced, that when we see it through Your eyes, when the darkness has been removed from our eyes, when the light shines bright in our hearts, and when You have given us wisdom and understanding, then, shall we see it as You see it. And we will rejoice and give You glory and give You praise. So our supplication is that You would continue to open up Your Scriptures to us. Give us understanding that You only can give. Give us knowledge You only can give, that we may see You as You desire us to and be convinced that we are prepared now to teach others as we have been taught. In the name of Jesus the Christ we pray, amen. Thank You, Jesus!

Scripture Study Assignment

Reference	Verse
John 5:24	"Truly, truly, I say to you, he who hears My word, and believes Him who sent Me, has eternal life, and does not come into judgment, but has passed out of death into life."
1 John 3:14	We know that we have passed out of death into life, because we love the brethren. He who does not love abides in death.
Ephesians 2:1-2	And you were dead in your trespasses and sins, 2in which you formerly walked according to the course of this world, according to the prince of the power of the air, of the spirit that is now working in the sons of disobedience.
Ephesians 2:4-5	But God, being rich in mercy, because of His great love with which He loved us, 5even when we were dead bin our transgressions, made us alive together with Christ (by grace you have been saved).
Colossians 2:13	And when you were dead in your transgressions and the uncircumcision of your flesh, He made you alive together with Him, having forgiven us all our transgressions.
James 2:26	For just as the body without the spirit is dead, so also faith without works is dead.
Matthew 8:22	But Jesus said to him, "Follow Me; and allow the dead to bury their own dead."
Romans 4:17	(as it is written, "A FATHER OF MANY NATIONS HAVE I MADE YOU") in the sight of Him whom he believed, even God, who gives life to the dead and calls into being that which does not exist.
Romans 6:13	and do not go on presenting the members of your body to sin as instruments of unrighteousness; but present yourselves to God as those alive from the dead, and your members as instruments of righteousness to God.
Romans 7:24	Wretched man that I am! Who will set me free from the body of this death?
Romans 8:6-7	For the mind set on the flesh is death, but the mind set on the Spirit is life and peace, 7because the mind set on the flesh is hostile toward God…
James 5:20	let him know that he who turns a sinner from the error of his way will save his soul from death, and will cover a multitude of sins.
1 Peter 4:6	For the gospel has for this purpose been preached even to those who are dead, that though they are judged in the flesh as men, they may live in the spirit according to the will of God.

7

BORN DEAD I

SCRIPTURE: Exodus 34:5-9, Nehemiah 9:1-20

Prayer: Father we thank You that You have awakened us this day with a renewed hope. You have inspired us to seek further understanding of Your awesome revelation. We thank You for You have taken care of us thus far. You have put a desire in our heart to learn of You so that we would understand You better and thereby truly appreciate You for the love You have showered upon us without measure. We thank You, Father. You have watched over our family members and friends. We thank You. You are working in our hearts and in the hearts of our families and friends (and even our enemies), although we may not see it now.

We thank You for being a forgiving God. We thank You for showering us with spiritual blessings in heavenly places. O' God, thank You, for You have truly been wonderful to us. You have shown us that You are righteous. You have shown us that You will not forsake us even though we are disobedient people.

We pray that You would be kind enough to visit us here in our study, that You would be in our midst, that You would touch the heart of each and every person here with us. O Father, penetrate our heart and spirit that we would indeed know that You are with us today. We thank You in advance for answering our requests. May Your name be forever glorified in the earth. In the name of Your Son Jesus, the Christ we pray, amen.

We read in our Exodus passage (above) where Moses says in his supplication to God, "let the Lord go along in our midst, even though *the people are so obstinate,* and *pardon our iniquity and our sin*" [Italics mine] (Exodus 34:9).

I wanted to get a clear understanding of the word "obstinate" in this context. What that word really means is people who insist on doing the wrong thing, the unreasonable thing in the face of extreme evidence that they ought not do it. There is reliable evidence all around. Yet, they insist on going the wrong way, doing the unreasonable thing, in disobedience to God. As I think about that, we are not much different from the Israelites. For oftentimes, we too insist on going the wrong way, doing our own thing in the face of voluminous evidence and reason insisting that we ought not do it. That is why the apostle Paul, in Ephesians chapters 4 and 5, entreats us to become imitators of God as His beloved children. He entreats us to walk as the Son also walked, forsaking our own selfish fleshly desires.

If you do not have a passionate desire to obey and commune with our awesome God, why not take some time right now to ask Him for that burning desire to take hold in you. Know in the depth of your heart that He wants you to walk hand in hand with Him each and every day.

∽

Did you perform the study assignment requested in the previous chapter? Would you like to share what you gained? Before you do, let us first review what the assignment is to ensure that we have the correct perspective.

I asked you to take the list of selected New Testament Bible verses and read at least five verses before through five verses after the selected passage. This should provide you at least a minimal context for what is being said or implied or what can be inferred or deduced in reference to death.

So now, share with us your notes by summarizing in your own words what you learned from studying the assigned verses.

Thank you. Great job!

Scripture Study Assignment

John 5:24—Truly, truly, I say to you, he who hears My word, and believes Him who sent Me, has eternal life, and does not come into judgment, but has passed out of death into life.

So often we read our Bible but we do not actually study to truly comprehend it. We read and notice what we want to notice and oftentimes we do not pay attention to what the Bible is actually saying and to its implications. Jesus says there in John 5:24, he who hears My Word and believes, "has passed out of death into life". What is life? Knowing the Father and the Son! So His audience must have been dead before they believed. And remember, he who confesses the Son has the Father also (1 John 2:23).

Please understand me. This verse is extremely significant! Why? Because, what have we been saying? Adam and Eve ate of the fruit and they died on the very day that they ate. They had their first child after they ate. What kind of children did they have? They had children some of whom were born dead (e.g., Cain) and others who were not (e.g., Abel/Seth). And now in the recent millennia and beyond, all their descendants are born dead. Remember, you must get that concept firmly planted in your head, in your heart and in your spirit. Because, without that confidence, you will not truly understand and appreciate what you read in your Bible.

To appreciate this single verse (John 5:24), it is critical that we reach the proper interpretation in Genesis. According to my reading of the Scriptures, this verse confirms that our interpretation of Genesis 2:17 conforms to Jesus' understanding of that verse. Jesus says, when one believes, they have passed out of death into life. Therefore, the one who believes must have been dead in their unbelief. She or he gained life (passed from death) only by believing Jesus Christ, the Son of the living God! Are you in agreement with me on that?

Note also that John 5:24 assumes that the reader knows he/she was born dead. Therefore it says, "he who hears My word, and believes Him who sent Me, has eternal life [or the life that is eternal], and does not come into judgment, but has passed out of death into life."

Now, if you do not know that you, and the rest of humankind, were born dead and its consequences, you do not have a proper appreciation for the word "death" in this verse.

So, when you are sharing the born dead Bible thread (the primary key to understanding the Bible) with your family members, friends and co-workers, they may say, "O, you don't know what you're talking about. That doesn't make any sense at all." You can go to John 5:24 and say, first of all, look at this Bible verse. What color is the print? "Red." What does that mean? "Jesus is speaking." Then you might say, if you believe anything, you certainly ought to believe what Jesus says. Right? And by implication, what has He said? Unbelievers are dead. When they believe Me, they gain life.

Any questions? Please append your notes now if necessary.

1 John 3:14—We know that we have passed out of death into life, because we love the brethren. He who does not love abides in death.

Looking at this verse, does it speak at all to our subject? In Genesis chapter 6 (which we cover in detail in Chapter 9), the righteous seed is assimilated into the unrighteous seed. Because the two people types intermarry, in time, the whole population ended up dead.

> So when time reached you, when your mommy and daddy had you, how were you born?

"I was born dead."

Therefore, what does this passage say to us?

"We were dead until we started to love."

That is good. But you only have it half right. And I want you to have it in full.

What does John 17:3 say?

"This is eternal life [or life eternal], that they may know You, the only true God, and Jesus Christ whom You have sent."

So Jesus says, this is life: knowing the Father and knowing the Son. That is life! So what is death?

"Not knowing the Father. Not knowing the Son."

And if you know the Father and the Son, you have life as well as love for the brethren.

"But John 17:3 only says that life is knowing the Father and knowing the Son. And that means truly knowing the Father and knowing the Son, i.e., having faith that the Father is, having faith that the Son is. It says nothing about love."

This 1 John 3:14 verse is addressing how we can be certain we know the Father and we know the Son. How? If we know the Father and the Son, we will demonstrate that knowledge and relationship by our love for the brethren. The manifestation of one's love is not what brings one into life. Rather, it is the factual evidence that you are now in life. What brings one into life is knowing the Father and knowing the Son. Notice, it does not say knowing of the Father or knowing the words of the Father, but knowing the Father, knowing the Son, i.e., experiencing the Father, experiencing the Son and their value system.

However, that is still not the main point I want you to see in this verse as it relates to the critical point we are making. If you will, read what it says in "part a" of verse 14.

"We know that we have passed out of death into life."

They were born dead! And they passed from their dead state into life.

That is the main point!

They were born dead!! And we know they are now alive because they have love for the brethren. One only loves the brethren because one knows the Father and the Son. For God is love.

If you are a believer in Jesus Christ, the main point here is, you were once dead and you were shaped in iniquity. You still carry the seed of death but you should not bear its fruit (Romans 7:14-25).

Additionally, all disbelievers abide in death, still destined for the lake of fire (Revelation 20:11-15). Make sure you get that reality firmly planted in your heart.

As you read the Scriptures, you are going to see many places referring to the fact that humankind is dead. You were born dead! That is the concept I want to get over. You were born dead to an awareness of God! Scriptures, New Testament Scriptures especially, speak to and assume that you, the reader, already understand that you and virtually all humankind were born dead.

The born dead thread (the foremost key to understanding the Bible) runs throughout the Bible from Genesis to Revelation. *It is the overarching thread and the backdrop to everything in the Bible.* So please, make a special and consistent effort to keep this understanding in the forefront of your mind. Remind yourself of it each time you read and study your Bible. Use it to grasp and illumine many mysterious concepts. And do not forget to share your new knowledge as often as you have opportunity.

This thread also helps you with many of your "why" questions. For example, one such question is, why is there so much evil in the world? It is because we are living in Satan's domain of darkness along with Satan's evil wicked dead children (<u>Colossians 1:13</u>, <u>John 14:30</u>).

So the question for you is, do you understand and accept what I am saying? Please pause now to document your answer, questions and concerns.

You must approach the Scriptures (the entire Bible) with the understanding that humankind is born dead. With the exception of the period up to Genesis chapter 6, all humankind has been born dead. The Scriptures and their authors assume you know that. This 1 John passage assumes that the reader knows that she or he was born dead. You were dead until God drew you to Himself and you believed Jesus Christ. When you believed Him, you passed from death into the life that only comes from knowing God the Father and knowing His only begotten Son. If one confesses the Son, then one has the Father also. The Son is the image and the exact representation of the Father, in human form (1 John 2:23, Colossians 1:15, Hebrews 1:3).

Knowing the Father and knowing His Son is a result of your concurrent spiritual transformation. For an interesting discussion on this subject (though a different perspective from this author), see the article, Spiritual Transformation Demystified by Hal Warren.

Questions or comments?

"Can you say then that we were spiritually dead?"

What do you mean when you say, "spiritually dead?"

"Not knowing the Father, not knowing the Word."

"So then does that mean when you are spiritually dead, you are not really dead?"

I am glad you brought that up because that is the very reason for the chart below—Humans Are A Trinity.

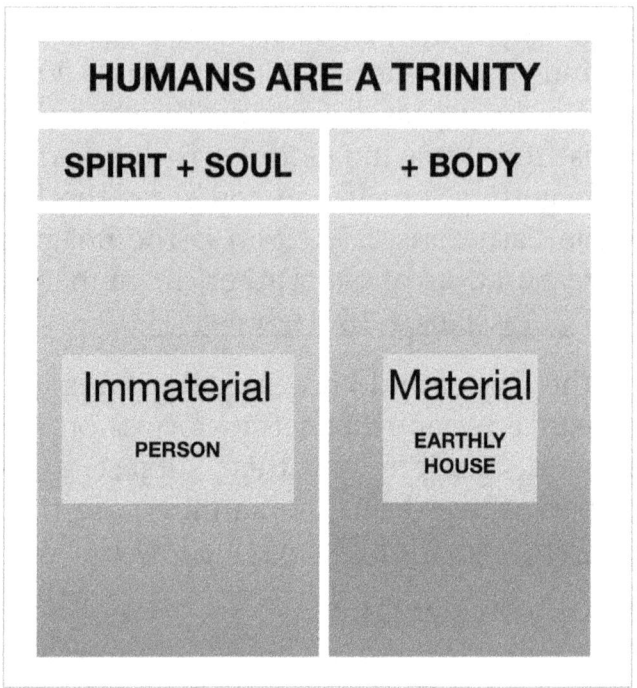

Take a look at our chart. Humankind is "spirit and soul and body" (1 Thessalonians 5:23). However, humankind is composed of only two major parts or substances. We have the *immaterial* or that which is not of a material substance. And we have the *material* part (the body). Within the immaterial part, we have the spirit and the soul.

Which of these—the immaterial or the material—is the real you? Which is the essence of you? The immaterial part is the essence of you. What is your body, the material part? That is the house you live in, what I like to call your space suit designed for propagation and earth's atmosphere. Scripture says that the Spirit gives life to the material part, i.e., the Spirit gives life to the body (Genesis 35:16-19).

At physical (natural) death, the two major parts or substances—immaterial and material—separate. The immaterial returns to the spirit world and the material remains. Because it is the spirit that gives life to the body, at physical death, when we separate, the body dies. It becomes lifeless.

> Your question dealt with spiritual death. So what is the answer to your question? If we say one is spiritually dead, what are we actually saying? The immaterial part (spirit and soul) is the true you or the true self. And the true you is spirit. So if you are spiritually dead, the true you is truly dead!
>
> We often hear people's response which in general is, "Oh, they were spiritually dead". And we move on without giving due consideration. Few ever talk about its true meaning in response to, "Oh, they were spiritually dead". So the implication is, let us move on and talk about the real stuff. However, that is the real stuff in God's eyes.

For greater depth, see the article, 2. Man A Trinity (Spirit, Soul, Body) by Lehman Strauss.

Any comments? Please make your notes now.

> Questions?
>
> "You know how people say you cannot take stuff with you when you die? Is that why material things don't matter because you cannot take material things with you? It is what's immaterial. It is what's going on within your spirit and your soul that is important. Is that the meaning?"

Let me answer you this way: As I was recuperating from a massive heart attack, I spent all my time with God. And God was speaking to me regularly. And on one particular day, God was telling me that all these things you have been seeking after—a house, a car, and all kinds of household items we struggle to have (to enjoy life) as well as things like great office buildings that the businessperson strives to own—have no value. He said to me, they are all toys. And I was like, God now, how can they just be toys? I mean, look at how much emphasis we place on them? Look at how we work so hard to get them! Look at how we value them so! And You are telling me they are just toys? But He simply said, "Toys". So I had to meditate on that for a long, long while so I could get God's perspective on what He was talking about. And what He showed me was this: Take little children and give them a toy. Let them find one that they really like. What does that toy mean to that child?

"Everything."

Exactly! If another child comes to the home and takes possession of that toy without your child's willingness to let them have it, what happens? They get really upset. And they are liable to hurt that other child because they love that special toy. That toy means a heck of a lot to your child. As a matter of fact, a child will literally put another child in the hospital because of his or her toy. Now as a parent, in your mind, what is that toy worth?

"Basically nothing."

Yes, we spend a little money for it. But even if we

spend one or two hundred dollars, it is still not of major significance to many of us.

"But to that child, it is worth much more."

And so what God was trying to show me, you see, is through His eyes, all this stuff we like so well and work so hard to have, is nothing but toys. So I said, well God, then why did you give us these things? And why do they mean so much do us?

"To keep you busy."

Something to keep us busy! Why?

"The same reason you give toys to your children—to keep them busy, to keep them entertained, to keep them from being bored."

And what else?

"To keep their minds occupied in order to keep them out of mischief."

What did the old folks say? "An idle mind is the devil's workshop."

When one looks back in Genesis chapter 3, after Adam and Eve sinned, what did God say to the man? He said to Adam, you are going to have little leisure time. You are going to have to work hard for the rest of your life. And much of the time you are going to work but the ground is not going to produce for you. We look at that and go, "What is God doing? Why is He making Adam (and us) work so hard?"

If the mind of a natural human is idle, the only thing it comes up with is sin. Therefore, work is an expression of God's compassionate grace.

Hopefully, I have addressed your point?

"You did."

Well, let me offer this final note. Physical objects are incompatible with the spirit world. Therefore, God has not made provision for transferring material objects or wealth into the spirit world. Sorry! It all must remain here on earth for those we leave behind.

Reference the above chart. We say Adam and Eve were spiritually dead. The immaterial part is you. While you are alive, you are composed of the three parts. But the real you, the essence of you is the immaterial—spirit and soul. On the right side of the chart is the material —physical flesh. When you die physically, the real you, the spirit you, ascends from the body, leaving the body lifeless. Because, it is the spirit that gives life to the body.

We usually say, when I die, I am going to heaven. Is the material part going to be in heaven?

"No."

So what is going to be in heaven?

"Spirit and soul."

Then, that must be the real you. So if the spirit should die, then you are in fact truly dead, totally separated from the loving presence and benefits of God the Father and God the Son, for all eternity!

We have an issue with spiritual death because at first the only concept we learn about death has to do with natural death—the separation of the immaterial from the material. And that is so deeply rooted in our minds that, when we hear the word "death", we cannot perceive of anything else.

"So death would be separation?"

Yes, death is separation. I first heard a pastor say that death is separation more than forty years ago. But he did not explain it.

"As we look at Adam and Eve after they ate the forbidden fruit, and God called out to Adam saying, 'Where are you?' one can see separation there because God called out to Adam who was hiding from God."

Correct!

Please take a moment now to document your questions and record your notes.

I urge you to ruminate on all you have learned up to this point. Recall that I said previously that each concept and commentary we present is important. One can listen to a pastor's sermon and much of what the pastor says you might say these pieces are not important, but I can still receive one or two valuable concepts from it. And that might be good because maybe he gave you all the rest so you could appreciate the few principle points you value. However, what I am doing here is not like that.

Everything that I am presenting to you is important, including documenting your questions and comments. I encourage you, therefore, to revisit all your notes several times in the coming months. Share, discuss and debate each concept with your study partners, friends and family, etc. That is why, since we started this journey, I have encouraged you to make copious notes in a spiral binder or digitize them. (Be sure to keep adequate backups.) That way you will have all your significant thoughts and questions in one location making it easy to locate and review them as often as you will.

Why am I presenting these concepts? So you will be able to read, study, understand and appreciate the Bible's message for yourself. That will encourage you to cultivate your own personal relationship with Jesus, God's Christ. That will lead you to frequently share the Bible's message with others. Hopefully, it will eventually inspire you to work diligently to keep the walking dead out of hell.

Additional reasons will become very obvious to you in part three. At that point, prayerfully, you will appreciate fully why I have spent all this time meticulously presenting this particular biblical perspective.

Renew Your Mind

Romans 12:2 tells us, "do not be conformed to this world, but be transformed by the renewing of your mind, that you may prove what the will of God is, that which is good and acceptable and perfect."

Psalm 51:5 says essentially that we were born in sin and shaped in iniquity. Therefore, our perception of God's reality is noticeably off-target. We are born without any knowledge or awareness of God's reality. Therefore, it is necessary that we renew our mind so that we perceive reality according to God's perspective and truth as opposed to the world's. If we do, we will be better able to appreciate the message of God's revelation.

Jesus expects you to actually read, study and meditate on His Word daily with understanding and with insight. Therefore, set as your immediate goal to read the Bible from cover to cover in twelve months or less. I estimate that one can read the entire Bible in 80 to 100 hours or less. That is a maximum of two hours per week, only seventeen minutes per day. But then, you need to read again and again more thoughtfully and meditatively. So an excellent goal would be to read the Bible twice in the coming year. Make your first read fast paced pausing only briefly to explore difficult passages. Then on your second read, take time to meditate on what you read and investigate difficult passages.

In closing, I encourage you to make Jesus Christ your true focus in every aspect of your life, i.e., to walk (live) in His will and in His way, day in and day out, as obedient children of the Most Hight God (Ephesians 4:17-5:33). In order to do that, you must become an avid student of God's revelation in the book known all over the world as the Holy Bible.

Let us pray: Heavenly Father, we thank You for the work You are doing here in our lives. We thank You for what You are doing in the hearts of your people. We thank You, Father, that You have chosen these Your humble servants to receive the deep treasures of Your Word. And we pray that it will not fall on shallow ground. We ask You, Father, to prepare the soil that it may receive Your seed and from it produce great fruit for Your kingdom.

Oh God, bless Your children to meditate on Your Word this week. Touch them in a special way. Give them all they need that they may truly understand what has been revealed thus far. Bring back to their remembrance all that we have said. And make it clear where there is cloudiness. And when they ask You to shed light, we beseech You, Father, to answer their prayers.

Put enthusiasm in their hearts for Your Word, not only to know it and understand it, but to teach it to others that they likewise may know, understand and desire to teach it to others. May Your name be glorified in the earth. May Your saints be edified. So that Your lost sheep will be evangelized and discipled. This we pray in the name of Your Son, Jesus. Amen.

8

BORN DEAD II

SCRIPTURE: Genesis 6:1-8

Prayer: Heavenly Father, let Your Word—the New Covenant and the Old Covenant—speak to our heart today. Help us to see that they are in fact one continuation of the same story where the central character is Your Son, Jesus, the Christ. Wherein the recipients of Your grace and mercy are the children of men. For You have loved us with a love we cannot comprehend. Being so deep in our sin, we do not understand how You could love us so! And yet, You loved us so much that Your Son was born a human to sacrifice Himself on our behalf that we may have a right and the access to the tree of life. And, in having that right, we shall indeed live with You and with Your Son forever.

In Your grace and Your compassion, cleanse our hearts and our spirits of all that separates us from You. We invite You to come near us now. Open our hearts and minds to receive what You have for us this day. Sow it not on rocky soil. But plant it in the rich soil of our hearts prepared by Your hand. In the name of Your Son, Jesus, the Christ we pray, amen.

∼

In your personal Bible study, particularly of major biblical concepts, you may interpret the Scriptures as providing a particular concept or message or principle. But you might not be absolutely certain that your interpretation is reasonably accurate. In that case, what you want to do is see if you can find other Scriptures that substantiate and confirm what you think the subject passage is saying. We call these proof or confirming passages or texts. In other words, the Bible explains the Bible.

> Up to this point, we have been exploring one primary concept. What is that one concept?
>
> "Life and death."
>
> What about life and death?
>
> "With a few possible exceptions early in the beginning, every man, woman and child has been born dead and dying."
>
> That is the point!

This Bible thread runs throughout the Bible. It is the one unifying thread that connects all the books, stories and prophecies. It is also the thread that explains society as we know it today, in every nation on earth. In chapter two of Genesis, God said, if you eat the fruit of the tree of the knowledge of good and evil, you shall surely die; you are going to die on the very day that you eat. And we have decided that we are going to believe God regardless of what we see or think. We may not understand the concept that God is presenting to us. But we are going to believe that God does not lie nor does He deceive.

The Bible is, in fact, the Word of God. Do you believe it? Second, do you believe that it is without error in its original manuscripts? And if you choose to believe this Bible, then, you must believe everything it says according to a literal interpretation of the Scriptures in accordance with standard literary conventions such as setting, context, hyperboles and metaphors. The sentence or concept may not make sense to you. That is OK. But God, the Creator of the universe and you, said it or inspired it! That should settle it!

Now, I have presented a picture depicting why humankind is born dead. And you may be saying in your heart, maybe not today, but somewhere along the way, "No one has ever told me this before. I simply do not believe it". Therefore, in the previous chapter and currently we are investigating the New Testament (by searching for the word "dead" or "death") to see if it agrees with our "born dead" conclusion. As we do, keep in mind the following truism:

> The New Testament is in the Old Testament proclaimed. The Old Testament is in the New Testament explained (Source: Dallas Theological Seminary).

One of the things I hope to accomplish with the various Scriptures in the assignment is to give you absolute confidence that the New Testament confirms the principle that all humankind who were born, were born dead and dying except for some of those born before and during the first part of Genesis chapter 6, e.g., Abel, Seth, Enoch, Noah, etc.

As we continue our investigation of the study assignment from Chapter 6, we are attempting to determine if these passages confirm and substantiate what we have concluded up to this point. And does our understanding of the born dead interpretation enlighten these New Testament passages? Make sure you pay attention to my words because the words are not what I say, but what is demonstrated to us in God's Holy Scriptures. Please do not go from here saying Arlington McRae says this or that. You should be able to pick up your Bible, the authentic Word of God, flip to the passages and say, "That is what the Old Testament Scriptures say. And this New Testament passage confirms it!" You do not need to use my name in your explanation. (But please encourage people to study all the books in this series for themselves.) You should simply say, this is what my Bible says.

Therefore, I have given you these verses (end of Chapter 6) to study as a demonstration to you that, in the New Testament, the fact that humankind is born dead is pre-knowledge to the New Testament authors and their audiences. That is to say, the authors write as if the letter or book recipients (and you) already know what the Old Testament says, particularly in regard to God's declaration and perspective of "death" in Genesis 2:16-17. This thread (this key to understanding the

Bible) contributes the overall setting and context for the entire Bible.

Nicodemus

Before returning to our study assignment, let us first take a look at another popular passage, John 3:1-11

> Now there was a man of the Pharisees, named Nicodemus, a ruler of the Jews; 2this man came to Him by night, and said to Him, "Rabbi, we know that You have come from God as a teacher; for no one can do these signs that You do unless God is with him." 3Jesus answered and said to him, "Truly, truly, I say to you, unless one is born again, he cannot see the kingdom of God." 4Nicodemus said to Him, "How can a man be born when he is old? He cannot enter a second time into his mother's womb and be born, can he?" 5Jesus answered, "Truly, truly, I say to you, unless one is born of water and the Spirit, he cannot enter into the kingdom of God. 6"That which is born of the flesh is flesh, and that which is born of the Spirit is spirit.
>
> 7"Do not marvel that I said to you, 'You must be born again.' 8"The wind blows where it wishes and you hear the sound of it, but do not know where it comes from and where it is going; so is everyone who is born of the Spirit." 9Nicodemus answered and said to Him, "How can these things be?" 10Jesus answered and said to him, "Are you the teacher of Israel, and do not understand these things? 11"Truly, truly, I say to you, we speak that which we know, and bear witness of that

which we have seen; and you do not receive our witness.

What is Nicodemus' problem? Why is Jesus so irritated with him? What do you think it is?

Well, I think Nicodemus' problem is he does not know that he and all humankind are born dead, completely separated from God. The passage says he is the teacher and/or ruler of the Jews. And Jesus is presenting something to him that a ruler and teacher should readily understand or accept. So Jesus says, how can you be the teacher and not understand this? Because Nicodemus does not know that humankind is born dead, he is therefore unaware of the need for a spiritual rebirth. Humankind will stay dead (never experience God's life) throughout eternity unless God Himself intervenes.

Jesus says to Nicodemus, "You must be born again". Perhaps you have heard that said many times. You have probably quoted it yourself. You have probably told someone, "You must be born again". What does that mean? Why is it necessary to be born again?

Because you were born dead to (i.e., totally unaware of) the knowledge and presence of God.

If you were talking to someone not acquainted with the subject, they would say, as Nicodemus did, "How can these things be?" Yes they were born, but not by the Spirit who provides God's life. Does that make sense to you?

> If one is not born to God's life, then, what is he or she born to?

> "Death!"
>
> You were born into death: "born in sin and shaped in iniquity".

We hear a great deal about God's blessings. What greater blessing can God pour out on us than "His life," eternal life in a love-filled relationship with Him and His Son (John 17:1-3)? There is no greater blessing He can bestow on us in our present depraved state. Hallelujah!!

Spiritual death is not a one-time event. Spiritual death is progressive separation moving us farther away from God, from a little sin to greater and greater sin. We go from bad to more bad, to worse to more worse, etc. (Romans 1:18-32). Excuse my English. But you do get my point?

> Then the Lord saw that the wickedness of man was great on the earth and that every intent of the thought of his heart was only evil, continually. And the Lord was sorry He had made man on the earth (Genesis 6:5).

Pause here for a moment. Please try to get in touch with that picture. I know you do not want to think about it. And probably you will not accept it readily because our hearts deceive us (Jeremiah 17:9). But this verse is talking about Noah's contemporaries and their foreparents. You are a descendant of these people through Noah's family. You have their DNA in you and so do your children and your grandchildren, and so will all your descendants yet to be born!

It is God who gives life to your spirit (John 17:1-3). And therefore, when one separates from God, when one loses that connection, one is dead and will continue to die, i.e., widen the gap between oneself and God. I am not talking about punishment or anything of that nature. I am speaking only to the consequence of disobedience, what the reality is, a broken relationship, not God's response to it.

So when Adam and Eve ate of the fruit, they began their separation from God. Therefore, God says Adam and Eve died. They and all of their descendants would continue to die. In other words, their death was not a one-time event. They, and their descendants (without God's intervention), would continue to move farther and farther and farther away from God and eventually would lose all connection to and knowledge of Him. And so we observe that truth in biblical and secular history reaching into the present day.

> "Why would they continue to get farther and farther away from God?"

> You can probably answer that question for yourself. Sin separates us from God. Think of the people you know who do not know God. Tell me about them. The people who do not know God do more sin and even greater sin with greediness (Ephesians 4:17-19). They cannot get enough of sin. And after doing all the sin they think they crave, they figure out even more sin to do. Then they will do more and more of that sin. Eventually, they will sit around and figure out even greater sins to do. Revisit Romans 1:18-3:18.

"If they have children, their children are born in sin. Therefore, those children are going to have children that are dead also. What is going to get them (and us) out of this cycle?"

"Knowing God and knowing His Son."

"How does that happen? Knowing God how?"

In John 6:65, Jesus says, no man can come to Me except the Father draws him. In other passages of Scripture (Romans 3:10-11, Psalms 14), we read, "There is none righteous, not even one; there is none who understands, there is none who seeks for God."

You see, once humankind is separated from God, it is impossible for us to return to God on our own merit or strength. So when you talk to people saying, "What are you doing about Jesus?", what good does it do? Yes, the question is designed to get their attention. But the real power is in God's Word, your prayers, your love and your witness. The Scriptures, your prayers, your love and your witness are your most potent weapons, the best thing you can do for unbelievers.

In other words, you must sow the seed (the Word) and pray diligently. The rest is left to the Holy Spirit. (Ref. True Evangelism: Winning Souls Through Prayer by Lewis Sperry Chafer.) In the same way, the farmer depends on God to turn his seed into a productive plant yielding a great harvest.

Our efforts to win souls for Christ must be high on our priority list. People are born on their way to hell! Therefore, our mission must focus directly at each and every man or woman or youth who is a disbeliever. However, as we move through life, we do encounter what I prefer to call the low-hanging fruit—those whose hearts are tender toward God, who are being wooed by Him. They already have a desire to learn more about Him. These we should give priority to and make a deliberate and determined effort to evangelize and disciple them to maturity. Then encourage them to do the same thing for many others by prioritizing disciple-making in their own lives as well.

Take some time now to meditate on the above presentation and to document your understanding and other thoughts on the matter. It is very likely Jesus is tugging on your heart right now. Please do not ignore Him. Record any new questions and thoughts this discussion has generated.

Keep in mind that the purpose of giving you these passages of Scripture is to confirm that the rest of the Bible confirms our born dead interpretation. The New Testament, is written from the perspective and viewpoint that the readers and hearers of that day (and also you and I) already understand that all humankind (with a few early exceptions before the flood) is born dead.

Why am I stressing this point? I want to be certain you see it in these Scriptures and have total, absolute confidence that the concept, the perspective, the principle and the theology that humankind is born dead is absolutely sound. It is critical that you accept and appreciate this perspective if you are going to obtain a proper interpretation of the Scriptures through God's eyes. Without acceptance of the born dead perspective, one cannot truly understand the Bible nor will one understand himself or herself or the character, values and actions of all humankind. Neither can one truly appreciate the glorious love the Father has poured out on us through His son, Jesus Christ, our Lord and our Deliverer from this death.

Scripture Study Assignment

Let us take a look again at pertinent Scriptures (end of chapter 6).

John 5:24—"Truly, truly, I say to you, he who hears My word, and believes Him who sent Me, has eternal life, and does not come into judgment, but has passed out of death into life."

If you believe, you have eternal life when? "Now!" Not one day. Not when you die. But you have it now if you believe Jesus. That is why Jesus could say, he who believes shall never die. Why? Because the life that Jesus gives is the life that is eternal. When you have that life, you can never die. And if you can never die, you can never lose your place in Christ Jesus. You cannot say I used to be a Christian but now I am so bad God will not accept me. Scripture says you will never die (John 11:23-26). Therefore, the only way you could possibly die would be for you to become separated from God. But what has Paul emphasized in Romans 8:28-38, "What can separate us from the love of God which is in Christ Jesus?" Nothing! No matter how high it is. No matter how low it is, no matter how wretched. Nothing can separate us from the love of God which is in Christ Jesus! Why would anyone want to live eternally separated from a God who loves like that?

"But has passed out of death into life." Now that is the phrase right there that lets us know the perspective of the writer of this passage. He is saying believers were dead. When they believed the Son, they passed out of death into the life that is eternal.

<u>1 John 3:14</u>—We know that we have passed out of death into life, because we love the brethren. He who does not love abides in death.

This passage here says we (Christians) know we have passed from death into life. It accepts that we were in death and that we know we were. So we passed from death when we believed. And it goes on to say that if you do not love, you are still dead because anyone who has the life loves. How can we be so certain of that? The life comes from God. And God is love (1 John 4:8). It is impossible to have God's life and hate what God loves.

I was listening to a young man testify on television yesterday about how he had died. A man shot him. According to his testimony, he went to heaven. But the thing that he truly emphasized was the love that engulfed him while in heaven. When you encounter God, when you are in His presence, the love of God takes over and permeates everything about you. It is in you! It is through you! It is all around you! It is what you crave! And you do not ever want to lose it! God's love is addictive.

<u>Ephesians 2:1-2</u>—And you [Christians] were dead in your trespasses and sin, in which you formerly walked according to the course of this world, according to the prince of the power of the air, of the spirit that is now working in the sons of disobedience.

Again, we see the Scriptures speaking from the born dead perspective saying you were dead before you believed. In your sins and in your trespasses, you were dead. Jesus makes one alive through faith in Him.

Ephesians 2:4-5—But God, being rich in mercy, because of His great love with which He loved us, even when we were dead in our transgressions, made us alive together with Christ (by grace you have been saved).

Again, before we were Christians, we were dead, born that way! But I want to emphasize here that it is by grace (unmerited divine favor) you have been saved. The point is, the apostle Paul can say this with absolute confidence because, what is the picture? When Adam and Eve died, they and their progeny went down, down, down, down into sin. All humankind keeps going down deeper and deeper into sin and away from God. Nobody looks back to see where God is or to seek His face. As a matter of fact, when I mention God to many who are dead in their sins, they do not want to hear anything I have to say. Some just turn and walk away. Therefore, the Scriptures say no human seeks God. No human can come to Jesus except the Father draws (or woos) them. That tells me that we (humankind) are helpless to find or even seek after God unless God on His own initiative decides to do something to rescue us.

Are you beginning to see the picture emerge?

Now, I know some are saying, "God didn't have to do much for me because I was already a good person". If you believe that, then you are calling Jesus a liar. How can I say that with confidence? Because Jesus said there is no one good but God alone. What you are doing is comparing your dead self to other dead people. Jesus is comparing Himself to the holy and righteous Father, something we all should do if we are going to acknowledge ourselves as we truly are.

<u>Colossians 2:13</u>—And when you [Christians] were dead in your transgressions and the uncircumcision of your flesh, He made you alive together with Him, having forgiven us all our transgressions.

Again, the perspective is, you were born dead. Jesus came and sacrificed Himself for your sins. Now, you are made alive if you in fact have faith in the name Jesus, the Christ (the Word of God) as He is presented in God's Holy Bible.

<u>James 2:26</u>—For just as the body without the spirit is dead, so also faith without works is dead.

The second phrase is saying, your faith is useless if it does not motivate you to do something that demonstrates you have it. What good is it to say, I am a child of God and not behave or act like it? How does that faith glorify God or influence others to seek after Him? You see, in Genesis chapter 1, God said let Us make humankind and let Us make them in Our image, according to Our likeness. Therefore, humans should be like Us, i.e., having the values and character that We have, having the perspective of life that We have, doing the deeds that We do, saying the words that We say.

Now, that ought not be a foreign concept to you because that is exactly what you want from your children. That is why you fuss at them when they do all their weird, outrageous and crazy stuff. They do not think like you think. They do not say what you say. And they do not do what you do. God is our Father. We are

His children if we have faith in Jesus. And we ought to act like it!

When God made humans, He made them to be like Him! So we should do the deeds that the Father does. Jesus provides us a new perspective in Matthew beginning at chapter 5 and continuing through chapter 7 (the Sermon on the Mount). He says, everything I do, I saw My Father do. Everything I say, I heard it from My Father. Jesus is letting us know by these words that He is the image and likeness of God, the Father. And if He is the image and likeness of God, what does that say about sin-filled disobedient us?

Please continue to study and analyze all the passages in the assignment until you are fully satisfied that they validate and confirm the born dead interpretation.

The Bible Is A Mystery

Do you agree that the Bible is indeed a mystery book? The Bible was a mystery to me until God opened my eyes to see the key Bible thread I call "Born Dead". It is the foremost key to understanding the Bible. And I thank God the Bible is not a mystery to me any more. But, I want you to understand. It took me more than twelve years of concentrated study to get here. And I do mean concentrated study accompanied by much prayer and meditation. I took the time to converse with God and to listen intently to what He spoke to me. What I have written for your consideration comes directly from Him and from His guiding my studies.

At this point you may be asking, what is all this leading to?

Many years ago, after I had written my first draft of this book, I went searching for a book at a used bookstore. I was looking for a Bible reference having two characteristics. One, I wanted to find books that were written long ago when humankind was not so overcome with self and things. And two, I was looking for something to help explain and confirm some of the concepts God had taught me. So the Holy Spirit led me to buy the book, "The Father and His Family" by E. W. Kenyon (1867-1948) . I had no knowledge of him and his writings. I later learned he is severely criticized for much of his theology. But I am convinced he got this concept right. In the first two chapters, his book introduces the reader to the concept that all humankind is born dead. Early in chapter 3, I found the other words I was looking for (what I needed to confirm what God had revealed to me): "The Bible is a mystery book until we find the key that opens it up."

The Bible will continue to be a mystery book until you find the keys that unlock its treasure chest for you. Born dead is the foremost key! Learn it; then use it to illumine your daily Bible study. Use it to draw you closer to God. Use it to teach others this foremost key to understanding the Bible. Then make it your goal to become a disciple maker just like our Master instructed us (Matthew 28:16-19).

There are indeed actual keys to understanding God's Bible. Once you understand and apply these keys, then it will stop being a mystery to you too and become your personal message from the God who created you. Born Dead is the primary key to understanding the Bible. It helps us to understand the essential biblical concept of death versus life.

Just as the Bible does, I have put the emphasis on the death first (Old Testament) and then the life (New Testament). With this born dead Bible thread, you have begun your accurate understanding of the message of the Bible and what makes you (and your fellow humans) the person you are.

Bible Threads And Sin

When we build our concept of sin using the born dead Bible thread as our foundation, we will come to realize that sin is but a symptom of a deeper sickness (or cause). When you have an infection in your body (as Satan's seed is in your heart), it may reveal itself on the top of your skin and infect other critical organs (your behavior and relationships). You can see the results of the infection (just as we see sin) in the form of a cyst or a fever (through what we value or devalue and how we comport or misbehave). Your skin (as with your heart) is all puffed up with puss (rotten wickedness) running out of it (through your thoughts, words and deeds). So you get some topical dressing (good deeds) and you put it on your skin (to hide your true heart). But the symptoms (sins) never go away completely. They keep returning again and again.

It may get a little better for a time. But it keeps coming back because that is not the true cause of the infection (your defect). The problem is deep inside (we were born with it). So you have to put some antibiotics (Word of God) through your mouth or skin (through your ears and your eyes) to go inside your body (your soul and your spirit) to cure (to reveal the true self and cause you to confess) the problem (your natural wickedness). Eventually, your skin (your rotten wicked thoughts, words and deeds) will heal (be cleansed) as well. But just like many viruses, the infection (Satan's seed) remains inside us repressed or inactive, but still present waiting to raise its ugly head at an opportune time or in an opportune circumstance.

Final Lesson

So what is the final lesson of this session? Read the words of the introductory Scriptures:

> "Then the Lord saw that the wickedness of man was great on the earth and that every intent of the thoughts of his heart was only evil continually" (Genesis 6:5).

These are your foreparents and mine. We descended from them. Like father, like son. Like mother, like daughter. No one is exempt (Romans 3:10-12)!

Let us pray: Father, in Jesus' name, we thank You. We thank You Father that You have made our way clearer. You have given us insight into the mystery of Your Word. And we know that the evil one has clouded our minds so we might not understand these basic truths. O' God, we thank You that You have opened our hearts to receive them. We thank You that You have removed the blinders, O' God. We thank You that You have given us the grace to understand Your Word.

And we Know, Father, that with this understanding comes responsibility. For You did not give it to us just to know it so we can walk around and proudly proclaim to others what we know; so we can puff ourselves up with the knowledge that we have that they don't have.

But You have given us these keys to unlock Bible knowledge. And You want us to use these keys to unlock and open biblical doors, not only for ourselves, but for everyone we encounter.

O' God, put a passion in our hearts to spread Your Word abroad. Put it in our hearts to spread Your wisdom and Your love. Put it in our hearts to spread the revealed truth about humankind and the good news of what You have done through the Gospel of Jesus Christ. Help us help others understand that it is Your compassion and Your grace; it is Your love and Your mercy that has brought us the life. And without You, we would be forever and eternally doomed to endure the fiery death, completely separated from Your presence and Your love which is in Your Son. Thank You for being so good to us! Hallelujah!! In Jesus name we pray, amen.

9

TWO TYPES OF PEOPLES

Scripture: Exodus 34:1-9, Psalm 34

Prayer: Thank You, heavenly Father, that You have given us the right to become children of the Most High God. And we know that it is not just children in name but children in reality. For we have been born again of the Spirit if we believe Your Son.

We have been born anew that we may have the image of God in us as Your Scriptures promised us. O' God, help us to allow that image to flourish in us. O' God, cause us to set aside what we want—our selfish desires and what we think is good. Help us to set it aside and reject it. Then, cause us to allow Your Holy Spirit to do its full and complete work in us that we may indeed walk in the image of Your Son. In Jesus' name we pray, amen and amen.

∽

In Genesis chapter 3, Adam and Eve ate from the tree of the knowledge of good and evil. On that day, they died. In John 17:3, the Scriptures say this is eternal life (or life that is eternal), knowing God and knowing His Son. So what is death? Death is the opposite of life. Adam and Eve's disobedience of Genesis 2:17 initiated the process by which humankind ended up not knowing God the Father and eventually murdering His Son (Ref. <u>Matthew 21:33-44</u>). Death, according to Genesis 2:17, is also the cause of all humankind being born in sin and shaped in iniquity (Psalms 51:5).

The Consequence of Sin

Genesis chapter 4 presents the story of Cain (first born) and Abel. As young men, they appear before God with each bringing their sacrifice. God accepts Abel and his sacrifice but not Cain and his sacrifice. Cain gets angry. Notice, while he may be angry with God, he is more angry with Abel, his brother. And why is he upset with him? Because Abel did the righteous deed and Cain did that which was evil as confirmed by 1 John 3:7-12:

> Little children, let no one deceive you; the one who practices righteousness is righteous, just as He is righteous; 8the one who practices sin is of the devil; for the devil has sinned from the beginning. The Son of God appeared for this purpose, that He might destroy the works of the devil. 9No one who is born of God practices sin, because His seed abides in him; and he cannot sin, because he is born of God. 10By this the children of God and the children of the devil are

obvious: anyone who does not practice righteousness is not of God, nor the one who does not love his brother. 11For this is the message which you have heard from the beginning, that we should love one another; 12not as Cain, who was of the evil one, and slew his brother. And for what reason did he slay him? Because his [own] deeds were evil, and his brother's were righteous [Brackets mine].

While keeping that passage in mind, let us go back to Genesis chapter 3. Verse 15 is one of the most important verses in the entire Bible. It is packed with meaning. In this verse, we find the first of many promises God makes concerning the salvation of His seed. The fundamental basis for our upcoming book—*A Hostile Environment*—is also found here in these three versions of Genesis 3:15:

> And I will put enmity Between you [the serpent] and the woman, And between your seed and her seed; He [Jesus] shall bruise you [the serpent,] on the head, And you shall bruise him on the heel" (NASB) [Brackets mine].

> And I will put hostility between you [the serpent] and the woman and between your offspring and her offspring; her offspring will attack your head, and you will attack her offspring's heel" (New English Translation (NET)) [Brackets mine].

> I will make you and the woman enemies to each other [place hostility/enmity between you and the woman]. Your descendants [seed] and her descendants [seed] will be enemies. One of her descendants [He] will crush your head, and you will

bite [strike; bruise; crush] his heel [Rom. 16:20; Rev. 12:9]" (Expanded Bible (EXB)).

Notice the word "seed". This word "seed" is both singular and plural depending on the context and is so translated in the NASB and the EXB. For example, the original language word (zera) is also translated child, children, offspring and descendants. So here, God is talking about a single seed for each—your seed and her seed—and seed plural for all of the descendants of the woman and of the serpent, i.e., their respective progeny.

In regards the single seed, her seed will bruise you (the serpent, the devil, Satan (Revelation 20:1-3)) on the head. You shall bruise Him (Jesus) on the heel. In the first instance, on the head bruise is designed to disrupt and destroy the works of the devil (1 John 3:8). In the second instance, on the heel, it is designed to harm, to cut off (Daniel 9:26), but not destroy the works of her seed (the Son of Man, Jesus).

So, what are we talking about?

I have provided you sufficient information for you to appreciate that God made a promise right there in Genesis 3:15. As He passed out judgments on those who sinned, He made a promise of redemption and salvation (from death and His wrath) in the midst of declaring their punishment. He promised to provide a deliverer, whom we now know is Jesus Christ. But our focus here is on another aspect of that same verse.

In Genesis 3:15, God is also saying there is going to be two kinds or types of seed. When we look at the main focus, we see that the emphasis is on the seed of the woman in contrast to the seed of the serpent, often translated or interpreted as singular. But there is also an indication that there will be two types of seed (often translated "offspring") coming from a single womb, i.e., two types (or kinds) of people coming from the same womb (see EXB version above). Because of the wording, it seems plausible that the serpent (Satan) thought his cunning plan would yield only one seed type, his own. Thereby, Satan would be spreading his own image all over the earth rather than God's. Instead, God is declaring that two types of seed will come forth from the same womb.

So, what am I saying?

Two Types of Seed

The word (zera) translated "seed" is a word with a dual nature—singular and plural. Therefore, Genesis 3:15 is not only speaking to us in the singular but also in the plural. It is not only a prophecy of the "single seed" of each (Jesus and the antichrist) but also of all seed (or fruit) coming forth from the womb. See diagram below, Genesis 3:15 - Two Types of Seed:

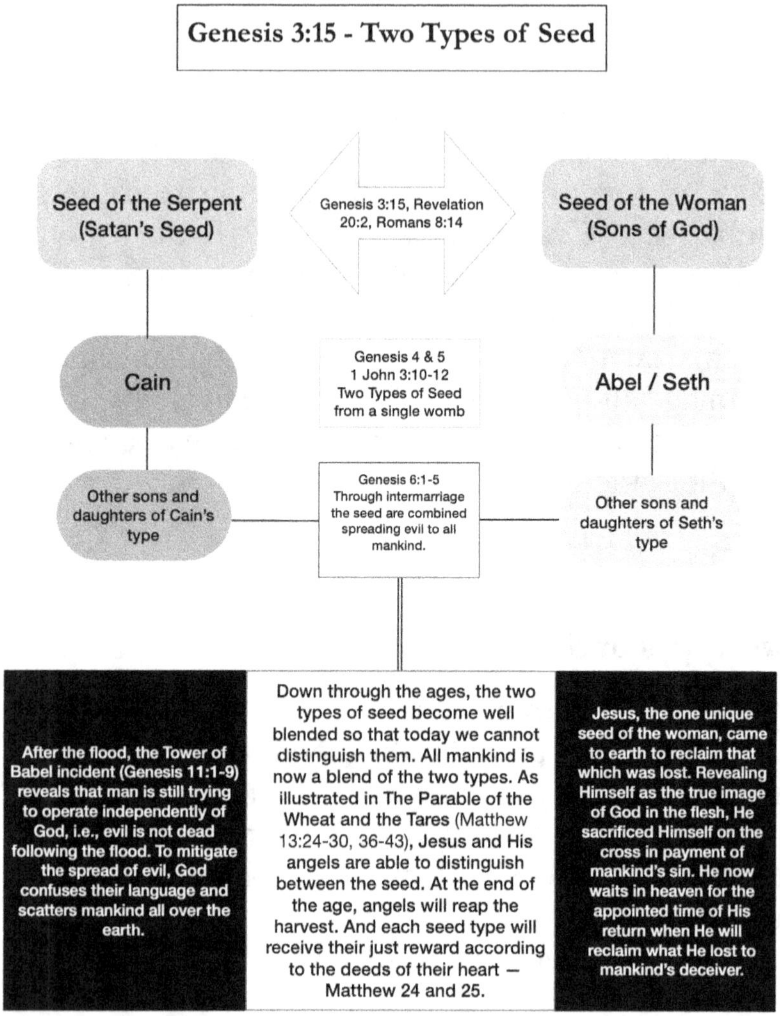

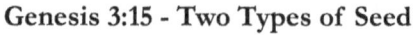

Illustration Depicting Two Seed Types

It is my contention that Genesis chapter 4 presents examples of the two types of seed coming from the same womb. We see the two types in Cain versus Abel. The Bible devotes nearly a whole chapter to Cain (the first born) and his descendants followed by a whole chapter (Genesis 4:25-5:32) on Seth (Abel's replacement, an offspring of the same type) and his descendants. The Bible invites us to focus our attention intently at the nature and character of these two individuals and their descendants (i.e., zera, seed).

But allow me a moment to interject a side note: I think this may explain in part the significance of genealogies in the Old Testament. However, the genealogies must be considered and interpreted in light of the nature of the forefathers and mothers.

As we read Genesis 3:15, Adam and Eve are already dead and dying for this death is a process, not a one-time event (Ref. <u>Romans 1:18-32</u>). When they committed the great sin, they acquired a new fallen (sinful) nature (image) while retaining a form of their original nature (image). In Genesis chapter 4, they have children. What kind of children do dead people have? Just like the plants and trees of Genesis 1:11-12, they bear fruit after their own kind with seed in them. When we get to Genesis chapter 4 (as confirmed by 1 John 3), we see that from the same womb/loins of dead people —Adam and Eve—came children of two types: children of God (i.e., seed of the woman) and children of Satan (i.e., seed of the serpent). And the Old Testament Scriptures go on to present a picture of what a life of "death" (with its disobedience, turmoil, conflict, wars and dysfunctional relationships) looks like.

In Genesis 3:15, God, speaking to the serpent, says I will put enmity between your (Satan's) seed and her (the woman's) seed. What is enmity? Hostility, malice and conflict. And we see its beginning in Genesis chapter 4 between Cain and Abel. And we see it continuing today even in our own families and communities. See for example the article, <u>Accepting That Good Parents May Plant Bad Seeds</u> by Dr. Richard Friedman.

When we get to the end of Genesis chapter 4, we see that Eve has another son and names him Seth saying, "God has appointed me another offspring in place of Abel [i.e., a seed of the same type or nature as Abel] for Cain killed him" (v25) [Brackets mine], thereby emphasizing the hostility and the two seed-types. Therefore, the chapter concludes by informing us that, after a righteous son (Seth) was born and he had a son (Enosh), then men began to call upon the name of the Lord. Following Abel's death, there was no mention of worship in regard to Cain and his descendants (who operated independently of God).

In chapter 5, the Bible continues to explore the nature and character of the offspring of these God (Yahweh) worshippers, e.g., Enoch.

The New Testament (1 John 3:7-12, see above) sheds more light on the two people types so that we may now understand them more clearly.

First John 3:7-12 informs us that there are children of God and children of Satan and how we can distinguish between them, i.e., the seed of the woman in contrast to the seed of the serpent (Ref. Genesis 3:15). First John 3:12 declares Cain is of the evil one. It also tells us that Abel's deeds were righteous, indicating that, if Cain is of the evil one (Satan), then Abel (the seed of the woman) is of God. Observe closely verse 10:

> By this the children of God and the children of the devil are obvious: Anyone who does not practice righteousness is not of God, nor the one who does not love his brother. 11For this is the message which you have heard from the beginning, that we should love one another; 12not as Cain, who was of the evil one, and slew his brother. And for what reason did he slay him? Because his deeds were evil, and his brother's were righteous (1 John 3:10-12).

So, in Genesis chapters 4 and 5, the Bible paints a portrait of the two types of people (or seed) who will populate the earth—the unrighteous and the righteous, the wicked and the upright—the people of Satan (chapter 4) and the people of God (chapter 5). The rest of the Old Testament adds to the portrait more detail (from the perspective of the righteous seed) via their interactions and reactions—the enmity or hostility between them—supplemented by God's providential interventions.

Document Your Thoughts

Take some time now to consider our assertions, the basis and the logic. Please, retrace the logical steps that got us to this point. Then meditate and ruminate on what you have learned. Ascertain if you agree or disagree with our reasoning and authoritative support. Then document your thoughts in your detail notes. Discuss it with your family, study partners and friends. Be persistent in asking them to read this book and the Scriptures for themselves so they too might become convinced and be more passionate about their daily

Bible study. Remind them also to draw near to God for He will surely draw near to you (James 4:7-8).

Questions?

After documenting your thoughts in your notes, please document your unanswered questions as well. If you cannot agree with my analysis and conclusion, document your issues in detail. Read and study this presentation again. Then take additional time to meditate and ruminate in regard to these assertions. Through persistent prayer, seek God's assistance to gain true knowledge and a clear understanding through God's eyes.

If you find you still cannot agree with me, do not give up! Please, diligently study this volume through to the end. Then continue your exploration of the Scriptures with even more determination to locate and identify God's satisfying truth. The grace (favor) of God and His Son, Jesus Christ, be with you. Amen.

Next Move: Checkmate?

Satan's plan to totally supplant God's image in the earth has now taken hold. But Satan is not yet satisfied. When it seems that things are already bad enough, Satan has another trick (chess-like move) up his sleeve to make matters even worst, i.e., absorb and assimilate the people of God into his family.

Turn now to Genesis 6:1-2:

> Now it came about, when men began to multiply on the face of the land, and daughters were born to them, 2that the sons of God saw that the daughters of men

were beautiful; and they took wives for themselves, whomever they chose.

Do you see a problem here? No? Let us look at this picture, carefully. Step back from the Scriptures and take an exploratory perspective of this picture. We have previously been informed of the two types of people coming from a single womb. And I have asked you to make a note of that. Do not forget it. You must take it with you into all of your future Bible studies, ruminations and conversations. No matter the passages of Scripture you are studying, this concept must inform your interpretation and understanding.

We see the two types of people in Genesis chapter 4 in Cain and Abel and later in chapter 5 in Seth, Abel's replacement. In Genesis chapter 6, we see that many sons (and daughters) have been born in the earth—seed of the woman as well as seed of the serpent. At the beginning of chapter 6, we see also two groups of people identified—"the sons of God" and "the daughters of men".

There is much disagreement among the experts on the proper understanding of these terms. For a summary perspective of the various interpretations, see the article, 7. The Sons of God and the Daughters of Men (Genesis 6:1-8) by Bob Deffinbaugh. See also additional articles below.

Taking into consideration our previous discussions, it is this author's conclusion that "the daughters of men" (plural, any or all men) are born of both the righteous and the unrighteous seed. However, the focus of the Scriptures in this passage is on the actions of "the sons of God". My conclusion is this term is referring to the sons of the righteous seed as demonstrated previously. It is my contention that this conclusion is confirmed in the New Testament.

For example, Luke 3 presents the genealogy of Jesus Christ. Beginning with Jesus, it traces His bloodline in reverse order through Seth and his descendants ending with the first man, Adam, "the son of God" (Luke 3:23-38). This little piece of information cannot simply be fortuitous (by chance) or coincidental. In the beginning, Adam surely was not the only "son of God". Some of his offspring were also sons of God, including Seth and his descendants.

Now, the sons of God are walking about, looking around and, no matter what direction they turn, they see beautiful women! They are attracted to their beauty without considering their ancestral lineage, i.e., that some are the seed of Satan. Their hearts are excited. "Wow! Look at that fine lady there! I've got to have that beautiful woman!" Another says, "Man, look at that! Do you see how beautiful she is? I am going to make that woman my wife!"

Do you remember the story of Samson and Delilah (Judges 16:4-22)? Samson had to have that certain beautiful woman from the midst of God's enemies. But she would be the cause of his downfall. He loves her but she has no concern for Samson's wellbeing. Therefore, she deceives him. And along with her compatriots, they destroy Samson.

Like Samson, the sons of God are only looking at the physical beauty. And they made their choice of wives based solely on their physical beauty without consideration of their nature, character, values and heart (Conf. 2 Corinthians 6:14-18).

So here is the deal: The sons of God beheld all the women they encountered, those of the seed of the woman and those of the serpent (Satan). They feasted their eyes upon the women and chose those that appealed to them visually, regardless of the women's ancestry or nature. They got married. They had children, i.e., they produced seed. What is the result?

The Sons of God had children with the daughters of men, i.e., the daughters of any of the men—sons of God, sons of Satan. Likewise, their sons married whomever they chose and they had sons who chose wives in like manner. Over time, what is the result?

Initially (up to and including Genesis 6), there were identifiable descendants of Cain (and Cain's brothers and sisters of the same nature as he) and of Seth (and Seth's brothers and sisters of the same nature as Seth) and so on to include all of Adam's sons and daughters and their descendants.

Over time, however, through intermarriage, the two seed types become intermingled and totally engulfed in unrighteousness (Genesis 6:5-6, Isaiah 53:1-7).

In the beginning, the righteous and the unrighteous seed were distinct. But as time progressed, because they intermarried, the God worshippers began to disappear. Therefore, it became more and more difficult to distinguish the righteous seed from the unrighteous, i.e., the sons and daughters of God (seed of the woman) versus the sons and daughters of Satan (seed of the serpent) as illustrated by the Parable of The

Wheat and The Tares (Matthew 13:24-30, 36-43). Consequently, following Jesus' visit to His own creation, the apostle John makes this harrowing declaration:

> There was the true light [Jesus] which, coming into the world, enlightens every man. 10He was in the world, and the world was made through Him, and the world did not know Him. 11He came to His own [Israel], and those who were His own did not receive Him (John 1:9-11).

And the apostle Paul, in Romans 3:10-18, quotes from the conclusion of King David in Psalm 14:1-3 and Psalm 53:1-3:

> As it is written, "THERE IS NONE RIGHTEOUS, NOT EVEN ONE; 11THERE IS NONE WHO UNDERSTANDS, THERE IS NONE WHO SEEKS FOR GOD; 12ALL HAVE TURNED ASIDE, TOGETHER THEY HAVE BECOME USELESS; THERE IS NONE WHO DOES GOOD, THERE IS NOT EVEN ONE." 13"THEIR THROAT IS AN OPEN GRAVE, WITH THEIR TONGUES THEY KEEP DECEIVING," "THE POISON OF ASPS IS UNDER THEIR LIPS"; 14"WHOSE MOUTH IS FULL OF CURSING AND BITTERNESS"; 15"THEIR FEET ARE SWIFT TO SHED BLOOD, 16DESTRUCTION AND MISERY ARE IN THEIR PATHS, 17AND THE PATH OF PEACE HAVE THEY NOT KNOWN." 18"THERE IS NO FEAR OF GOD BEFORE THEIR EYES."

At this point, God has no more naturally born children in whom His image dominates. And there is no one from whom the promised righteous seed can come (Genesis 3:15) because there is no one righteous. So, in Satan's mind, this last move (Genesis 6) is checkmate! God has no more countermoves He can make. He may as well give up!

But God!

Remember those two words: "But God".

Today, Satan continues to follow this same strategy against God's people which is, if you cannot kill or deceive them, then, absorb and assimilate them through marital or cohabitational relationships.

Any questions?

Please document your current questions and comments now. Also fill in answers to any of your previously unanswered questions.

For even greater enlightenment, see the articles, Lesson 14: Sin's Full Course (Genesis 6:1-8) by Steven J. Cole, The Meaning of "Sons of God" in Genesis 6:1-4 by Trevor J. Major, M.Sc., M.A. and the scholarly article, The Sons of God in Genesis 6:1-6 by Ayantunde Olaoluwa Meshach and Kolawole Oladotun Paul. Use these references to draw your own conclusions on this extremely critical portion of the Scriptures.

Assess Your Thoughts

Everything we cover in this entire presentation is critical. It is intended to reshape your mind—your perspective and your thought process with regard to the Scriptures. Our goal in this series is to equip you to study and interpret the Scriptures for yourself, and then, for you to equip others to do likewise. Therefore, remind yourself of this fact daily.

Please make an effort to follow along and understand the logic of every point and concept, including those in the referenced articles. Get comfortable with the logic. Then make an effort to prove or disprove our assertions and those in referenced articles. Remember, in our previous volume, I said that the first eleven chapters of Genesis are a window (the setting) to the rest of the Bible. Consequently, if you do not fully understand and appreciate the perspective given in that portion of the Scriptures, you cannot understand, appreciate and fully accept the truth revealed in the rest of the Bible.

Before We Close

Let me ask you a question, "Considering what we have discussed so far, does it make sense to you?" "What are your uncertainties?" Another question for you is this: "Is there anything that is causing you to doubt what you have read so far?" I encourage you to address these questions honestly for yourself before moving on to the next chapter.

I would also remind you to write out your responses in detail for future reference. It is important that you make current detailed notes of your thoughts on the evidence presented herein. These notes will prove to be extremely valuable in your ministry obligation to teach and train others to do likewise.

Remember Jesus' parting instructions to His disciples (that includes us who believe today) in Matthew 28:16-20:

But the eleven disciples proceeded to Galilee, to the mountain which Jesus had designated. 17And when they saw Him, they worshiped Him; but some were doubtful. 18And Jesus came up and spoke to them, saying, "All authority has been given to Me in heaven and on earth. 19" Go therefore and make disciples of all the nations, baptizing them in the name of the Father and the Son and the Holy Spirit, 20teaching them to observe all that I commanded you; and lo, I am with you always, even to the end of the age."

Please commit yourself to doing your part to keep the people you encounter out of hell! Please! Hell is an evil wicked torturous place not fit for even your worst enemies!

Let us pray: Heavenly Father, we thank You once again. We are thankful that You take time to notice Your children. We are thankful that You love us so much that You want us to know who we truly are but not to stay as we are. You want us to grow and mature, to mature into the likeness of Your Son, Jesus, So that we would become true disciples of His and walk as He walked, love as He has loved us, forsake ourselves as He forsook Himself, do Your will as He did Your will, even unto death.

Jesus has commanded us to deny ourselves and take up our own cross each day and follow Him. And we confess to You, Father, that we have not done as He has commanded. So we ask You, Father, to forgive us and create in us a desire and a willingness, even a passion to walk as Your Son also walked. So that in what we do in this body, we may bring glory, honor, praise, and thanksgiving to Your holy and righteous name. Give us the grace to contribute mightily to the advancement of the Kingdom of Your Son on the earth. In the name of Jesus the Christ, who loved us enough to die for us, a distressfully agonizing death, in that one and only name we pray, amen!

10

HUMANS: THE IMAGE OF GOD?

SCRIPTURE: Galatians 5:16-24

Prayer: O' Lord our Father and our God, the Creator of the heavens and the earth, the God of compassion, the God of love, the God of unending mercies, before You O' God we come first of all to give You thanks for seeing another glorious day that You have made for us to enjoy. But most of all You made it so we would enjoy You. O' God, forgive us of our sins and our trespasses. Cleanse us so that we may have uninhibited fellowship with You and with Your Son today, that we may walk hand in hand, talking with one another, speaking to one another in love.

Let us hear from You today. Speak to our hearts, speak to our spirits that our minds might be renewed and enlightened. Visit us this day. Cause us to experience Your presence. Prepare our hearts as the farmer prepares the soil that You may plant Your seed (Your Holy Word) in rich soil prepared by You to receive it and thereby produce a bountiful harvest in and through us. We praise You in advance. We honor You. We revere You. In the name of Your Son, Jesus, we pray and ask these blessings, amen.

∼

I have a question for you. It is a simple yet a very intense question. And the question is this:

Are you, were you born in the image of God?

"Yes!"

You say, yes. On what do you base your "Yes"?

"Genesis chapter 1 verse 26."

All right, anybody else?

"Yes. He said, 'let Us make man in Our image'. So man is made in the image of God."

So you are essentially saying the same thing she said, right? Anybody else?

"I would like to make a comment."

Please.

"It depends on what you mean in the word, "born", because, you were made in His image. And of course, the Bible says you must be born again of the Spirit. So it depends on what you mean by 'born'".

I mean, when you came from your mother's womb.

"So natural birth?"

Yes.

"Was I made in God's image?"

Right. Did you come forth from your mother's womb in the image of God?

"What do you mean by image, physical appearance?"

Whatever Genesis 1:26-27 means is what I mean.

"In that instance, then, yes."

So you say, "yes"?

Then here is my second question: We read a passage of Scripture at the start of this chapter, Galatians 5:16-24. Looking at verses 19 through 21, about whom is this passage speaking? And is this passage referencing the image of God?

"It refers to the flesh, therefore, natural man. So no, not the image of God."

Then about whom is it speaking?

"No, that's not the image of God. My interpretation of Genesis 1:26-27 is that God put us on earth and gave us dominion over the earth. Not that we would have the nature of God. But He put us in position in the garden so we would have dominion over the world. But He would have dominion over the universe. So not necessarily His image for the image does not have to have, necessarily, all the characteristics. That's the way I look at it."

All right, anyone else?

"It seems like since we were born in sin (Psalm 51:1-5), we could not be born in His image."

All right, sister!

Who disagrees with this sister?

"I agree with her."

So you are retracting what you said?

"Yes."

OK. So this sister has retracted her initial statement and she is now saying she agrees with that bold sister over there.

Anyone else?

"Does that mean we were born in darkness?"

That is the conclusion of the Scriptures in Psalm 51:5 and Colossians 1:13 and elsewhere.

Psalms 51:5 says I was conceived in sin and I was brought forth in iniquity. That seems to confirm what Genesis 5 and Romans 5 are pointing out—humankind is born in the image Adam acquired after eating the forbidden fruit. When Adam chose to disobey God, he began to lose God's image. Plus he received the seed of Satan (a fallen sinful nature, i.e., "the flesh," passed on to all of Adam's descendants).

Up to this point, we have focused on one primary concept, i.e., death and life. And that primary concept is summarized as follows: All humankind (with a few exceptions at the beginning (Ref. Genesis 4, 5 and 6)) is born dead. And that reality will continue at least until Jesus returns. And, we have talked a little bit about what that "death" looks like. It is my contention that the Old Testament paints a picture of that death and darkness. While we are on the subject, I have indicated that, unlike natural death, the death that

Adam and Eve suffered in Genesis chapter 3 was a **regressive** and on-going death. If you will, they became deader and deader and deader. Are you with me on that?

This is a good time for you to make your notes. If you disagree, please state the basis of your disagreement (based on the Scriptures) in detail and the fallacy you see in our logic and conclusions.

The question on the table is, "Did you come forth from your mother's womb in the image of God?" And about half of us say, "No I didn't". And the other half says, "Yes". But are you certain?

Look again at Genesis 5:1-3:

> This is the book of the generations of Adam. *In the day when God created man,* He made him in the likeness of God. 2He created them male and female, and He blessed them and named them Man *in the day when they were created.* 3When Adam had lived one hundred and thirty years, he became the father of a son in *his own likeness, according to his image,* and named him Seth [Italics mine].

All right, let us dig a little deeper into this passage. The first thing that the author tells us is, go back to Genesis 1 and 2. That is what the author says, right? Well, you see, he said, "In the day when God created man, He made him in the likeness of God." So he is saying look back to Genesis chapters 1 and 2 ("In the day when God created man", i.e., in the beginning) and observe what God did one hundred and thirty years ago. Then he says, God made them (Adam and Eve) in the likeness of God. "He created them male and female, and He blessed them and named them Man <u>in the day when they were created</u>." This underlined phrase appears twice because the author wants to impress this point upon your mind.

Then the author says, let us observe Adam presently. When Adam was one hundred and thirty years old, "he became the father of a son in *his own likeness, according to his image* and named him Seth"[Italics mine].

So, why would the author send us back to and stress Genesis chapters 1 and 2, and then, direct our attention to Adam's person one hundred and thirty years later?

When Adam was created, he was in the image of God. But when Adam was one hundred and thirty years old, he had a son in Adam's own likeness, according to Adam's image.

Why did the author direct our attention to that? Why did he stress to us that Adam was created in God's image, then tell us that Seth was born in Adam's own image? Why would he focus our attention on that? Why did he not simply say, Adam had a son? For we would naturally conclude (as most of us already have) that son is the image of Adam who is the image of God.

> Oh, you want to answer that question? Well, go for it sister.
>
> "God made Adam in His image, OK. And after God made Eve and they bit the apple, then sin came." (Please note: "Apple" is not a biblical term in Genesis chapters 2 and 3.)
>
> So, it was the woman's fault?

"After a hundred and thirty years, all this time, everything has changed now. Sin has gotten their souls. OK now, Adam is now living in a sinful world. They have this child. Then this child grew in sin. And now this child is different from the child made by God."

Just remember now, Adam was not created a child. He was created a full-grown human.

"Ok."

Now, Mrs. W has stepped out there and told us, boldly I might add, what she thinks. Who agrees with her? Miss AK agrees with her. Miss MK agrees with her. Well, you have the children on your side.

"I don't agree or disagree with her. But I think it is a very plausible and mature viewpoint."

All right. So he is straddling the fence. Anybody else?

So what do you (the reader) think? Please take some time to document your thoughts at this moment.

Now, let us see if we can dig even deeper into this passage so we can draw a Bible-centered conclusion.

In chapter 5, the author says go back to Genesis 1 and 2. That is the creation of man and woman. Then, he jumps back to chapter 5 and he says, at this point in time, Adam has lived one hundred and thirty years and God has blessed him with a son. However, that son is born in Adam's own likeness according to Adam's image. (Please note that the terms "image" and "likeness" are reversed in Genesis 5:3 in relationship to Genesis 1:26. Do you feel this is significant?)

Let me pause for a moment and interject something here. It is not pertinent to our discussion. But I just want to throw this in for your consideration. If you will, notice in verse one, the Bible says, "This is the book of the generations of Adam". What happened in chapter 4 of Genesis? Cain and Abel were born and grew to adulthood. But in chapter 5, Cain and Abel are not even mentioned! Yet chapter 5 says, this is the book of the generations of Adam. One would think that Cain and Abel would be significant members of the "generations of Adam". This appears to indicate that the author is presenting only the righteous, godly generations in this chapter. Adam starts out righteous. Abel (the righteous seed) is dead and Cain, who is of that evil one, and his generations have already been addressed in chapter 4. So they are not the focal point moving forward. The righteous seed is.

Getting back to the Bible, let us dig even deeper into this passage. In chapter 5, the author says first, go back to Genesis 1 and 2. That is the creation of the first man and woman. Then, he returns to chapter 5 and he says, at this point in time, Adam has lived one hundred and thirty years and God has blessed him with a son. That son, however, is in Adam's own likeness and image.

What happened between Genesis chapter 2 and Genesis chapter 5 that may shed light on the issue before us?

So what do you (the reader) think? Please take some time right now to document your answer and your other thoughts at this point.

> May I help you out? What happened in Genesis chapter 3?

"The man and the woman disobeyed God?"

They committed the great sin, right?

That is the major triggering or pivotal event that began the fall of humankind. In Genesis chapter 5, the author says, here we are 130 years after creation. Go back to chapters 1 and 2 and get that picture well-anchored in your mind. Now observe what is taking place in the present. Then contrast the two and you will obtain an astounding perspective of humankind through God's eyes.

What is your (the reader's) conclusion? Make your analysis and comparisons now. Then document your conclusion.

In the beginning, God made Adam in His image, according to the likeness of God. When Adam had a son, he had a son in the likeness of Adam. Why did the author not say simply that Seth was born in the image of God, or, simply leave the matter alone? Why say anything? Because Adam was no longer the full image of God. The wording suggests that Adam had his own image instead of God's. Why? Because, when Adam ate of the fruit, he opened the door for Satan to infiltrate his person and pour out his sin nature (Satan's likeness) upon him. God's image (already impaired and diminished because of Adam's sin) is in decline. Satan's nature begins to take hold, grow and will eventually takeover. Satan is never satisfied in having just a portion. He wants the whole thing. That is why he likes to rule your entire life. And if you do not agree with me on that last point, I suggest you read Romans 1:18-3:21. What is the source of this condition?

Dead People's Children

In their dying state, Adam & Eve had both the partial image and likeness of God and the seed of the serpent (a fallen sinful nature, what the Apostle Paul calls the "flesh"). The two types of seed (Genesis 3:15) presented in the Cain and Abel story (supplemented by Seth) provide the evidence for this conclusion. Since Cain and Abel were born after the sin was committed, they too and their siblings would project the likeness (one or both of the two divisions) of Adam. But keep in mind that the main purpose of Genesis chapter 4 is to introduce the two types of seed (coming from the same womb) who will populate the earth. Chapter 4 also paints a detail picture of Satan's seed, the firstborn child, and his contribution to the development of the world's (society's) systems and structure.

Chapter 5 then presents details of the seed of the woman (the righteous seed). And finally, chapter 6 presents the two types of seed uniting in marriage to form a single race leading to the proliferation of evil in the world (v5). Eventually, that evil permeated all humankind. That is why Jesus could say, there is none good but God alone (Luke 18:18-19).

For deeper insight, see the article, Lessons From the Garden: Dying You Shall Die by Mike Boling. This particular article provides original language translation. But regarding its other theological conclusions, I do not necessarily agree with them all.

For a modern day homily (sermon) taken from this portion of the Scriptures, see the article, Lesson 13: The Epitaph of Sin (Genesis 5:1-32) by Steven J. Cole.

Humans: The Image of God? | 219

For an expanded presentation on Genesis 5:3, see the <u>various translations</u> and the two parallel commentaries —<u>Pulpit Commentary and Matthew Henry Commentary</u>—located near the middle of the page (Parallel Commentaries) on the Biblehub.com website using the reference "Genesis 5:3".

See also the article, <u>Adam Before And After the Fall</u> by Pastor A.W. Weckeman.

So! There you have it—the complete born dead Bible thread, the essential key for a valid understanding of the Bible. And it is extremely important that you take note of this interpretation and store it in the forefront of your mind. Rehearse it over and over. Critique it! Debate it! But please, do not leave it behind! Whether you believe it or not, take it with you for as long as you read and study your Bible. Remind yourself of it daily. Search for its validity as you study your Bible. You shall surely find its truth throughout the biblical text. I urge you to observe its truth as you study your Bible from cover to cover. In your daily Bible study, be certain to notice how it informs your perspective, context and biblical interpretation.

Ask God regularly to reveal His insights to you so that you might see the Scriptures through God's eyes. Then make it your life goal to teach as many as you can. Invite them to read this series and to share it with others.

> "So you are saying that Adam was made by God. As long as he was not sinning, He was alive. But once he sinned, he was in a dying state. But his offspring were

born some dead and others at least partially alive as opposed to what it would be if he had children before the sin. In that case, all his children born before the sin would have been born fully alive."

Precisely!

Please document any comments or thoughts you may have right now. Do you take issue with this presentation? If so, please detail your issues and state your views with biblical support in your notes.

You now have a comprehensive understanding of the born dead Bible thread. It is the primary, the foundational key for truly understanding the Bible through God's eyes.

So what now? There is still at least one more question to be addressed. Initially, Adam and Eve were the image of God. And one question we need to ask is, "What is the image of God?" There is a host of articles written on the subject. But I wonder, "Does the Bible clearly describe the image of God for us?"

Humans: The Image of God?

Adam and Eve began to die the day they ate. Originally, they were like God—in His image, according to His likeness. When they sinned, they and their offspring began the process of losing that image, losing that likeness and increasing in the likeness of Satan. Genesis 6 reveals that this process is further precipitated or fueled by the intermarriage of the two types of seed (offspring). The sons of God (righteous seed) married the daughters of either people type (revisit the chart in chapter 9, "Genesis 3:15 Two Types of Seed") without considering their genealogy or family values and character. Along the way, they had children in their own (mixed) image. Due to the commingling, the image of God eventually all but disappeared. In that process, humankind proceeded to lose (reject) their knowledge of God and increase in the likeness of Satan. This process and its consequences are further explained in Roman's 1:18-3:21. Remember, "death" is not knowing God and not knowing His Son. So here in the twenty-first century, we were all born ignorant of God and His Son (John 1:9-11) because Adam chose to disobey God in the Garden of Eden (Romans 5:12-15).

Today, are the two types of seed still identifiable? Has the Holy Spirit given us the means to distinguish the two different seeds presently?

> "By this the children of God and the children of the devil are obvious: anyone who does not practice righteousness is not of God, nor the one who does not love his brother. 11For this is the message which you have heard from the beginning, that we should love one another; 12not as Cain, who was of the evil one, and slew his brother. And for what reason did he slay him? Because his [Cain's] deeds were evil, and his brother's [Abel's] were righteous [brackets mine] (1 John 3:10-12).

This New Testament passage is looking back to Genesis chapter 4. And this passage specifically tells us that Cain was of the evil one (Satan). You may recall from our previous studies that chapter 4, the Cain and Abel story, presents the two types of people born into the world—children of God and children of Satan—Cain, child of Satan, Abel / Seth, sons of God (or seed of the woman).

In Genesis chapter 6, the sons of God chose to marry the beautiful women. Together they began to dissipate or destroy, through their offspring, what remained of the image of God. So that now, here in the twenty-first century, we are having children among whom we seemingly can no longer distinguish between the image of God and the likeness of Satan. The image of God in humankind is so diminished that the Scriptures tell us that all humankind is born in sin and shaped in iniquity (Psalm 51:5). And all have sinned and fall short of the glory of God (Romans 3:23). But the most significant evidence of our state is in John 1:10-11 that tells us pointedly:

> "He [Jesus, the Creator] was in the world, and the world was made through Him, and the world did not know Him. 11 He came to His own [Israel], and those who were His own did not receive Him [Brackets mine].

Any questions? Please document your thoughts now.

Why Humans?

OK, I am going to wrap it up with this. In Genesis 1:26, God says: "Let us make man in Our image, according to Our likeness."

He created humankind, male and female, in the image and according to the likeness of God. He blessed them. And He commanded them to multiply and fill the earth.

What was God doing? What was His objective with humans? Or, what was humankind's eternal purpose?

Adam, who was created in God's image, had the responsibility of spreading God's image and likeness all over the earth. Satan (if you want to get a look at his thought process, read Isaiah chapter 14) looked at this and said, I am going to "be like God!" I am going to spread my image and likeness all over the earth. Using his craftiness, he enters the serpent and confronts Eve in the garden. And essentially he says to Eve, God is holding back on you because if you eat of this fruit, you are going to "be like God" knowing good and evil, implying that this is a good thing. Satan loves to paint a picture of sin as good and exciting. Then he accuses you of violating God's law.

Deceived by Satan, Eve says, oh, that fruit looks good, umm. It looks like it will taste good too, umm. And it will make me wise, double umm!! I think I need this fruit. So she eats. And she gives it to her husband who is with her. He keeps his mouth closed until she gives him the fruit. When he (God's mediator and ruler on the earth) does open his mouth, it is to disobey God by eating the forbidden fruit instead of leading his wife. He chose (he was not deceived) to listen to the voice of his wife instead of God's voice.

Satan's plan to spread his own image and likeness all over the earth is now put into action but with a significant flaw. He apparently was unaware there would be two types of seed instead of one. Eventually, however, all humankind (beginning in Genesis chapter 6 and beyond) is born in the likeness of Satan (or the fallen image Adam acquired after he disobeyed God).

God's original plan is to spread His image all over the earth. Satan says no, I am going to spread my image all over the earth. Now, at this point, it looks like God has no way out, no way to prevent Satan from accomplishing his goal, no way of getting humankind back on God's original plan. And as far as Satan is concerned, this is checkmate (for those of us who play chess)! God is defeated! Satan (the god of this world) is now fully in possession of God's own creation.

So God allows Satan's rule to continue uninterrupted through the centuries and millennia until He displays His awesome power and wisdom. Because no natural human could ever qualify, God Himself became the sinless human, the righteous sacrifice (the sacrificial Lamb of God) to satisfy the wrath of God and meet the requirements of God's justice. He could then justify humankind while they are still in their sin. That was done with the appearance of Jesus and His self-sacrifice on the cross to pay the cost for all of humankind's sins for all time. He is our substitute who paid the price we could not pay.

By justify, we mean to declare righteous those who believe and place their confidence (their faith) in the good news (the Gospel) of Jesus Christ, i.e., acquitted, no longer guilty, all charges dismissed and their records expunged. Hallelujah!!

Turn to Colossians 1:13-15:

> "For He [God] delivered us [believers] from the domain of darkness [Satan's domain], and transferred us to the kingdom of His beloved Son, 14in whom we have redemption, the forgiveness of

sins. 15And He [Jesus] is the image of the invisible God, the firstborn of all creation" [brackets mine].

So, what were Adam and Eve like at creation before they sinned?

"They were like God, in His image."

And what was that like? Do we have a picture in the Bible of what the image of God is?

What one human can we point to and say, He is in fact the exact image of God?

Read Colossians 1:13-15 again.

"JESUS!!"

So what were Adam and Eve like at their creation?

Adam and Eve were created like the human (excluding His deity, of course), Jesus, who is God's image abiding in human flesh. Unfortunately, Adam and Eve failed to retain that state by disobeying the true and righteous God.

What About Christians?

In whose image are we Christians? If we believe the apostle Paul, we are the new human created in the image of Jesus Christ, the Son of Man. Old things have passed away. Behold, new things have come! (2 Corinthians 5:16-17). Unfortunately, however, the old human, though now diminished, is still with us until our final redemption at the second coming of Jesus Christ.

For a beautiful description of the Christian state, see the article, Created to Become Like Christ by Rick Warren.

For a careful, scholarly study of the image of God in Christians as presented in the New Testament, see the article, The Image of God as the Resurrected State in Pauline Thought by Eric R. Montgomery.

Where do you (the reader) fit in this picture? If you are not yet a believer, now would be a great time for you to consider seriously how you would like to experience life after this earthly life—fire and brimstone in eternity with Satan or in the loving presence of Jesus Christ?

Questions or comments? Please make your explicit notes now.

Let us pray: Father, we thank You. We thank You that You have seen fit to show us deep insights into Your Word; things hidden from the mind of humans for centuries. But You have chosen to reveal it to us in this day, in this time. O' God, we thank You for Your light has shone brightly in us. You have made our way clearer. You have given us great understanding. Thank You, Lord, for being so good to us! Thank You, Lord, for blessing us! And we pray, Father, that You would show us the way to use what You have taught us to the glory of Your name, to the edification of Your saints, to the evangelization of Your lost sheep, so that Your kingdom may be made bigger and that hell might be made smaller. This is our prayer in the name of Your Son, Jesus, the Christ. Amen.

PART 2—THE PERSON OF GOD

Then the LORD passed by in front of him [Moses] and proclaimed, "The LORD, the LORD God, compassionate and gracious, slow to anger, and abounding in lovingkindness and truth; 7who keeps lovingkindness for thousands, who forgives iniquity, transgression and sin; yet He will by no means leave the guilty unpunished, visiting the iniquity of fathers on the children and on the grandchildren to the third and fourth generations" (Exodus 34:6-7).

11

GOD'S NATURE AND CHARACTER

SCRIPTURE: <u>Nehemiah 9</u>

Prayer: Heavenly Father, we, a few of Your humble servants, have gathered here in Your name once again to seek Your face, to know Your presence, to experience Your visitation. Forgive us, Father, for we have committed sins against You. We have acted arrogantly before You. Pride has overtaken us.

We have not loved one another as You have commanded us. And we have not spread Your gospel as Your Son has commanded. Forgive us, Father, forgive us and cleanse us from all unrighteousness. Create in us a clean heart and renew in us the right spirit that we may walk according to Your will and Your way.

We ask You, Father, to visit us here now. Touch our hearts. Touch our minds. Make us receptive vessels. Remove the cloudiness in our eyes that we may see clearly. Teach us that we may surely know. Give us understanding. Teach us how to see Your Word through Your eyes. Help us to know You the way You desire and deserve to be known so that as we go forth from here this day, our lives will never be the same. This is our prayer in the name of Your Son, Jesus we pray. Amen.

Our Scripture for this session is the whole of Nehemiah chapter 9. So we encourage you to read and meditate on the whole chapter to broaden your perspective. However, for our purpose here, we shall first look at the setting in verses 1-5 to prepare us for our primary focus on verses 16-20.

This section of Nehemiah takes place some twelve to fifteen years after the second group of exiles led by Ezra had returned to Jerusalem from the Babylonian exile. Nehemiah led the third company of exiles and supporters to Jerusalem to rebuild the city walls. Recall that God sent the Israelites into exile because of their gross disobedience and outright rejection of and separation from God (i.e., they broke their covenant relationship with God). And so we observe that Israel (God's chosen people) is dead, too, just like the rest of humankind (the Gentiles).

> Now on the twenty-fourth day of this month the sons of Israel assembled with fasting, in sackcloth and with dirt upon them. 2 The descendants of Israel separated themselves from all foreigners, and stood and confessed their sins and the iniquities of their fathers. 3 While they stood in their place, they read from the book of the law of the Lord their God for a fourth of the day; and for another fourth they confessed and worshiped

God's Nature And Character | 231

the Lord their God. 4 Now on the Levites' platform stood Jeshua, Bani, Kadmiel, Shebaniah, Bunni, Sherebiah, Bani and Chenani, and they cried with a loud voice to the Lord their God. 5 Then the Levites, Jeshua, Kadmiel, Bani, Hashabneiah, Sherebiah, Hodiah, Shebaniah and Pethahiah, said, "Arise, bless the Lord your God forever and ever!
O may Your glorious name be blessed
And exalted above all blessing and praise!
(Nehemiah 9:1-5).

They go on to declare who God is. They rehearse the experiences of the previous generations with Him. He delivered them from bondage in Egypt and gave them the Promised Land just as He had promised to father Abram (Abraham). In their prayer, they go on to declare:

"But they, our fathers, acted arrogantly;
They became stubborn and would not listen to Your commandments. 17 "They refused to listen, And did not remember Your wondrous deeds which You had performed among them; So they became stubborn and appointed a leader to return to their slavery in Egypt.

But You are a God of forgiveness, Gracious and compassionate, Slow to anger and abounding in lovingkindness; And You did not forsake them. 18 "Even when they made for themselves A calf of molten metal And said, 'This is your God Who brought you up from Egypt,' And committed great blasphemies, 19 You, in Your great compassion, Did not forsake them in the wilderness; The pillar of cloud did not leave them by day, To guide them on their way, Nor the pillar of fire by night, to light for them the way in which they were to go. 20 "You gave Your good Spirit to instruct them, Your manna You did not withhold from their mouth, And You gave them water for their thirst (Nehemiah 9:16-20).

∽

We began this journey by asking the question, what is the church doing? What should the church be doing? And in line with that, we first asked the question, do you believe the Bible is the Word of God (your Creator)? And secondly, we asked the question, do you believe the Bible is without error in the original manuscripts? Now, if you say, Arlington, I believe the Bible is the Word of God and I believe it is without error, then the next question I have for you is, what role does the Bible have in your life?

A Quick Review

We said in a previous session, if your mother told you as a child, if your father told you, if you go out in that busy street, with all that traffic, you are going to be hurt, maybe killed. Then if you believe your father, if you believe your mother, you will not go out in that street because you are convinced that if you do, you could be hurt. That means, you have decided to order your life based on your belief in what your father and mother told you.

Likewise, if you truly believe the Bible is the Word of God, if you truly believe it is without error, then you will surely modify your life to conform to its imperatives, precepts, instructions and commandments. Why? Because God's unfailing love is overwhelming or to keep yourself out of hell for all eternity!

Our primary study is in the book of Genesis chapters 1 through 6. We have focused on Genesis 1:26-27 where Scripture says, "Let us make man in our image, according to our likeness; and let them have dominion over the earth." Then we moved on to Genesis 2:16-17, where "the LORD God commanded the man, saying, "From any tree of the garden you may eat freely; 17but from the tree of the knowledge of good and evil you shall not eat, for in the day that you eat from it you shall surely die."

That passage asserts that in the very day that he eats he shall surely die. So the question before us was, "Do you believe that if they eat they will die on that day?" We wrestled with that because some of us perhaps had some issues with it. But we have come to realize and appreciate that this is God's Word. And if God said they were going to die on that day, then they would in fact die on the day they should eat the forbidden fruit.

So we went on to Genesis chapter 3 where Adam and Eve did in fact eat the forbidden fruit. Therefore, they died on the day that they ate. And of course the question is, if they died, how is it they are still walking around? And if they died, how can we be here?

Then we went over to John 17:1-3. In that New Testament passage, Jesus is praying to the Father. And

He says, "And this is eternal life, that they may know Thee, the only true God, and Jesus Christ Whom Thou has sent." So Jesus is telling us what life is. Life is knowing God and knowing His Son. If that is life, what then is death in Genesis chapters two and three? We concluded that death is the opposite of life. Therefore, death is not knowing God and not knowing God's Son. If you do not know the Son, you do not know the Father:

> Whoever denies the Son does not have the Father; the one who confesses the Son has the Father also (1 John 2:23).

This Is Who I Am

Now, here we are today and we had an assignment given to us at the beginning of chapter 6. Our assignment was to spend some time on the passage, Exodus 34:5-9, to study this passage, not one time, but make it your daily time with the Lord for at least a week. Spend fifteen to thirty minutes in meditation and rumination on each of God's character traits (a glimpse of His person) and how it is partially quoted or referenced throughout the Bible. You were to ask God to show you, through His eyes, what that passage is saying to His people today. So do you have anything you would like to share with us on what you gained from your study and meditation on Exodus 34:5-9?

Please take some time now to review and summarize your observations in your mind or verbally. Refer to your notes, if necessary. Please detail your current

God's Nature And Character | 235

response in your notes now as well and record any other observations.

Thank you for sharing.

Let us back up a little bit and look at the context of Exodus 34:5-9. If you go back to Exodus chapter 33 and you read all the way through to our passage (34:5-9), you will observe God and Moses interacting with one another. And Moses is saying teach me who You are. Show me who You are. Help me to understand Your character, Your nature. And God tells Moses He is going to pass by him and declare His glory. But He tells Moses you cannot see My face because if you look Me in the face, you will die. Therefore, you can only see My back. When I pass by you, I will declare who I am.

Now, this is God Himself telling His obedient servant, Moses, who He is. You must get your mind firmly around that concept. God, the Creator of the universe, is saying this is who I am. To help you appreciate that, remember, He is the God who cannot lie. Therefore, it seems to me that, if God is declaring this is who I am, we ought to stand still and take special note of it. He does not say, I am the God who made the heavens and the earth. He does not say, I have all power, etc. Instead, He says here in chapter 34 verses 6-7:

> Then the LORD passed by in front of him and proclaimed, "The LORD, the LORD God, compassionate and gracious, slow to anger, and abounding in lovingkindness and truth; 7who keeps lovingkindness for thousands, who forgives iniquity, transgression and sin; yet He will by no means leave the guilty unpunished, visiting the iniquity of fathers

on the children and on the grandchildren to the third and fourth generations."

Do you see it? God is saying this is who I am. And do you see that "thousands" there? When we go deeper into the Scriptures, we will see that He is referring to thousands of generations. So, when you ask yourself, why am I so blessed? Why has God chosen to bless me? Why has God chosen me? And if you tend to get in your head that there is surely something truly great about me that God has chosen to bless me so, do not deceive yourself. It is because of who God is and who your forefathers and foremothers were. It may have absolutely nothing whatsoever to do with the person you are in the midst of this corrupt generation.

So God says, *I am compassionate and gracious, slow to anger. I abound in lovingkindness and truth.* And I keep lovingkindness for a thousand generations. *I forgive iniquity, transgression, and sin.* But *I will by no means let the guilty go free.* Not only do I punish the guilty, I also punish their children and grandchildren to the third and fourth generations.

We read a passage at the beginning of this session from Nehemiah 9. Do you see a relationship, a correlation, between our Exodus passage and Nehemiah 9?

Before verse 16, the sons of Israel (through the Levites) are recounting their history with God. Then they say in verses 16 and 17:

> "But they, our fathers, acted arrogantly; They became stubborn and would not listen to Your commandments. 17"And they refused to listen, And

did not remember Your wondrous deeds which You had performed among them; So they became stubborn and appointed a leader to return to their slavery in Egypt. But You are a God of forgiveness, Gracious and compassionate, Slow to anger, and abounding in lovingkindness; And You did not forsake them.

So where does that last sentence come from? How do the Levites know that? How did the people know, "You are a God of forgiveness, gracious and compassionate, slow to anger and abounding in lovingkindness; And You did not forsake them". How did the Levites know that? They read what Moses wrote in Exodus and they believed it! Not only that, they have observed what God has done historically in the lives of His people. Consequently, they concluded that God's actions line up with who God says He is. Therefore, even though the people have done all these horribly disobedient things, having committed all these sins, they observe that Yahweh is a forgiving God. He is compassionate. And therefore, He did not forsake them even in the midst of their disobedience.

Recall that I said of the Exodus 34 passage that you will see it quoted partially throughout Scripture. So as you read Scripture, you want to keep in the forefront of your mind the reality of who God is. This is who He is directly from the mouth of God Himself! And this is the passage Jesus used as the basis for His earthly ministry. One of the goals of Jesus' earthly ministry was to reveal the reality that God actually exists, and the true nature of His person, to this dead world. <u>(For details, see volume 1.)</u>

When you are talking to someone and they say, "God can't forgive me for what I did!" How should you respond? A great response would be, "Oh child, look at Exodus 34 verses 1 through 9!"

As we move deeper into Exodus 34, begin at verse 8. After God says this is who I am, verse 8 tells us Moses' response to who God says He is. Then verse 9 reveals how Moses reacts to this new insight into the person of God. So what does it say?

> And Moses made haste to bow low toward the earth and worship. 9And he said, "If now I have found favor in Your sight, O' Lord, I pray, let the Lord go along in our midst, even though the people are so obstinate; and do You pardon our iniquity and our sin, and take us as Your own possession."

Think about that for a moment! Formulate a picture of Moses' reaction in your mind.

When we look in chapter 33, we see that the people are stubborn, stiff-necked. As a matter of fact, God says to Moses, these are the people *you* brought out of Egypt. Prior to that, God had said, I brought them out of Egypt. But He was so angry with them, He says to Moses, these are the people *you* brought out of Egypt. (That was the obvious belief of the people since they gave God no credit for their deliverance.) So you take them. I am not going with them. If I go with them, I may destroy them. So it is best for them that I not go with you.

But look at what Moses says after God reveals Himself. God says this is who I am. Moses says, OK, then! If this is who You are, this is my prayer and supplication. Notice, he does not pray based on who the people are neither based on who he is. Instead, he prays in spite of who the people are. Moses says to God, look at these people. Look at how wicked they truly are. Look at how messed up they are. Look at how sinful and disobedient they are. But go with us anyway because of who You are! And take us, even in the midst of all our disobedience, disrespect and sin, take us as Your own prized possession. Is this the picture of your God? Is your God one who forgives iniquity, transgression and sin?

Take a break and ponder the two previous paragraphs for a moment. Anchor these concepts in your spirit. Experiment with their application to your own life.

A Closer Look

There is, however, much more to the *person* of our God, another group of spiritual and personal attributes belonging solely to our sovereign God. They tell us what we need to know to realize that He truly is holy and He truly is the Creator God of the universe. Included in this group of attributes is the fact that God is omnipotent (all-powerful), omniscient (all-knowing), eternal (having no beginning and no end), omnipresent (everywhere present at all times) and sovereign. Not only that, He is the King of kings and the Lord of lords.

For more insight into these and other qualities of our God, refer to the article, <u>6. Characteristics of God, Part Two</u> by Dr. Gregory Brown. See also the article, <u>4. The Nature of God</u> by Charles T. Buntin. Finally, review the article, <u>Names of God</u> by J. Hampton Keathley, III.

For a broader understanding of the nature, character, person and divine attributes of God, see <u>Theology You Can Count On</u> by Dr. Tony Evans. See also all the articles within the <u>Bible Teacher's Guide: Theology Proper</u> by Dr. Gregory Brown.

When I consider the totality of what we know about who God truly is, all His qualities and attributes, "What is man, that You do take thought of him? And the son of man, that You do care for him?" (<u>Psalm 8:4</u>).

After all has been said and done, "what does the Lord your God require from you, but to fear the Lord your God, to walk in all His ways and love Him, and to serve the Lord your God with all your heart and with all your soul, 13 and to keep the Lord's commandments and His statutes which I am commanding you today for your good" (Deuteronomy 10:12-13)?

It is my hope and my prayer that you too will come to truly know and greatly appreciate, glorify and honor the magnificent and awesome person of Yahweh, our holy and righteous God and Father of our Lord and Savior, Jesus the Christ.

Let us pray: Heavenly Father, You have truly been good to us! You have loved us with a love we did not earn, a love we cannot lose. You have looked down on the earth to consider our need in spite of our faults. You have sent Your Son to pay our sin penalty and to reveal Your existence to us for our good. Your mercies are new every morning. And we just want to say thank You, Lord, for all You have done for the children of humankind, amen and amen.

12

JESUS: THE IMAGE OF GOD!

SCRIPTURE: 1 John 4:7-11, Colossians 1:13-23

Prayer: Our Father in Heaven, hallowed be Your name. Your kingdom come and Your will be done on earth and in our hearts today, henceforth and forevermore! In Jesus name we pray, amen.

∼

In this session, we want to continue our focus on the person of God but with emphasis on the image of God. In Part One, our primary focus was on the nature of humankind (according to the Scriptures), being in the image of fallen Adam (or Satan). And I pray you have taken some time to meditate on that presentation and that the Holy Spirit has shown you that the ugliness we discussed there describes all of us before we came to know Jesus Christ (Ephesians 2:1-6).

The Work of God

When the Holy Spirit regenerated us (who are now Christians) through a new birth resulting in the new human, He did not destroy the old human (2 Corinthians 5:16-17, Romans 7:14-25). He simply added to us the new human, who is the image of God (Colossians 3:5-13). Therefore, our original natural self is still distorted in its manifestation of the image and likeness of fallen Adam (or Satan). That fallen nature (what the Apostle Paul calls the flesh) is striving diligently to supplant the new self (Galatians 5:16-24, Romans 7:14-25—"The Conflict of Two Natures"). But we must strive to overcome it beginning with our constant obedience to Jesus Christ.

Our regeneration and renewal is all the work of God (Ephesians 2:8-10). Jesus tells us in John 6:44, "No one can come to Me, unless the Father who sent Me draws him." We are born in sin, shaped in iniquity, born into death (with no knowledge of God). Therefore, without Jesus, we know nothing but death. And we love this death. We love it so much that when our Creator, Jesus Christ, came to visit His own creation, we did not even know Him. For the Scriptures tell us that, "the world was made through Him, and the world did not know Him". Not only that, even God's chosen people did not receive the Father's Son (John 1:10-11). They even went so far as to instigate His demise. This is also a picture of the current state of "death", the consequence of Satan's deception in the Garden of Eden.

Questions? Please document your thoughts and questions at this time.

"Did I understand you to say we have the image of Satan?"

Yes ma'am. A lot of us find that hard to receive because of what we are taught by Hollywood and because our heart deceives us. But that is not my word. That is God's Word. I did not say it. The Bible says it. I am merely proclaiming God's revelation. Are you not convinced? Study Ephesians 2:1-3, Romans 1:28-32, Galatians 5:16-21, 2 Timothy 3:1-9 and Genesis 6:1-13. Whose character is being proclaimed in these passages? How many of these character traits apply to you? And how many apply to God or His Christ?

The Image of God

In contrast to the foregoing, we want to take a good look at the image of God according to the Scriptures.

Adam and Eve were created in the image of God according to His likeness. But since the beginning of time, humankind has been portraying everything but the image and likeness of God. Therefore, when Jesus came to earth, He taught us that we should represent the Father always, in all we think, say and do.

So how are we to get a good picture of the image of God? Does the Bible provide an example to follow? The definitive manifestation of God's image in the Bible is found in the person of that one distinct seed of the woman (Genesis 3:15), born of a virgin, that one unique human, Jesus the Christ.

Jesus is that picture! Jesus is the visible image of the invisible God—the radiance of His glory and the exact representation of His nature (Hebrews 1:3). All His words and deeds were directly and specifically done to demonstrate that He is the exact image of God the Father as expressed in Exodus 34:5-7 in contrast to you and me.

> Jesus said to him, "Have I been so long with you, and *yet* you have not come to know Me, Philip? He who has seen Me has seen the Father; how *can* you say, 'Show us the Father' (John 14:7-11, Colossians 1:15)?

Therefore, if Jesus is the image of God, the exact representation of His nature, what does that make unregenerate you and me and the rest of humankind? We Christians, the children of God, who are born again to the image of God by the power of the Holy Spirit, should strive earnestly to imitate Jesus in thought, word and deed, day in and day out (Ephesians 5).

The Person of God

God has declared: I am compassionate. I am gracious. I show favor, divine favor, to those who do not even deserve it. I am compassionate. So I have compassion even on those who are my enemies. I give it freely to them anyway. I am slow to anger. You do many things that displease and upset Me. Yet, I am not easily angered. It takes a long time for Me to manifest My anger at the things you do. But once My wrath is released, it will be an horrific thing. I am abounding, filled up and overflowing in lovingkindness and truth. My lovingkindness reaches to a thousand generations of those who love Me. I am forgiving of all your sins and transgressions. But I will by no means leave the guilty unpunished, reaching even to the third and fourth generations of those who hate Me.

When the scholars were translating the Bible, they came upon the Hebrew word, "hesed". And there was no word in the English dictionary which could adequately describe the word "hesed". So they coined a new word, "lovingkindness". Now, hesed says I love you unconditionally. I love you even though you did not do anything, not one thing, to earn that love. I love you endlessly. Therefore I am merciful, steadfast and faithful to those I love. That is why Paul could say in Romans 8:35-39, what can separate us from the love of God in Christ Jesus? Nothing!

For a detail discussion on the full meaning of hesed, read the article, God's Hesed: Its Meaning and Its Theology by Kenneth Banks. Scroll down until the article is displayed. Or, sign up to download the pdf file.

See also the article, Lovingkindness—Definition of Hesed on the Precept Austin website.

As a Christian, when you examine yourself and recall all the evil you have thought of and done, when you look at how **ugly and hateful** you have been to your brothers and your sisters, when you recall how you have misrepresented and ignored God, remember, He has chosen to love you anyway. You are His child. And you might say to yourself, there must have been something good in me that God saw for Him to choose me as His child. But the Exodus passage declares that He is blessing you because of the faithfulness of your forefathers and mothers. Plus, Exodus says that God will do things for you even though you do not deserve it. It may have absolutely nothing whatsoever to do with who you are (with your bad self) and everything to do with who God is.

God goes on to tell Moses, He "...forgives iniquity, transgression and sin". Simply put, whatever does not conform to God, He will forgive it; whatever, except your unbelief and blasphemy of the Holy Spirit! "Yet He will by no means leave the guilty unpunished, visiting the iniquity of fathers on the children and on the grandchildren to the third and fourth generations." So the sin, the iniquity you commit, your children and your grandchildren may suffer for it.

God says to Moses, this is who I am. I love you with a love you did not earn. Therefore, you can do nothing to lose it. I keep My lovingkindness even to a thousand generations for those who love Me. I will forgive all your sins; whatever you have done. But I will not let the guilty (disbelievers) go free. The guilty must and will stand before the Divine Judge. If you commit the crime, you will pay or your substitute (Jesus) must pay. In the end, someone must and will pay!

Believe Jesus

Throughout His ministry, Jesus worked purposefully and diligently to demonstrate beyond a shadow of a doubt that He is in fact the exact image and the Son of the true and living Creator God (Hebrews 1:1-3).

God has made it easy for us to avoid The Day of the Lord, a day when God will deal with those who reject Him. He sent His only begotten Son (that one special seed of the woman) to earth to be sacrificed on a cross for our sins (i.e., be our substitute). His Son is the sacrificial lamb giving God the justification to forgive our sins according to His justice system. God has left us (everyone who has been born) with one thing to concern us—believe His Son! If you choose to believe His Son whom He sent to earth with God's Word in His mouth (Deuteronomy 18:18-19), then all your sins are forgiven. But if you choose not to believe His Son, then the wrath of God rests on you. These are the guilty. He will not let the guilty go unpunished (John 3:16-21). But, if the guilty (if you) choose(s) to believe His Son and repent, their sins and your sins are forgiven. God will remember their (and your) sins no more. If, however, the guilty chooses not to believe His Son, if you choose to go your own way, then, you have no forgiveness and the wrath of God rests upon you.

Please take a moment now to document your thoughts, questions and comments.

True Disciple

Have you ever thought about striving daily to be as much like Jesus as you possibly can? He is the visible image of the invisible God! Therefore the primary goal of every Christian (as a disciple of Jesus Christ) must be to become more and more like Jesus, i.e., to talk like Jesus and walk (live) like Jesus in total obedience to God, the Father (Matthew 10:24-25).

Jesus tells us, I do what I have seen My Father do. I say what I have heard My Father say. So Jesus made it a point to disclose to us (by word and deed then and now by the Scriptures) what He learned from the Father. Our goal must be to learn from Jesus and emulate Him. We Christians should set our sights high, to attain "to a mature man [or woman], to the measure of the stature which belongs to the fullness of Christ" (Ephesians 4:7-16).

Take a look at Galatians 5:22-23:

> "But the fruit of the Spirit is love, joy, peace, patience, kindness, goodness, faithfulness, gentleness, self-control; against such things there is no law".

That verse is saying this is the fruit one ought to see when he or she observes a true disciple of Jesus Christ —a manifestation of the values, nature and character of Jesus.

1 John 4:8 says very simply,

> "The one who does not love does not know God, for God is love".

So then, if I were to ask you, what is the primary character trait of God, what would your answer be? What is the one thing that best describes who God is?

"God is love!" So if He is love, how can one better describe Him? That is who He is and His actions and reactions reflect that love, His *hesed*. Yet He is also just! Therefore, lawlessness will surely be punished in the coming Day of the Lord.

The apostle John tells us that if we receive Christ, He has given us the right to become children of God (John 1:10-12). As believers, we are born of God by the power of the Holy Spirit. We are the children of God! Therefore, we are also children of love for God is love.

Therefore, put on the new human and walk in love (agape) in the image and likeness of Jesus Christ.

Take a look at 1 John 3:16-24:

> We know love by this, that He laid down His life for us; and we ought to lay down our lives for the brethren. 17But whoever has the world's goods, and beholds his brother in need and closes his heart against him, how does the love of God abide in him? 18Little children, let us not love with word or with tongue, but in deed and truth. 19We shall know by this that we are of the truth, and shall assure our heart before Him, 20in whatever our heart condemns us; for God is greater than our heart, and knows all things. 21Beloved, if our heart does not condemn us, we have confidence before God; 22and whatever we ask we receive from Him, because we keep His commandments and do the things that are pleasing in His sight. 23And this is His commandment, that we believe in the name of His Son Jesus Christ, and love one another, just as He commanded us. 24And the one who keeps His commandments abides in Him, and He in him. And we know by this that He abides in us, by the Spirit whom He has given us.

This passage is telling us how we can identify love, how we can observe love in others and in ourselves. As Christians, our Father is the God who is love. Just like you expect your children to do the deeds and have the values that you have, so God expects His children to have His values, speak His words and do His deeds. Therefore, this passage is asking us who are believers, the children of God, the children of love, a penetrating question. If you have the world's goods—food, clothing, shelter, means of subsistence—and behold your brother in need, and close your heart against him, how does the love of God abide in you, the child of love?

Ruminate on that for a moment.

You see, God has demonstrated His love toward you. He saw you in your sin with your back turned to Him and no desire to know Him. Yet He Himself is your greatest need. He saw your need. He knew that "life" was better for you than "death". He did not shut up His heart against you. In His compassion and love, He opened up His heart and poured out His grace and His mercy upon you. He became a lowly man to die a horrific death on your behalf, so that you can have "life".

Therefore, God is saying to us who believe, "As My child, how can you look at your sister and brother, whom I love, see them in need and shut up your heart against them? Have you considered what I did for you? Have you given attention to My power and image now living inside of you?"

Any Questions?

> "So you are saying then that we should show love, walk in love. Our actions should speak love always?"

Exactly! What she is asking is, should our actions speak (i.e., shout out) love always?

The answer, of course, is absolutely!

Agapao

This is a good point for me to explain Jesus' definition of "love".

The English language in many ways is simple yet complex. Often, we have one word to say a number of things and the only way we can know what the word is saying is through an understanding of the context in which it is being used. For example, if I tell Brother Andy that I love him, he has one picture. But if I tell my wife, Pauline, that I love her, she has a different picture. However, in the Greek language, there are several words for love. When Jesus walked on the earth, He often used the word "agape" for love, a word that was seldom used in the Greek. And when it was used, it was used in regard to the love of gods. What does that kind of love look like?

I have looked at a number of definitions of the word "agape"(noun) and "agapao"(verb) because I like to keep things simple. After studying a number of references, here is my simple definition I believe captures the essence of "agape" love: *Acts in the best interest of the other person.*

For a detail look at a description of "<u>agape</u>" love, please see the article, <u>Love-Agape (Greek Word Study)</u> on the Precept Austin website.

Now, you probably have two problems with what I just said. First, I said love is "acts" or action. We think love is this warm fuzzy stuff: "Ooh, I feel so good when I am with you." But the love we are talking about goes beyond feelings, being motivated by a conscious choice born of the heart. Jesus says, if you see a person in need, knowing that you are My child, knowing what I have done for you, you ought to have compassion and be gracious to him or her. That is who I am and that is who you should be. Agape (love): *Acts in the best interest of the other person that result in acts in the best interest of you.*

The second thing you are likely to have a problem with is "the other person". Why? We think about self first and foremost. When we talk about love, we often say, do you love me? Our first thought is about self. "Look at what she did to me." Why does he do that to me?" "How come she did not give that to me?" God's kind of love does not simply think about "me". God's love looks outward and says, hey, they have a sin problem. Let us see what We can do about that.

Galatians 5:22-23 says that we should manifest love, joy, peace, patience, kindness, goodness, faithfulness, gentleness and self-control.

God says He is slow to anger. Therefore, strife and contention should be nearly extinct amongst the children of God. This is who God is. This is who He expects His children to be, as those born again, in His image.

> "For those whom He foreknew, He also predestined to become conformed to the image of His Son, so that He [the Son] would be the firstborn among many brethren" (Romans 8:29) [Brackets mine].

Loving Churches Grow

When one goes to many churches on Sunday morning

and looks around, what do they see? One sees lots of empty pews! Is that right? Why aren't they filled up?

Here is the thing: When you have someone that truly loves you, you really want to be around him or her don't you?

> How much do you want to be around them?
>
> "Most of the time."
>
> And if something gets in the way of your being around them, how do you react?
>
> "I get anxious or upset."
>
> "I've got to get it out of my way so I can go be with the one I love."
>
> "Honey child, I do not have time to talk with you. I've got to go be with my boo!"

Now, look at the empty pews and think about that. If yours were a church of love, God's kind of love, the pews would be filled to overflowing. You could not keep the people away. Rick Warren, in his anointed book, "The Purpose Driven Church" page 210, puts it this way: "Growing churches love; loving churches grow."

Are you hearing me? I am going to say it again. If yours were a church (not the building, the church is the people), if yours were a loving church, you could not keep the people away. Now, that ought to tell you something. The pews are not filled. That suggests to me that we may not be living the love life God has commanded us to live.

I know you do not want to hear that. But I pray that as you relax at home, you will think about it. Talk about it. Pray about it. And if your heart is telling you, "He is not talking about me because I know I have the love in me," that is OK. In that case, talk to God. Say, God, show me if I have the love in me that You want me to have. And, after You have shown me and I am not what You want me to be, then God, please, do a new thing in me! Renovate my heart that I may love others like Your Son has loved us.

Reconsider all the discussions we have had concerning the truth of who we are. Then consider this: If you are going to demonstrate the love that God wants you to, you cannot do it on your own, in your own strength. The first step is a willing heart. You see, the problem is, we love the ugliness and selfishness. It makes the flesh feel good! We do not want to give that up. Therefore, for most of us, we cannot project the image of God because we are not willing. Make sure you get that. We do not demonstrate the love of God because we are not willing. One big reason why we are not willing is because we think the worldly people will consider us weak and foolish. Therefore, you must decide whom you will please.

Understand me, please! We were born with the desires of Satan within us. Satan has his seed (the flesh) in us. If we are believers, the Holy Spirit regenerated us and placed Jesus' Spirit in us. And now we have both. Yet we do not look and behave like Jesus because we love the flesh more. We love the deeds of the flesh. The Holy Spirit is in us. And when He is speaking to us quietly saying, no child, don't do that, what is our response? "Huh, I'm not going to let them get away with that!" Therefore, what are we saying? Holy Spirit, You sit back and let me handle this one. My point is, yes, the Holy Spirit is in us. Yes, the seed of God is in us. But we repress Him. Paul says so in Romans chapter 1. We know the truth of God, but we repress it because satisfying this flesh feels sooo so good. Are you hearing me?

You do not want to hear this? It is hard to accept. I know it is. I know it is very hard. For <u>Jeremiah 17:9-10</u> talks about how deceitful the heart is. Most likely your heart is telling you now, "He is not talking about me". Your heart is deceiving you! Hear me now! If your heart is speaking those words to you, your heart is deceiving you!

So, are you willing to give up the good feelings and the deceitfulness of the flesh? Luke 9:23 instructs us,

> "If anyone wishes to come after Me, let him deny himself [the flesh], and take up his cross daily, and follow Me."

Deny yourself! Deny what the flesh (your sin nature) wants. Deny the ugly selfish desires of the flesh. Deny the pride and selfishness within you.

We step all over people trying to lift ourselves up. It is not that we hate people but that we care so much more for self. That is not God's love. God's love says, think as much about the needs of others as you do about self:

> Do nothing from selfishness or empty conceit, but with humility of mind let each of you regard one another as more important than himself; 4do not merely look out

for your own personal interests, but also for the interests of others (Philippians 2:3-4).

God wants you to know: "I love you. You already have all the love you could ever need. I love you! If you want to experience the love that I have for you, then love (<u>agapao</u>) others and stay in My face (delight yourself in the Lord not in the things of the world)! Then you will know the love I have for you. And when you experience the love I have for you, you are able to pour out that love on other people without thinking so much about self."

Do not allow unwillingness to stop you. You must cross over into the realm of the willing. Let God know, even though I have Your Spirit in me, I still sin. I sin against You. I sin against my brothers. I sin against my sisters. Confess all your sins to God, even your secret sins. Then ask God to forgive you. Ask God to give you a clean heart. Ask God to renew the right spirit within you. Let Him know, "I cannot do it in my own strength, God, but I am willing to allow You to do what You will in and through me."

Please take some time right now to pray that prayer from your heart. Then document your current thoughts and feelings.

We say we love God. But we do not want to be like God. We want to walk in the ways of the world and stick our prideful heads in the air to satisfy the flesh. And God's heart is broken because His children do not revere Him enough to desire His presence and His likeness. So God is crying out to you today, "Give up the flesh. Give up what you want. Surrender to Me. Seek My face. And walk in My will and in My way."

Walk in love in the image of God's Servant, Jesus Christ. He is the image of God. He is also our example. Let us, therefore, imitate Him in our words and our deeds.

Image of God
(JESUS / LIGHT)

Exodus 34:6-7	Galatians 5:22-24
John 17:1-3	1 John 4:7-12

1 John 3:16-24	1 John 4:20-21
1 John 5:1-5	Philippians 3:20-21
Philippians 2:3-15	Colossians 1:13-14
1 John 2:3-6	Colossians 3:1-4
1 John	Colossians 3:12-14

Image of Satan
(DEATH / DARKNESS)

Romans 1:18-32	2 Timothy 3:1-5
Galatians 5:19-21	Colossians 3:5-9

Let us pray: We thank You, Father, that You are not like us. We thank You that You did not throw us away because we were no good. We thank You, Father, that You saw the ugliness in us and yet You loved us anyway. You loved us so much that You decided to give Your only begotten Son to pay the price that we could not pay.

You knew without Your sacrifice, without His sacrifice, we would be forever separated from You. Therefore, You poured out Your love on us to save us from the consequence of our sins. We just want to thank You. We want to praise You. We want to give You all the glory because You are deserving of all thanksgiving, all praise!

And we are asking You to forgive us now and do a new thing in us. If we are not willing, Father, we ask You to make us willing. If we are walking down the wrong path, we ask You to turn us to the right path. O' God, renovate our hearts. O' God, cleanse us. O' God, bless us and be gracious to us according to Your compassion and Your lovingkindness.

Pour out Your grace upon us. We want to know You like You really are. Please God, do a new thing in us. Manifest Your presence here with us. Let us not leave this place like we came. Let us never again be what we were when we came here, that we may truly walk as children of God, children of Love. In the name of Your Son, Jesus, we pray, amen.

13

THOROUGHLY HELPLESS!

Scripture: Psalm 40, Romans 7:14-25

Prayer: Heavenly Father, with humble hearts, we come before You, the King of kings and the Lord of lords, asking You first of all to forgive us of our sins and our trespasses. And we ask You to reveal Yourself to us today and that You would indeed speak to us. Speak to us so that we may gain greater insight into Your Word so that we would understand You better. And in understanding You, Father, we would come to love You the way You deserve to be loved.

Reveal to us the person of Yahweh, Your nature and Your character, that we would comprehend fully what it means to be in Your image. So that we would desire to walk in that image. Thereby, we would lay aside the sinful desires and lusts of the flesh and put on the garment of righteousness.

O' Father, we pray that You would anoint us anew this day with a fresh anointing. Enlighten us to know that You have great plans for our lives. Your Son has instructed us to set aside what we want and take up what You want for us. Make this a reality in our lives. O' Yahweh, the God of compassion, the God of daily new mercies, hear our prayer. Hear our hearts and answer us. In the name of Your Son, Jesus the Christ, we pray, amen.

∽

Can you tell me the primary idea presented in chapter 10? Look back to that chapter and refresh your memory.

So what is your answer?

> What was the primary question in that session?
>
> "Are we born in the image of God?"

Before I ask my questions for this session, do you have any questions you would like to ask? If you have questions that you must find answers to, please jot them down in your notes now and look for answers as we press on toward our journey's end.

Whether you have questions or not, you can relax. In this session, we are going to have a calm lightweight discussion, no heavy stuff. Most of our attention is going to focus right on the illustration presented below.

Before we proceed to our illustration, I would like you to read Galatians 5:19-24 and keep it in the forefront of your mind:

> Now the deeds of the flesh are evident, which are: immorality, impurity, sensuality, 20idolatry, sorcery, enmities, strife, jealousy, outbursts of anger, disputes, dissensions, factions, 21envying, drunkenness, carousing, and things like these, of which I forewarn you just as I have forewarned you that those who practice such things shall not inherit the kingdom of God. 22But the fruit of the Spirit is love, joy, peace, patience, kindness, goodness, faithfulness, 23gentleness, self-control; against such things there is no law. 24Now those who belong to Christ Jesus have crucified the flesh with its passions and desires.

In this session, we are going to talk about some concepts you already know, especially if you are a Christian. Our objective is to make these concepts clearer so they may go deeper into your heart than in your head. The way we are going to do that is by way of contrast and comparison. So are you ready to explore a little deeper?

Top Line / Bottom Line

As we begin our discussion, carefully review the illustration below, Dome: The Bible Story, Part 4:

262 | BORN DEAD

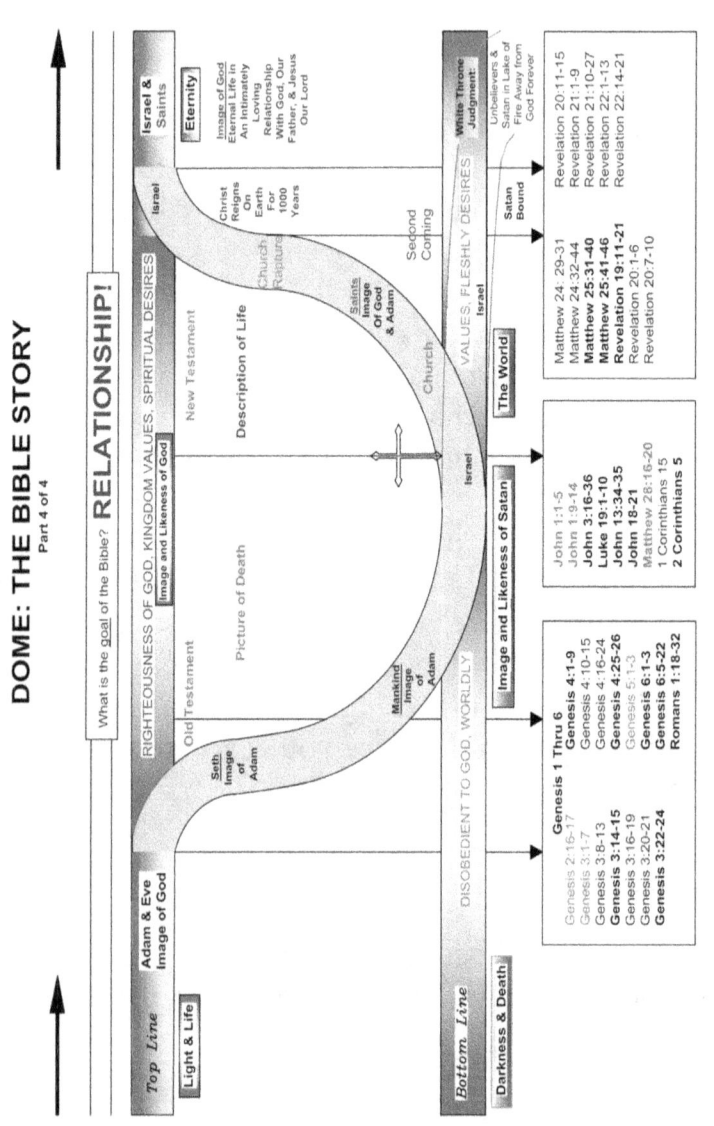

Bible Story

This illustration is adapted from the "Top Line / Bottom Line" concept of Dr. Charles P. Baylis, Professor of Bible Exposition, Dallas Theological Seminary. For a more in-depth understanding of the biblical story as presented by Dr. Baylis, see the Biblical Story on his website at thebiblicalstory.org. Click the book image for a free download.

The original of our illustration containing four parts is presented in volume 1 of this series. Part one contains the least detail of the story. Each succeeding part includes additional detail with part four providing the most detail. For our current discussion, we shall use only Part 4. For a full discussion of the entire illustration, see volume 1, chapter 5.

Each of the four parts includes a subheading generally in the form of "question / answer", a contrasting top line / bottom line section, a graphical rendering of the fall and redemption of humankind and a Scripture reference section at the bottom that is identical in each part.

Each scriptural passage makes a specific point. Each succeeding passage builds on the points made in the preceding passages. You should study the passages in the sequence presented, keeping in mind the cumulative message of the previous verses. The sequence begins in the left most block with a study of Genesis chapters 1-6. Then flows to the top of the first (left most) column and continues down that column over to the top of the next column, down that column to the top of the next column, and so on.

The Top Line / Bottom Line presentation contrasts the image of God with the image of the unregenerate (natural) human, a major Bible thread and perspective. For example, read and meditate on Psalm 1.

On the top line is the image and likeness of God—righteousness, compassion, kindness, unconditional love, favor, forgiveness, mercy, justice, etc. (Exodus 34:6-7, Galatians 5:22-23).

On the bottom line is the fallen nature of the natural human—ungodliness, selfishness, pride, arrogance, anger, "lovers of pleasure rather than lovers of God", "disobedient to parents" and disobedient to God in the image and likeness of the fallen nature of Adam (Genesis 6:5-6, Galatians 5:19-21, 2 Timothy 3:1-5).

In the day God created Adam and Eve, He created them in the image of God. In the upper left corner of our illustration, on the top line is the space titled "Adam & Eve Image of God". This is where Adam and Eve were created.

In Genesis chapters 1 through 5 there is no definition or explanation for the image and likeness of God. We only know that Adam and Eve were created (without sin) in the image and likeness of God.

God told Adam, and Eve through Adam, if you eat from the tree of the knowledge of good and evil, dying you shall die. Not only will you die but on the very day that you eat of it, you shall surely die. The Bible says Adam and Eve ate the forbidden fruit from the tree. Therefore, we are certain they died on that very day because God said they would die that very day.

In Genesis chapters 3 and 4 and following, we see that Adam and Eve were still what we call "alive". God says they are dead. Therefore, when Adam and Eve ate of the forbidden fruit, they began to progressively lose the image of God. For when God said Adam and Eve would die, it was not a one-time event. Instead, it would also become all of humankind moving deeper and deeper into sin and death and away from their God who created them. They died on that day and they continued to die.

Genesis 3:15 informs us that there will be two types of seed—seed of the serpent and seed of the woman—with deep-rooted hostility (enmity) between them. For a clearer picture, revisit the diagram, <u>Genesis 3:15 – Two Types of Peoples</u> in chapter 9.

In this death, Adam and Eve first had children—Cain and Abel/Seth along with other sons and daughters. Cain is the seed of the serpent while Abel/Seth are seed of the woman. Adam's other descendants are born seed of the serpent or seed of the woman as well. Both seed types continue to propagate and fill the earth. However, in Genesis chapter 6, everything changes. The two seed types intermarry eventually combining into a single race, a dead race, fully separated from God.

God's Program

Turning to our illustration, Dome: The Bible Story, Part 4, Adam and Eve ate of the forbidden fruit. They died up on the top line and began their fall. And they continued to die on their way toward the bottom line. We, the descendants of Adam and Eve, are born dead and we will continue to die as well unless we decide to trust Jesus. You and I, our mothers and our fathers, our grandmothers and our grandfathers, our great grandmothers and our great grandfathers are all born down on the bottom line.

Therefore, we all were born in whose image?

"The image of Satan?"

And if you do not accept that designation, if that is too strong, too bitter for you to swallow, we can say we were born in the image and likeness of fallen Adam, if that makes you feel better (Romans 5:12-14).

In Genesis 5:1-3, the author tells us:

"This is the book of the generations of Adam. In the day when God created man, He made him in the likeness of God. He created them male and female, and He blessed them and named them man in the day when they were created. When Adam had lived one hundred and thirty years, he became the father of a son in his own likeness, according to his image, and named him Seth."

In whose image did Adam have a son?

"His own."

In Adam's own image.

In our illustration, Adam and Eve were created on the top line in the image and likeness of God. But after they sinned, they began their fall toward the bottom line. Below the top line, their God-like image was diminished. The Bible, in the Old Testament, does not tell us much about what humankind—Adam and Eve—was like up on the top line. But in the New Testament, the Bible provides a vivid picture of what Adam and Eve were like.

Can you help me out with that? Can you provide a New Testament reference for the image of God?

What person in the New Testament do we know for certain is the image and likeness of God?

"JESUS CHRIST!"

Jesus is the image of God according to Colossians 1:13-15. Therefore, if we want to know what Adam and Eve were like before the sin, we need to look directly at Jesus Christ. Jesus demonstrated that He is just like His Father. If Jesus is the image of God in the flesh, then, He is also who Adam and Eve were created to be (excepting His deity, of course) before they disobeyed God.

Questions? Please document them in your notes now.

When the Bible talks about "flesh", it is talking about the sin nature (values, nature and character according to the likeness of Satan). When the Bible speaks of "light", it is speaking of traits according to the image and likeness (values, nature and character) of God. When the Bible speaks of "life" in the New Testament, it is often referring to one who knows God and His Christ. When the Bible speaks of the Spirit and fruit of the Spirit, as in Galatians 5:22-24, it is referring to characteristics according to God, the Father and His Son (their values, nature, and character).

The story of the Bible, therefore, is a story of God's love for humankind and God's program of redemption to return those who believe Him to the top line.

Fruit of The Spirit

Here is an interesting thing about Galatians 5. Paul says, these are the "deeds of the flesh" (the sin nature inherited from Adam), and it is all evil. Then he says these are the "fruit of the Spirit". He did not say these are the fruit of you nor of godly ones. He says these are the fruit of the Spirit abiding in you. So if one is to comprehend what Paul is saying in Galatians 5:22-24, then know that the fruit does not originate with you. Its origin is the Spirit of God dwelling inside you, if you are a Jesus believer and disciple. And if one does not see that fruit of the Spirit coming from within you, then, one will tend to wonder if the Spirit is filling you (i.e., controlling you). If He is in you, one should see some indication of it in your words, your deeds, your values and your worldview, no matter how small.

Let us talk about the Spirit indwelling you for a moment. Paul tells us that, when you receive Jesus Christ as your Savior, then the Holy Spirit comes to dwell in you (Ephesians 1:13, John 14:16-17). Paul also talks about being filled with the Holy Spirit. And when he uses that term, he is talking about people who are Christians. So what is Paul saying? Is he saying get some more Spirit? What is he talking about? Theologians tell us that once you get the Holy Spirit, you have all the Spirit you are ever going to get or need. Then, why do I not always see the fruit of Galatians 5:22-24 pouring out of you? That is because the phrase, be filled with the Spirit, is encouraging you to allow the Spirit complete control instead of you having control of you. The Spirit is not your co-pilot. He is your pilot if you allow Him to be. Consult with Him, therefore, in all circumstances.

Let us say, for example, you have a serious argument or a point of contention with your spouse or your children. What is your first reaction? "I am going to handle this right now!" Right? "I have to deal with this." So, who is dealing with it? You are dealing with it down there on the bottom line.

What should your first reaction be instead? "I need to let God handle this." Therefore, before you react, you need to pray and say, "God handle this for me, please". Or, before you open your mouth, you might say, "Holy Spirit take control and kill my flesh, because, if I do it my way, it will make matters worst. Therefore, I want You, God, to do it Your way and bring us peace, amen."

Back to our illustration: We have the image of Adam in his fallen state and the image of Jesus who is the image of God. It must be noted that Adam and Eve committed the sin before they had any children. All their children were born after their sin. Therefore, all humankind is born on the way to, or down on the bottom line. Adam and Eve were created (not born) on the top line. But everybody else was born after Adam's disobedience, after he fell from the top line. Therefore, everybody who has been born was born in the image of fallen Adam, who had a dual image after he sinned. However, his progeny eventually ended up in the likeness of Satan. That is why the Bible can say I was born in sin. I was born down on the bottom line. I was shaped in iniquity, by the bottom line. I was shaped into bottom line characteristics in accordance with the culture of darkness (Colossians 1:13). And the domain of darkness is ruled by Satan.

Pause, close your eyes, take a deep breath and relax for a minute or two. That was quite a discussion, wasn't it? So rest a little. Please!

Deep Trouble

Let us talk a little bit about being shaped. Have you ever noticed that children tend to act a lot like their parents? Have you ever noticed that? For the most part, children tend to have the value system of their household. We are not talking in an absolute sense because of DNA. Children are shaped also by their neighbors, by their colleagues and their peers at school. But at the core, they have the values of the household.

How do they get that? They observe everybody. They observe every household member. When I consider my granddaughter, for example, we observe that she behaves much like her mother. She has concentrated her efforts on making herself behave like her mother behaves. One of the things we observe about her is she also likes to look at us and imitate us. She wants to be able to do what we do in the way we do it. That is what children do. So, when the Bible says I was shaped in iniquity, I was shaped by the value system of my household and culture. And that value system, for the vast majority of us, was down here on the bottom line.

Do you get the realization that down here on the bottom line, we are in deep trouble with the omniscient, omnipotent, omnipresent, righteous God?

Questions and comments?

Now turn to John 3:16-17. I just want to give you some perspective on our deep trouble.

> "For God so loved the world, that He gave His only begotten Son, that whoever believes in Him should not perish, but have eternal life. 17"For God did not send

the Son into the world to judge the world, but that the world should be saved through Him."

In Romans chapter 5, Paul says, while we are down there on the bottom line, we are enemies of God. Try to grasp that picture. On the bottom line, we are enemies of God! And if you do not think so, think back to before you knew Jesus and people would talk to you about Him. How many times did you say, "I'm tired of you talking to me about God". "I don't want to hear that." "Oh man, get away from me with that." Or, did you say, "Every time I see that lady, the only thing she talks about is God. It looks like she would have something else to talk about." Notice, that is the enemy of God speaking.

Here is the picture God wants us to focus on. Look at what John says: For God so loved the world, that He sent His only begotten Son into the world that the world might be saved through Him. Here is the problem though: dead people love this darkness, this death! Do not simply focus on what I am saying. Look around you. Look at your own children. Look at your brothers and sisters. Look at your parents and neighbors who do not know God. (Look at yourself.) We love this darkness (i.e., the world system and values, society at large) and relish in it. We love this death! Why? See <u>Ephesians 4:17-24</u>.

We love what this darkness offers the flesh. Because we were born in and love this darkness, we do not care about anything on the top line. And what is on the top line? The character and nature of God and His righteousness. Righteousness is an idea that is foreign and contrary to our natural self. That is why Jesus says in John 6:44, "No one can come to Me, unless the Father who sent Me draws him". Listen! This is what Jesus is saying: No human can come to Me unless the Father first does something about that person's heart. So when you start thinking, "Oh, I'm a pretty good person. I'm a Christian because I was not a bad person to begin with." No matter how good you were, Jesus is saying you were not good enough to find God on your own. You were helpless! And if you are not by now a believer, you are so thoroughly helpless!

But God!

Take some time to meditate on this picture until it is a reality in your spirit.

You were born, according to the apostle Paul, a child of wrath (Ephesians 2:1-3), i.e., condemned to suffer at the wrathful hand of God. So Jesus looked down here on Earth, saw your plight, saw that you were forever helpless to extricate yourself from this darkness (Romans 7:18-24). You were doomed to hell! In His compassion and love, God decided to become a human to die a horrific death so that you—having been born in darkness—could experience His life and His light.

No One Is Good

The picture I am trying to paint for you is this: From Genesis 6 through today, dead people are having dead children and they will stay dead, forever (for all eternity!), unless our compassionate, gracious, merciful, forgiving, and loving Father chooses to do something about it. He has no reason to do anything about it based on you or me or anyone else. He did not look at you nor me and say, You know you are a pretty good person; I think I am going to do something about you and your situation. No! We were (and many still are) His enemies! When the man came to Jesus and said, "Good Teacher, what shall I do to inherit eternal life?" Jesus said what to him? "Why do you call me good? No one is good except God alone" (Luke 18:18-19).

So if you think you are so good, then you are saying Jesus is a liar. And when you think, "God saved me because I was not that bad", that is Satan deceiving you, influencing your thoughts. Therefore, especially at those times, refocus your attention to John 3:18-20:

> "He who believes in Him [the Son of God] is not judged; he who does not believe has been judged already, because he has not believed in the name of the only begotten Son of God. 19"And this is the judgment, that the light is come into the world, and men loved the darkness rather than the light; for their deeds were evil. 20"For everyone who does evil hates the light, and does not come to the light, lest his deeds should be exposed."

Therefore, forget every thought of your own goodness. Just know that God's goodness and His mercy are sufficient for you. So humble yourself and accept His free gift if you have yet to do so!

Good News

Now, John 3:16-19 is the Gospel, the good news! No matter what sins (except for disbelief and blasphemy of the Holy Spirit) you have committed, if you believe in and trust Jesus, you are not judged by God. That is a shouting concept right there! If you are a Christian, know that you were helpless! You were once God's enemy as well! You could not find God. As a matter of fact, you had no desire to even seek after God. You were doomed to eternal death and darkness. You were destined for eternal torment in the lake of fire (hell!).

But God, in His infinite love, in His awesome, unfathomable compassion decided to do something about your sorrowful and woeful situation. He brutally sacrificed His only begotten Son on a cross to pay your sin penalty, a penalty you could never pay. He drew you to Himself. He regenerated your heart. Therefore, you believed. And now, you are not going to be judged. Hallelujah!!

But, "He who does not believe has been judged already, because he has not believed in the name of the only begotten Son of God" (v18).

So, what is John saying here according to our perspective? You were born on the bottom line. You have already been judged, down on the bottom line. You have the sentence of death pronounced over you. And that death is an eternal death wherein you would never experience the ecstasy of God's loving and overwhelming presence! But God! Keep that in the forefront of your mind.

When believers talk to people about Jesus, some want to run us away. They hate it. Therefore, we must try to impress upon them that God's love still remains open to them:

"For God so loved the world, that He gave His only begotten Son, that whoever believes in Him shall not perish, but have eternal life. 17 For God did not send the Son into the world to judge the world, but that the world might be saved through Him (John 3:16-17).

For a thorough discussion of this subject, see the article, <u>The Helplessness of Humanity</u> by Bob Deffinbaugh.

Any questions? Please jot them down in your notes now.

Before We Close

Before we wrap this up, we should regain our perspective. In this volume, our primary purpose is to provide you the overarching key to truly understanding the Bible. Once that objective is accomplished, the next big question is, what are you to do with your new biblical knowledge and insight? Therefore, a part of our goal is to seek answers to two critical questions: a) what is *the universal church* (and *your* church family) doing? That is, what has the church been doing in the not so distant past through today, i.e., what is your church's view of its divine purpose? And b) what should the church be doing according to what the Scriptures say (<u>Matthew 9:35-38</u>, <u>Matthew 28:16-20</u>)?

Now, if the answers to these two questions are the same, then we say let us move forward, in the power of the Holy Spirit, even more aggressively. But if these two pictures are different, then we must make a decision about the direction in which we, the church of Jesus Christ, will go from this point forward. Otherwise, we risk being a rebellious generation as Israel was during the Creator's visit to the earth.

Let us pray: Father, we thank You for making Your Word plain. We thank You for making it clear. We thank You for touching our hearts. We thank You for giving us the realization of how great and wonderful You are and how awful and wrathful we are. O' God, thank You for sending Your Son to the earth to die for our sins. Bless us, Father, that we may know You and that we might have a right to the tree of life and that we may be called children of the Most High God.

O' God, we thank You for You have truly been good to us. You have poured out Your love on us. And we do not yet know how great a love You have given us. But we do know that one day Your Son shall return and we shall be like Him for Your Word says so. Thank You for Your mercy, for You did not give us what we truly deserved. Thank You, Father, for Your grace, for You gave us what we did not deserve. For we had no expectation, even any right to it, but You gave it to us anyway. O' God, we want to thank You and we want to praise Your name for the goodness You have showered on us. In the name of Your Son, Jesus, we pray, amen.

PART 3—MAKE DISCIPLES

And Jesus came up and spoke to them [the apostles], saying, "All authority has been given to Me in heaven and on earth. 19"Go therefore and make disciples of all the nations, baptizing them in the name of the Father and the Son and the Holy Spirit, 20teaching them to observe all that I commanded you; and lo, I am with you always, even to the end of the age" (Matthew 28:18-20).

14

ARE YOU WILLING?

SCRIPTURE: Matthew 9:35-38, Psalm 103

Prayer: Heavenly Father, in the name of Jesus, we confess we have sinned against You. We have not done what You have commanded us to do. We have spoken lies. At times, we have misled others. And we have not loved our neighbors as Jesus instructed us. Father, please forgive us and cleanse us and give us a pure heart. Renew the right spirit within us.

We confess that we are unable to do what You require of us in our own strength. We need Your grace. We need Your Holy Spirit. Help us, and do not depart from us. Let not our words fall on deaf ears, but make Your ears attentive to our prayer. Hear us and answer us.

We invite You to come near and commune with us today. Open our hearts and minds to receive Your message that we may go forth into the world a changed people, ready and willing to be obedient children of the

Most High God. In the name of Your Son, Jesus, we pray, amen!

~

Having read the Scriptures above, keep their messages in mind as we turn our attention to Genesis 6:5:

> Then the Lord saw that the wickedness of man was great on the earth, and that every intent of the thoughts of his heart was only evil continually.

Genesis 6:5 is a picture of the consequence of humankind's descent into wickedness and death resulting from Adam's transgression.

One of the points we stressed previously is that "death" (Genesis 2:16-17) is not a one-time event. The death that God is proclaiming in Genesis chapter 2 is a continuously progressive (or regressive) event. It will continue forever unless God should intervene and interrupt it. We are descendants of these evil people.

The New Testament confirms the Born Dead thread. Born dead is the primary and foremost key to truly understanding the Bible. Without the perspective and context it provides, one cannot truly appreciate the message of the Bible. Nor can one appreciate the magnitude of God's love and mercy given to undeserving sinners.

Get this point into your knower and keep it there through repetitive meditation, rumination and use. And just to shed a little more light on it, let me give you something else to meditate on these next few weeks—the Old Testament is a portrait of that "death". The book of Judges is a prominent example. The Old Testament presents a picture of death or a dead environment for both the people of God (the Israelites or Jews) and everyone else (the Gentiles).

Any questions? Please document them now. Additionally, make a note of your understanding or thoughts in your heart right now as well.

The Problem

What we are going to do now is see how this death is played out in the lives of people currently and what should be done about it. If you will, please take a few minutes to view the movie by New Tribes Mission. As you are viewing <u>Ee-Taow! The Mouk Story</u> on Vimeo or on <u>YouTube</u>, take notes, please, on the significant points in this evangelistic documentary. Following your viewing, we shall discuss its implications for us who are alive today.

Welcome back. Did you enjoy the movie?

The Taliabo had no knowledge of God. The whole tribe and their neighbors lived in utter darkness. They lived in fear. They were dead! "We don't know why we are born. We don't know why we live. And we don't know why we die."

They believed eternal life existed on their island some time in the distant past. So they decided to search for it.

They did not know why they were here in the earth until they heard the Bible story and accepted Christ into their lives.

At some point in the past, it appears that a previous generation had been told of God but the current generation did not know anything about Him. So they did not think about Him. They just wanted to live forever. But not like you and I think about living forever with Jesus. They just wanted to live in their corrupt bodies here on earth, forever in their current sin-sick state. And they were seeking a way to make that happen.

So how about you? Do you know why you were born and why you die and what eternal purpose your life serves?

> This story takes place in Papua New Guinea, but what about China? Do we have anybody like those people in India or Pakistan? What about here in the Americas—north, south or central?
>
> "Yes, we do."
>
> Do you know any of those people?
>
> "Yes!"

We Christians used to be just like them. And in many ways we are too much like them still.

We did not see many terribly violent things in this video. But there are people out there (you may be one of them) doing some really terribly vain and horribly vicious things. They are walking around in darkness just like the Taliabo and they are trying to figure out why they live, why they die and what this life is all about. They have no answers because these people who do not know are spending their time talking to other people who do not know.

There are many, many people who know of Jesus of Nazareth. They went to church with their parents or grandparents. But they sat in church and thought about everything but what was going on inside the church house. Because they paid little attention to what was being taught, they walked out of church actually ignorant of God. Now they are walking around trying to figure out why their life is what it is.

Why were they born? They get up in the morning and follow their normal boring daily routine. They come back home and watch a little TV or play a video game. They go to sleep. They get up in the morning and do their daily routine again. They have nothing to look forward to. Some of them probably say, "Why don't I just go ahead and die? What good is this?" In desperation, many commit self-murder (suicide). Like the man said in the movie, the sun comes up; the sun goes down. The sun comes up; the sun goes down (Conf. Ecclesiastes 1:1-11). For the many, nothing truly meaningful to life happens in between these two events. Therefore the question, "What good is my being here?"

When I try to talk to people about Jesus, some say, "Get out of my face. Don't talk to me about that." They do not want to hear it. They are truly dead! So does that mean I am going to stop telling them? No! I am not. But I am going to spend more time praying for their salvation instead of annoying them. Why? When I see them in eternity, I want my conscience to be satisfied that I did the best I could to keep them out of hell and safe from God's wrathful Judgment Day.

For example, several years ago, I was on a long trip by car. One young man I met was sitting on the curb at a fast food restaurant. He was cordial until I started talking about Jesus. He was not rude. Without saying a word, he simply got up and walked away. My feelings were not hurt. I did not feel insulted. Instead, I felt compassion for him. Therefore, I prayed for him then and I continue to pray for him, even now, that God would bring him to repentance before he dies. When death is eminent, I have requested that God would give him, and others like him, a few minutes to call on the name of Jesus. I encourage them, when death is eminent, to call on the name of Jesus before it is everlastingly too late. Usually I am able to leave them with that prayer message. And I urge them to simply say, "Jesus save me!" If you cannot say anything else, say that. For the Scriptures tell us, "...whoever will call on the name of the Lord will be saved" (Romans 10:8-13).

The Solution

Up to this point, we have discussed the concept that all humankind is born dead with no knowledge of the living God or His Son, Jesus. We have presented to you a portrait of the person of God, the only righteous One. You have seen in the historical documentary what kind of torment is going on in the hearts of men and women who do not know Jesus Christ exists. You now realize that the walking dead are helpless to receive life in their own strength. And you understand that, without God's help and yours, their woeful circumstance is permanent, eternally permanent!

> So the question I would like for you to ponder for the next few days is this: you have this knowledge. You have seen the video. You can look around you and observe the walking dead in your own home, in your extended family, on your job and in your daily encounters. Therefore, the question is,
>
> *What are you willing to do for the walking dead?*
>
> That is the question Jesus is presenting to you today.
>
> "I'm going to pray for them to come to know Christ before they die."
>
> Thankfully, some are going to pray for them.

But I want you (the reader) to think about this over the coming days and weeks. Knowing what you know about the plight of humankind—your parents, your brothers and your sisters, your aunts and uncles, your nieces and your nephews, your cousins and your neighbors, your co-workers and strangers you encounter—knowing what you know, what are you willing to do for them? Keep in mind that we are all born on our way to hell through no fault of our own.

Are you willing to do whatever is necessary to keep them out of hell for all eternity? As you ponder that question, keep in mind there are no exits in hell, neither is there any water to cool one's tongue, nor is there any godliness in hell! Hell is a place of extreme suffering with **no hope** of ever escaping (Conf. Luke 16:19-31).

If you are a believer, you have experienced the reality of God's grace and His mercy, His forgiveness and His lovingkindness. You are obliged, therefore, to sow the same seed-blessing you have received into the lives of those around you. You are their light in darkness.

Please take the time you need to hopefully make a life altering decision. If necessary, take several days or weeks to explore the implications of this question for your life and what you are willing to do for the walking dead, i.e., decide on a new focus and purpose for your life. Then, set new life priorities for the remainder of your years here on earth (Acts 1:7-8, Matthew 28:16-20).

To encourage you, Jesus has established His incentive program—with rewards now and more benefits in eternity—should you choose to be obedient and submissive to His will (Luke 18:28-30).

Please pause now to make your notes.

After carefully considering our challenge, document how you will prioritize your life moving forward. Will your focus be only self OR are you willing to prioritize saving the helpless from eternity in a fiery hell?

Let us pray: Heavenly Father, we thank You for opening our eyes. Thank You for allowing us to see deep into Your Word and to understand it better. Thank You, Farther, for touching our heart and our mind. And now we pray that You would help us wrestle with what we know and help us come to a conclusion as to what we will do with what we know.

Father, we give You permission to take control of us now. Touch our hearts and spirits in a way that we would become whatever Your eternal desire is for us. Help us, Father, to throw away what we want and to pick up what You want for us, that our lives may indeed bring glory to Your name. May we live the life that You have called us to live. In the name of Your Son, Jesus the Christ, we pray and give thanks, amen and amen!

15

CHILDREN OF GOD!

SCRIPTURE: Colossians 1:19-29

Prayer: Father, our Lord, our God, our Savior, the provider of salvation, the God who loves us beyond our understanding, beyond measure, an endless love, a love we did not earn, a love we cannot lose. For nothing can separate us from Your love that is in Christ Jesus, our Lord.

To You, O' God, we come asking You to commune with us here today. Make Your presence known, make Yourself at home here with us now. Remove from our hearts, from our minds anything preventing us from communing with You, anything weighing on us that is causing our minds not to be in tune with Your purpose for the moment. Cleanse us, Father, that we may indeed walk hand in hand with You this day, even all day, today.

Grant us grace that we might recognize exactly who we are, children of the Most High God (i.e., if we believe Jesus). Bless us, Father, with knowledge, bless us with wisdom, bless us with insights, bless us with understanding. And we will be careful to give You the praise, to give You the glory, to give You the honor. In the name of Your Son, Jesus the Christ we pray, amen!

Most of the apostle Paul's letters (epistles) are addressed directly to the church in various cities from which the books get their names. The following passage, Philippians 2:1-16, speaks directly to issues in the church at Philippi. As we read this passage, please note that it deals with a heart problem still prevalent in Jesus' church today:

> If therefore there is any encouragement in Christ, if there is any consolation of love, if there is any fellowship of the Spirit, if any affection and compassion, 2make my joy complete by being of the same mind, maintaining the same love, united in spirit, intent on one purpose. 3Do nothing from selfishness or empty conceit, but with humility of mind let each of you regard one another as more important than himself; 4do not merely look out for your own personal interests, but also for the interests of others. 5Have this attitude in yourselves which was also in Christ Jesus, 6who, although He existed in the form of God, did not regard equality with God a thing to be grasped, 7but emptied Himself, taking the form of a bondservant, and being made in the likeness of men. 8And being found in appearance as a man, He humbled Himself by becoming obedient to the point of death, even death on a cross. 9Therefore also God highly

exalted Him, and bestowed on Him the name which is above every name, 10that at the name of Jesus EVERY KNEE SHOULD BOW, of those who are in heaven, and on earth, and under the earth, 11and that every tongue should confess that Jesus Christ is Lord, to the glory of God the Father. 12 So then, my beloved, just as you have always obeyed, not as in my presence only, but now much more in my absence, work out your salvation with fear and trembling; 13for it is God who is at work in you, both to will and to work for His good pleasure. 14Do all things without grumbling or disputing; 15that you may prove yourselves to be blameless and innocent, children of God above reproach in the midst of a crooked and perverse generation, among whom you appear as lights in the world, 16holding fast the word of life, so that in the day of Christ I may have cause to glory because I did not run in vain nor toil in vain (Philippians 2:1-16).

∽

Our focus for this session is a single subject but from two perspectives: the image of God and the children of God.

You may recall that when we began this adventure, we indicated we would be taking two simultaneous paths leading to a single destination. I informed you then that the focus of the first path is humankind, who are we really—our values, nature and character—through the eyes of God? The focus of the second path is the person of God—His values, His nature and His character.

I pointed out that we would explore these two paths in parallel. Thus far we have walked these two paths alternating between them. I further indicated that in the end (and we are nearing the end) these two paths would converge and eventually merge into one.

You understand all that. So, in order to provide perspective and context for our ensuing discussion, we are going to do a quick review.

Nature of Humankind

On the path dealing with humankind, we spent most of our time in the books of Genesis and John demonstrating primarily that humankind is born dead, according to the Scriptures. And so we wrestled with appreciating that truth and its implications. Peering through the eyes of God, it is obvious that humankind is indeed born dead! And the various writers of the Bible presume that you, the Bible student, already know and accept that truth. So we spent some time talking about how the born dead thread is interwoven in and serves as a backdrop throughout the pages of the Bible. We also discussed how it plays out in the lives of humans today.

If you would truly understand the Bible and its message, you must take with you (always) what you have gained from these lessons into your Bible study and into your thought process. In everything you do, in every conversation, in every prayer, in your time of meditation, you must take this knowledge with you. The Bible is presented in such a way that it presumes you know and accept the truth that humankind is born dead. The Bible is written under the presumption that you (the reader) know that you too were born dead. Therefore, if you do not accept in your knower that you were born dead, when you go to the Scriptures, you will not appreciate what the Scriptures are telling you about yourself and your fellow humans. Therefore, we spent a great deal of time discussing the implications of that death and how to identify it in the Scriptures.

Following Adam and Eve's disobedience, we observed in Genesis chapter 4 that Cain and Abel represent the two types of seed (or peoples, as indicated in Genesis 3:15) coming from the same womb. Chapter 4's focus is the seed of the serpent (Cain) while chapter 5 is focused on the seed of the woman (Seth, Abel's replacement). In Genesis chapter 6, we explored how the "sons of God"—who were the righteous seed (people) at the beginning—looked at (lusted after) the "daughters of men". In the word "men" (i.e., all men) Scripture is informing us that there are daughters of the righteous seed and daughters of the unrighteous seed. And the sons of God did not consider nor give attention to the righteous versus the unrighteous. They simply saw beautiful women. And what did they do? They took for themselves wives (whomever they chose) based on their beauty, their physical appearance, not their heart, just like so many are doing today in contrast to what the Scriptures say (2 Corinthians 6:14-17).

Therefore, the sons of God married the daughters of unrighteous men as well. Eventually that resulted in a blended people—the sons (or people) of God and the sons (or people) of Satan becoming blended into a single people group. Stated more succinctly, the sons of God married the daughters of Satan producing a blended posterity. So that today, as in the millennial past, all humankind is blended (though not evenly so) and born dead, i.e., without the knowledge of God and His Christ. Therefore today, we have come to a point where natural humans cannot distinguish one people group from the other as confirmed in the parable of the wheat and the tares (Matthew 13:24-30, 36-43).

Please study and ruminate on this parable until its revelation is firmly anchored in your spirit.

In the book of Romans, chapter 1, Paul describes the process for how humans sank deeper and deeper into death and what this death looks like. And today we see the evidence of this truth all around us, in every home, village, town, city and nation. That is, we see both chosen (Colossians 3:9-14, 2 Thessalonians 2:13-14) and unchosen (Ephesians 4:17-19) children being born into a single family or household though we may be unable to clearly distinguish between them.

One of the points we emphasized in discussing the human path is that death is not a one-time event. When God specified death in Genesis 2:16-17, He said if you eat of this fruit, "dying you shall die". That death is not a one-time event. It is a progression, perhaps more appropriately a regression for humankind. That is what Paul is describing to us in Romans chapter 1. Humankind went from bad to "badder" to worse to "worser", if you will.

At this point, you understand all that.

Person of God

On the God path, we spent the majority of our time in one passage.

Do you recall what that one passage is?

"Exodus 34:5-9."

Have you committed this passage to memory?

If not, please make a genuine commitment to plant this seed verbatim in your heart within the next thirty days. Reading, writing and speaking it out loud several times each day over the next month is a good way to accomplish that.

Thank you very much!

In all of the Old Testament, I believe this passage, these few words, give us the greatest perspective of the person (nature, values and character) of God, i.e., His image and likeness that God wants to replicate in us. These are the words directly out of God's own mouth. God Himself is declaring (to His obedient servant and friend, Moses) who He is as the sovereign ruler and standard for righteousness. They are quoted in various forms throughout the Old Testament. And Jesus used this passage to formulate a pattern for His earthly ministry since His goal was to reveal the Father (John 17:6-26) to this world of darkness without the knowledge that God, our Creator, even exists.

In Exodus chapter 33, Moses says to God, show me Your glory. God responds to Moses, I will pass by you; you cannot look Me in the face. But you may look at Me from the back. And I will declare to you who I am.

God says to Moses, this is who I am: "I am compassionate". That is the first thing out of God's mouth: "I am compassionate". I empathize with those who need empathy. I relate to your pain. I feel your brokenness. I appreciate your disappointments. I feel your sorrow. And I fully appreciate the extent of your sins and your predicament. Yet, I am compassionate.

I do not give you what you deserve. "I am merciful and gracious." I show divine favor to those who do not deserve it. I give strength even to those who may misuse and abuse it.

"I am slow to anger." Every intent of the thoughts of your heart is only evil continuously; you have turned your back to Me; you want nothing to do with Me. Yet I am slow to be angry with you. Therefore, I will not be angry with you always.

"I am abounding in lovingkindness". This is a loyal love, a love that is poured out on us though we do not deserve it. We did nothing to earn it. In fact we have done the opposite. It is the righteous God giving His love to us without measure. And we cannot do anything to lose that love which is in Christ Jesus (Romans 8:37-39).

Now, are you glad God is not like us? Where would we be? What hope would we have? He keeps lovingkindness to a thousand generations. So your blessings today, as God pours out His love on you, may have nothing whatsoever to do with who you are or your goodness. It could be because of your great, great, great grandmother and grandfather. So do not get so happy and puffed up and say, it's because I am such a good person; God sees something good in me. However, Jesus says, "there is NONE GOOD but God alone"!

Even so, God still pours out His compassion and lovingkindness on evil people, even us. Who could not love a God like that?

"I am abounding in truth." I never lie (Numbers 23:19). What comes out of My mouth is right and true. You can trust it. You can stake your life on it. What comes out of Satan's mouth (the world at large) is nothing but lies for he is a liar and the father of lies (John 8:37-47). Much of what he has told you, what you have learned outside of what you have learned from God's revelation (the Bible), is a lie, often presented as half-truths. Satan was a murderer from the beginning. For he, the thief, comes only to steal, kill, and destroy (John 10:10). The world system as we know it is formulated by and in the likeness of Satan.

"I am forgiving." I will forgive iniquity, transgression and sin. Basically, He is saying, I will forgive anything that is not like Me. I will forgive you. But I will in no way let the guilty go free. So we look to the God who is love, the God who loves just because He chooses to love. That is who He is. He loves the unlovable. Yet, He declares, I will still maintain My system of justice.

Therefore, there is an appointed day of reckoning for unrighteous (unbelieving) people. For us Christians, our righteousness is solely the work of Jesus Christ who declares us righteous when we choose to believe (trust in, have faith in) Him instead of Satan's lies. For those who choose not to believe Jesus, the wrath of God rests upon them (John 3:16-21).

Today, while you are still in your body, choose life; choose to believe and trust Jesus Christ if you have yet to do so. Please surrender your life to Him right now.

Do not wait another moment. Make the righteous choice. Do it now (Romans 10:8-13)! Talk to Him. He is waiting to hear from you. No matter your sins, He will receive you with open arms (Revelation 3:19-22).

Two Becoming One

So we have traveled these two paths—the path of the nature of humankind and the path of the person of God. Therefore, our goal now is the two paths becoming or converging into one.

In that regard, we know that Adam and Eve were created in the image and likeness of God. One way of looking at that is they had everything in common with God. They were created for relationship and fellowship with God. With pleasure, they were to spread God's image and likeness all over the earth. But instead, they have ended up spreading Satan's image all over the earth.

But now, in this age, through the church, God is at work putting humankind back on His original plan and intent. He is conforming the elect (those whom He has chosen) to the image and likeness of Jesus Christ, His Son Romans 8:29, 1 John 3:1-2).

So what does the image of God look like? I believe we have demonstrated that Jesus is the image of God in all its fullness. So if we want to know precisely what the image of God is, if we want to know what the likeness of God is, we have only to look at that one specific human, that one unique seed of the woman, Jesus, the Christ. Take some time to think about that to get your mind around it. I contend the Bible is telling us that

Adam and Eve were created in the same image as the human Jesus, the Christ, and vice versa (excluding Jesus' deity, of course). Jesus is the genuine image and likeness of God (Colossians 1:15).

Adam and Eve chose to sin. Jesus (the second Adam) chose to obey. He also chose to be the righteous sacrifice (the submissive Lamb of God) to pay sin's penalty for all humankind for all generations. Jesus says no man takes My life. I lay it down of My own free will (John 10:17-18) because unlike Cain, **I AM My brothers' keeper** (Genesis 4:3-10, John 15:12-17). It is My choice. I could choose not to. He also says, if I desire to, I could call twelve legions of angels to come rescue Me (Matthew 26:51-54). He did not call them because that was not in your best interest.

He could choose to do what He wanted to. He did not have to go to that cross. But in His compassion and love, His abundant grace and mercy, He chose of His own free will to be obedient to the Father.

Jesus tells us, I say what I heard My Father say. And I do what I have seen My Father do always in obedience to Him. Now that is the likeness God has planned for us who believe. Eventually, when Jesus returns, we will be just like Him (except for His deity of course)— "Beloved, now we are children of God, and it has not appeared as yet what we shall be. We know that, when He appears, we shall be like Him" (1 John 3:1-2).

Any questions? Please document your innermost thoughts now. Please, do not put it off to another time.

Children of God

In John 1:12 we read, "But as many as received Him, to them He gave the right to become children of God, even to those who believe in His name." Now, if you are in fact a child of God, what kind of person ought you to be? Who should you be in your home, in your neighborhood, on your job and within your culture? You should be like that one specific and unique human, Jesus Christ!

If you believe and have received His Son, you are a child of God just as Jesus is. God has placed His seed in you. What is His seed? His Holy Spirit. His Holy Spirit is in you to empower you, to counsel you and teach you so that you would live the rest of your life according to the image and likeness of Jesus Christ, not perfectly but actually striving toward that goal with a sincere heart. That is what believers are created to be.

You should be "compassionate and gracious". You should have compassion on those in need. Look at God's compassion. God observed His enemies. He looked at our plight. We could never ever see life. In His compassion, He decided to pay the penalty for our sins so the requirements of His justice system would be fulfilled. That gave Him the freedom to shower us with His grace and love, His presence and His blessings. So, for those who could never find their way out of death, He decided to show compassion on them. Therefore, He became a human and sacrificed Himself on a cross for your sins and mine.

When we look at 1 John 3:16 (I am paraphrasing), Jesus loved us so much that He became a human and died for us on a cross. And if *Jesus was willing to give up His life for us*, we ought to be willing to give up our lives for the brethren (i.e., brothers and sisters) including those yet to be saved.

So what does that mean? I know that Bible students smarter than I will disagree with me on this because they interpret the word "brethren" there to apply to Christians only (Ref. <u>Greek Dictionary (Lexicon-Concordance)</u>). Therefore, they interpret that verse to mean one should give up his or her life for the benefit of other Christians. I do not believe that is the primary message of that verse. Context (<u>1 John 3:15-16</u>) does not suggest that. Rather, the context suggests that we ought to give up our lives for the chosen (<u>the elect of God</u> which includes those yet to be saved) who are still walking amongst those who are perishing. That is what Jesus did for us while we were in unbelief and walking amongst those who were perishing. And since we cannot identify the chosen, of necessity, we must focus our attention on all humankind, again, just like Jesus did in His ministry.

There are two types of unsaved people in the world and we cannot distinguish between them (<u>Matthew 13:24-30, 36-43</u>). Therefore, we ought to be self-sacrificing to save all who are perishing, which of necessity will include those not chosen. Just like Jesus sacrificed His life for the benefit of all humankind, we are obliged to make sacrifices in our lives to save all that we can. <u>Imagine the impact if each Christian (through the knowledge of Jesus Christ) was striving to save just five percent of those we each encounter in life.</u>

Therefore, we ought to have compassion for the people who are perishing. Just like God loves us, He also loves His lost children. And we should love what God loves. He is our Father. *We are His children.* We should love just as He loves (John 13:34-35). God, the Father, loves us so much. He also loves the world so much that He gave His only begotten Son so that whoever chooses to believe the Son should have life and have it eternally (John 3:16-18).

Look at how simple God made it. All one has to do is believe and trust (have confidence in) the Son, i.e., have faith. And to that person He gives eternal life, plus the promised Holy Spirit as a down payment on current blessings and **His future promises**. So Jesus is saying to us who believe, come join Me in what I am doing. Come join My ministry of reconciliation (2 Corinthians 5:18-21) where we can work together as one with a single objective—*keeping billions of lost souls out of hell for all eternity*!

When I took a course on church planting, the author said in the included materials, what one needs to do in planting a church is find out what God is doing and join Him in that. In other words, do not go out and do your own thing. Find out what God is doing and join Him in doing whatever it is God is doing.

And I believe Jesus is telling us today, what I am doing is saving those who are perishing. The end of this age is drawing near. The signs are all around us. The Times of the Gentiles is nearing a close. I am seeking for all those whom the Father has chosen to come in. And I am inviting you to join Me in that work, to bring them in, not only for their benefit but also for your own current and eternal rewards (Mark 10:25-31).

If you pay attention to many of the televangelists, those who are on TV and radio, you will see the emphasis of many is on discipleship—evangelism, saving souls and making disciples. I saw on TV several years ago a guy from the Assemblies of God denomination who said that the Assemblies of God is growing by leaps and bounds, not in the United States but elsewhere in the world. Remember that the Assemblies of God started here in the US. But the US churches are but a small portion of the total number of Assemblies of God churches (Statistics), less than 4% (13,000 churches) currently. The other 96% (370,000 churches) is outside the United States. I believe the guy said in less than a month, they planted about 200 churches. They are planting plenty of churches. That is what God is doing all over the world under various umbrella organizations and individuals. That is what God is blessing. God is blessing the work of those who are willing to give up what they want, give up seeking after things and wealth for themselves, give up their selfishness and sacrifice themselves to save the souls of those who are on their way to hell (John 15:12-17)! That is what God is blessing today and what He has always blessed. In the book of Acts, take a look at the work of Jesus' apostles following His ascension.

Forgive Others

As His children, God expects us to be "forgiving". That is who we should be, not holding grudges. Here is a good reason why you can be forgiving. Think about the unbelieving person toward whom you are holding ill will. As you think on them, think about who they are. They are born dead. The seed of Satan is still active in them. They do things they do not want to do, just like you. They say, I'm going to do good. And then they turn and do just the opposite. The Scriptures tell us that, right? In Romans chapter 7, Paul says, the good that I would do, I find not. But the very thing that I say I am not going to do, that is what I do.

Therefore the Scriptures are saying to us, when you have something against someone, look at who they are. Look at what is in them. Oftentimes, they cannot help it. They would do better if they could. However, they cannot do what they do not know. Instead, look at who is in you. First take the log out of your own eye so you can see clearly how to get the speck that is in your sister or brother's eye. So do not hold a grudge against them. Remember always, God does not hold a grudge against you in your sin! He has chosen instead to love you in spite of you.

Just think about that. I know we Christians can sit around at church in our nice clothes and act like we have always been the great person we portray. As a matter of fact, as far as we are concerned, we do not do anything seriously bad right now, just little stuff. We tell a lie and we label it a white lie. That means it is not really sin because it is a "white lie". Just look at yourself, though. God forgave you! You did not deserve to be forgiven. And the thing about it is, He has not forgiven you just one time either. He keeps on forgiving you. How many times has He forgiven you just for today's sin? So be like your Father and your Lord and forgive others.

One of the things I have tried to do over the last few years (and I strongly recommend you do the same) is to remind myself to not speak so much of God as "God" but as "Father". Father because I want to be reminded that He is my Daddy. And He wants His children (you and me) to be like Him. He wants us to love what He loves. He wants us to hate what He hates. He wants us to do what He does. He wants us to say what He says. And He wants us to bear fruit for the kingdom of His beloved Son whom He has appointed heir of all things.

Read these Philippians verses to make my point:

> "Do all things without grumbling or disputing; So that you may prove yourselves to be blameless and innocent, children of God above reproach, in the midst of a crooked and perverse generation, among whom you appear as lights in the world" (Philippians 2:14-15).

So what is God saying here in this passage? What is He saying? Do not look and act like the world! If you are like Me, you will not be like the world. If you look like the world, there is no light in you. And, if there is no light in you, the world will see no light. But if they see the light in you, they will come to the light for your love will draw them to you.

> 'For I am the LORD your God. Consecrate yourselves therefore [separate yourself unto God for His purpose], and be holy [unique, separate and distinct from the culture of the world] for I am holy (Leviticus 11:44).

Any questions? Please document them now along with any comments on your mind right now.

Two Paths Merging

So, we have these two paths coming together. In the beginning, humankind fell into sin and death—violence, wickedness, evil. Throughout the Scriptures, however, God is manifesting love, being what love is for He is love.

Thus far we have travelled the two paths. In uniting them as one, the goal for you, O' man or woman, is to become totally submissive to Jesus Christ, striving to be conformed to His image and likeness. That is who we were created to become so that God might be all in all. If you are His child (a Jesus believer), you are obliged to work toward that final goal that the apostle Paul describes in 1 Corinthians 15:

> But now Christ has been raised from the dead, the first fruits of those who are asleep. 21For since by a man came death, by a man also came the resurrection of the dead. 22For as in Adam all die, so also in Christ all shall be made alive. 23But each in his own order: Christ the first fruits, after that those who are Christ's at His coming, 24then comes the end, when He delivers up the kingdom to the God and Father, when He has abolished all rule and all authority and power. 25For He must reign until He has put all His enemies under His feet. 26The last enemy that will be abolished is death. 27For HE HAS PUT ALL THINGS IN SUBJECTION UNDER HIS FEET. But when He says, "All things are put in subjection," it is evident that He

is excepted who put all things in subjection to Him. 28And when all things are subjected to Him, then the Son Himself also will be subjected to the One who subjected all things to Him, that God may be all in all (1 Corinthian 15:20-28).

Any questions?

One of our passages of Scripture for this session is Philippians chapter 2. And I just want to remind you of a couple of things in that passage.

As God instructed me, I have gone around to various churches to experience church people firsthand. I have observed many issues in the various churches. And, I believe that this passage speaks directly to the cause of many of those problems and issues. Those of us in the church must give consideration to these verses and ask God to help (i.e., cause) us to walk in His pure light.

> "Do nothing from selfishness or empty conceit. But with humility of mind, let each of you regard one another as more important than himself" (v3).

This is another way of saying love (agapao) others.

Now, think about that for a moment. Do you have a problem with that verse? Tell the truth now. Do you have a problem with that verse? Just say yes. You may as well say yes. Even if you think you do not, just say yes, anyway, because none of us likes to consider other people as more important than ourselves. We may as well admit it. That is not who we are.

So you say, I am a good person. I do a host of good deeds for others regularly. However, it may be that the only reason you are doing those so-called good deeds is for what you want; what you can get out of it, for your own self-glory or self-gratification. If your motives are wrong, there is no blessing in it for you (Matthew 6:1-8). If you need more Scriptures for what we are saying, meditate on the entirety of Matthew chapter 6. In that chapter, God makes it plain that people who are doing things for their own glory, for their own selfish reasons, have received all the reward they are ever going to get.

Are you hearing me? I see church people doing all sorts of unrighteous deeds. We want higher positions. We want the position so people will look up to us. Intense pride says you ought to have that position. This position is mine. I am in charge of this. In these circumstances, we are getting our glory. Once one gets this earthly glory that is all they are ever going to get. Do not look for Jesus to give you heavenly rewards when your good deeds are not about Him but are all about self.

If you believe, be concerned about your position in heaven instead of your glory here on earth. This earthly life is only temporary. But your standing in heaven is eternal. So we ought to be working for our rewards in heaven, building up our stock in heaven, not building up self and things here on earth. *If we believe Jesus, we are children of God!* Therefore, let us strive to imitate His Son, our senior brother.

We are all selfish. We are all conceited. We all lack humility in many situations and circumstances. And we are puffed up with pride. So you say, OK. That is I. What am I to do about it? Here is the point I would make to you. You cannot change yourself. You may take issue with me on that. But I use Romans chapter 7 as my support. Here we have, I believe, the greatest apostle and saint of all time saying, I have a problem and I cannot fix me (Romans 7:14-24).

Therefore, what are you to do? Get down on your knees. Call on God and confess your sins. Submit yourself willingly to Jesus Christ saying, Thank You, Lord, for showing me who I truly am. I do not want to be who I am. Release me from the bondage of this flesh! Do whatever You will in me. Tear from me everything that is not of You. Put in me only that which is pleasing to You. Do in me whatever needs to be done. Do Your mighty work in me. And mean what you say. Pray until you receive it. Then give Him the praise at every opportunity both publicly and privately! "For it is God who is at work in you both to will and to work for His good pleasure" (Philippians 2:13).

You exist for God's good pleasure, not yours. Work, therefore, so you are pleasing to God. Work to please God and not yourself. Work to please God, not a man or a woman. Work to please God. Work to please Jesus Christ and your heavenly Father! *You are a child of God, if you believe and trust Jesus.* As His child, you are obliged to strive to be just like your Daddy and like your Lord and savior, Jesus Christ, your eldest brother (John 8:29). Therefore,

> "Do all things without grumbling or disputing [i.e., causing conflict, creating confusion] that you may prove yourselves to be blameless and innocent children of God" (v14).

Satan is having a field day in Jesus' church because we refuse to practice the wisdom of this verse. Why? Because the world tells us, if you look like this verse, that is weakness. And we do not want the world to see us as weak. That is another one of Satan's great deceptions.

> "Therefore be imitators of God, as beloved children; 2and walk in love, just as Christ also loved you, and gave Himself up for us, an offering and a sacrifice to God as a fragrant aroma. 3But do not let immorality or any impurity or greed even be named among you, as is proper among saints; 4and there must be no filthiness and silly talk, or coarse jesting, which are not fitting, but rather giving of thanks. 5For this you know with certainty, that no immoral or impure person or covetous man, who is an idolater, has an inheritance in the kingdom of Christ and God. 6Let no one deceive you with empty words, for because of these things the wrath of God comes upon the sons of disobedience. 7Therefore do not be partakers with them; 8for you were formerly darkness, but now you are light in the Lord; walk as children of light 9(for the fruit of the light consists in all goodness and righteousness and truth), 10trying to learn what is pleasing to the Lord (Ephesians 5:1-10).

> And He gave some as apostles, and some as prophets, and some as evangelists, and some as pastors and teachers, 12for the equipping of the saints for the work of service, to the building up of the body of Christ; 13until we all attain to the unity of the faith, and of the knowledge of the Son of God, to a mature man, to the measure of the stature which belongs to the fullness of

Christ. 14As a result, we are no longer to be children, tossed here and there by waves, and carried about by every wind of doctrine, by the trickery of men, by craftiness in deceitful scheming; 15but speaking the truth in love, we are to grow up in all aspects into Him, who is the head, even Christ, 16from whom the whole body, being fitted and held together by that which every joint supplies, according to the proper working of each individual part, causes the growth of the body for the building up of itself in love (Ephesians 4:11-16).

Any questions? Please jot down your final thoughts and questions now.

Let us pray: Heavenly Father, help us to flourish in Your kingdom according to Your image, in accordance with Your likeness, that we may indeed appear as children of light in a world filled with darkness.

Help us, Father. Help us! Help us, Lord. Do not turn a deaf ear to us. We confess to You that we are unable to do it in ourselves in our own strength. We have tried, Father, and we have failed. We have failed miserably. So, Father, we ask that You would take charge of our lives, that You would do Your work in us according to what pleases You.

Cause us to appear as light in this dark world. Cause us to work as You are working. Cause us to strive for what You are seeking to obtain, for what Your focus is. Cause us, Father, to do all things from a heart of love, from a heart of compassion, and a heart of forgiveness. In the name of Your Son, Jesus, the Christ, we pray, amen, amen and amen.

16

WALK IN HIS IMAGE

Scripture: 1 John 4:7-11, Exodus 34:6-9

Prayer: Heavenly Father, in the name of Jesus, we thank You that You have been so loving and kind to us. We thank You that You have seen fit to shine Your light on us and be gracious to us.

We thank You that You have enlightened us. And we know that You did not enlighten us just so that we could simply have knowledge, so that we could have knowledge that puffs us up, just so we can walk around and proclaim how much we know. But You are revealing it to us, Father, so that we would put that knowledge into action in demonstrating our love for You by following the commandments and doing the work your Son has assigned to us. May our obedience to Your Word bring joy to Your heart, joy that is manifested on Your countenance. In the name of Jesus we pray, amen.

I would like to ask you, please, to read the entire book of 1 John. Your assignment is to read it perhaps daily over the next week. Make it a part of your daily devotion. It can be read entirely in less than thirty minutes. Supplement that reading with Philippians 2:1-16. Meditate on the theologies and messages of these passages. For each chapter, summarize what you have learned. Then, incorporate this knowledge into your life's purpose and into all your interactions and relationships. Begin by developing an even deeper relationship with Jesus Christ, our Lord and Savior, by spending daily *quality* time with Him.

∽

Pause for a moment right now and take a really deep breath. Allow your mind to wander as you take a stroll through chapter 12 (Jesus: The Image of God!) and chapter 15 (Children of God!). Ruminate on our discussion regarding God's image (Exodus 34:5-7). As you meander through those chapters, you may have some questions or thoughts at this time about those discussions. If so, please document them now. Go back and review those chapters if necessary to refresh your memory.

As you ponder your own questions and comments, would you please tell me, what was our point really in those two chapters?

> What was the mental picture we attempted to paint?
>
> "The Lord is crying out to us to give up our flesh and walk hand in hand with Him?"

Do you (the reader) agree or disagree with that observation?

I think she put it precisely.

> Tell us that again.
>
> "The Lord is crying out to us to give up our flesh and walk, i.e., live our lives, in His image according to His likeness."

Give up the flesh. Walk according to His image and likeness!

Why would God want us to give up the flesh?

> "The flesh is what makes us sin."
>
> "Give up our flesh because it is not about us; it is all about Jesus."

Wonderful!

Now, the question is, Do you have that concept (that we should give up our flesh and live our lives in His image according to His likeness) deep down within your soul and spirit?

Does your life, day in and day out, reflect that understanding?

As you ponder those questions, look back over the past few chapters and ask yourself, "Do I have God's concept for my walk (the way I should live my life) deep down within me?"

> "Deep down? I think I do."

You think you do?

"Yes".

Let me ask you another question as you pause your response. Would Jesus say you have that concept deep down within you?

"I think so because He knows us inside out. He knows our heart. And if we have it in there, He would say we have it."

And if you do not have it?

"Then He would say we don't have it. For He knows what is deep down within our hearts."

Like the rich young ruler of Luke 18, one can believe he or she has solid biblical concepts deep down in their heart but actually have them only superficially (based on tradition instead of the Bible) in their mind, not in their heart and walk.

> A ruler questioned Him, saying, "Good Teacher, what shall I do to inherit eternal life?" 19 And Jesus said to him, "Why do you call Me good? No one is good except God alone. 20 You know the commandments, 'Do not commit adultery, Do not murder, Do not steal, Do not bear false witness, Honor your father and mother.'" 21 And he said, "All these things I have kept from my youth." 22 When Jesus heard this, He said to him, "One thing you still lack; sell all that you possess and distribute it to the poor, and you shall have treasure in heaven; and come, follow Me." 23 But when he had heard these things, he became very sad, for he was extremely rich. 24 And Jesus looked at him and said, "How hard it is for those who are wealthy to enter the kingdom of

> God! 25 For it is easier for a camel to go through the eye of a needle than for a rich man to enter the kingdom of God." 26 They who heard it said, "Then who can be saved?" 27 But He said, "The things that are impossible with people are possible with God." 28 Peter said, "Behold, we have left our own homes and followed You." 29 And He said to them, "Truly I say to you, there is no one who has left house or wife or brothers or parents or children, for the sake of the kingdom of God, 30 who will not receive many times as much at this time and in the age to come, eternal life" (Luke 18:18-30).

You see, the young man did not realize he had positioned his idol (his wealth) above the righteousness of God, who is the giver of wealth.

Surely, we all agree that Jesus knows what is deep down in our heart. But the question is not whether Jesus knows what is deep down within us. Rather, since He does know what is deep down within us, would He say that we have His concept for our walk deep in our knower? It is all about Jesus and what He expects of us. So would He say you have that concept deep down within you? Then, the question becomes, is your walk (i.e., the way you live your life) screaming that you do? Another way of looking at it is, would the people around you say you have put Jesus and His mission first and foremost?

You and I were God's enemies. We were born in sin. We have been shaped in iniquity (wickedness, immorality, etc.). Before we came to believe Jesus, all we knew was sin. We turned our backs to God. What we cared about first and foremost was self.

But God looked at us and observed, "My people are doomed to damnation in hell, forever! They have no way out, none! They cannot find their way to God." Yet He had compassion on us even though we were His enemies.

"They cannot find their way to Me. They do not even want to know Me. But I am going to love them with an insatiable agape love. I am going to do what is best for them."

Walk In His Image

Therefore, when you see the woeful plight of those who are perishing, where is your compassion? Are you saying, as God said, I am going to make provision to keep these people (even my enemies) out of eternal damnation?

God says, "I am gracious." That means He is giving and He shows favor even to those who are undeserving of favor, even His enemies. In chapter 5 of Matthew, Jesus says, "Love your enemies. Pray for those who persecute you." Is that you? That is the question. Is that you?

God says I am slow to anger, "sloooooow" to anger, truly slow to anger. You see the flesh loves to rise up against the offender. God says, "I am slow to anger". How about you?

God goes on to say, "abounding in lovingkindness and truth." We talked about that in a previous chapter. We talked about the fact that the translators coined the word "lovingkindness" in order to translate the word "hesed".

Do not forget the kindness in lovingkindness. We gave you a definition of the God kind of love in the New Testament. Do you recall what that definition says?

Can you provide our definition of agape love?

"Acts in the best interest of the other person."

All right. Talk to me about that somebody. Give me a picture of what that love looks like.

"Showing compassion. Instead of thinking about me, I should be thinking about somebody else. Instead of always thinking about myself, I should be concerned for the welfare of somebody else."

When God showed His compassion for you, about whom was He thinking?

"Somebody else."

Was He thinking about Himself?

"No."

He was thinking about those undeserving of His love. When God poured out His grace on us, He sacrificed His Son to make it easy on us to get out of the deep devilish pit we were born into. One can have God's eternal life simply by believing and trusting His Son, Jesus. That is all one has to do. Think about that. You do not have to jump up twenty feet to prove how much you trust Him. All He asks you to do is believe and trust (have faith in) His Son (the Prophet of Deuteronomy 18:15-19). Jesus spoke the words God placed in His mouth. He was and has been continuously thinking about you and your need, instead of Himself.

As you revisit these past lessons, whom have you been concerned about? Many of us would have to say, "Mostly, I was concerned with 'me' and my welfare". If we are honest, most of us would have to say, my focus was I. What can I get? How can I manipulate (or negotiate) this situation to benefit me, to get me into Heaven? Keep me out of hell.

Let me tell you an interesting thing about our thought process. There is a concept in the Bible few of us have been taught, that few of us know anything about. It is called "motive" (<u>Proverbs 16:2-3</u>, <u>James 4:1-4</u>). If you really want to know what you are about, seek out your true motive.

Jeremiah tells us in chapter 17 verse 9,

> The heart is more deceitful than all else and is desperately sick; who can understand it?

Our heart deceives us. It makes us think we are one thing when we are actually the opposite. Let me give you an example: You have a husband. Or, you have a wife. You have a boyfriend or girlfriend. Go back to the dating and courting period. Do you remember how you would do things for them while you were dating and courting? You would regularly go out of your way to do something special for that other person, ostensibly unselfish things. But then, you got married or you moved in together. Six months later you do very few special things for them. And they ask you, what happened? Why aren't you as attentive to me anymore? Have you experienced that?

You see we must first look at the motive.

> When we are courting, our motive is all about what?
>
> "Me! How can I get what I want?"
>
> "How can I make them fall in love with me?"

But we want them to think we are all about "them". So we do all sorts of (what appears to be) nice little selfless things to impress them. Can you relate to what I am saying? But when we get married or move in together, they soon begin to think who is this person I have married or this person I am living with? I thought I had married or united with a loving, generous, kind, gentle and unselfish person. Now I don't know who this person is.

You see our motives were all messed up. We portrayed the image that we were all about the other person by manipulating them, when in fact, we were all about self. We only did those things so we could get what we wanted. The sad part is the other person was likely doing the very same thing to you. Can you relate to what I am saying?

So, we can sit here and say, oh yes, I love this person and I love that person. But what we do (in fact) is love them enough to get what we want, because we are all about self. That is right! We are selfish like that. As a matter of fact, when we speak the word "love", we are mostly speaking of the love that comes to us. And whatever we do, it is designed to get the love in them to come to us. No matter how we try to make our actions sound really nice and pretty, what we are truly about is getting the love in others to come to us.

After we get their love, what do we argue about? "You don't love me! If you loved me, you would not have forgotten our anniversary! If you loved me, you would not have said those cruel things!"

You see, our love is all about us. We erroneously think love is what comes to us. God says love is what goes forth from us and is manifested in the care, kindness and compassion we show others. "But God demonstrates His own love toward us, in that while we were yet sinners [enemies of God], Christ died for us" (Romans 5:8) not to give us what we want, but to give us what we need.

Lovingkindness (hesed) is loving and also showing kindness even to our enemies, showing kindness to those who do not agree with us, showing kindness to those who do not look or act like us, showing kindness even to those who hate us, loving and showing kindness when we do not feel like it.

God says He "forgives iniquity, transgression, and sin." For you it means forgiving those who have transgressed against you, forgiving those who have hurt you bitterly, those who have upset you so much you can hardly contain yourself. You want to explode! Can you forgive them in such circumstance? Do you think maybe God, as He observes humankind, do you think that over time He has arrived at the point where He was furiously angry? Oh yes! God gets very angry. And the day is coming when we are going to see the explosion of God's anger (wrath) upon the guilty—disbelievers.

What God says is, He is slow to anger not that He does not get angry. In the meantime, for those who believe and trust His Son, He has chosen to forgive all the sins (past, present and future) committed against Him.

Jesus' image and likeness is what God expects us to desire and strive diligently to become.

Questions or comments?

There was a time many years ago when I would read Exodus 34:5-7 over and over again on a regular basis. I would read all the way down through the point of forgiveness in verse 7 with no concern for the guilty. My focus was always on the forgiveness of my sins. Thank You Jesus! That was all I needed to know. And I would stop there. That was my vision of God. That is who God was to me. He was the God who forgives my sins! Hallelujah! Thank You Jesus!

But that was only one side of God. I was only looking at one side of His true nature. There is another side to God that we must not miss. God says, "yet He will by no means leave the guilty unpunished, visiting the iniquity of fathers on the children and on the grandchildren to the third and fourth generations" (v7b).

So we go back to the concept we talked about at the beginning of these sessions. We said the Bible is the Word of God, that we believe it is true. We believe everything written in its original manuscripts. And God is saying He is going to punish the guilty. Then who are the guilty? The guilty are those who are the disbelievers, those who refuse to believe and trust Jesus. Those who have chosen to go their own way. God says the disbelieving sinners are going to be punished with an everlasting punishment (Matthew 25:41-46).

Do not forget that! The guilty are going to be punished with an everlasting punishment! He is talking about our children, our grandchildren, all of our progeny, aunts, uncles and cousins who do not believe Jesus. He is talking about our friends, our neighbors, our coworkers, our parents and siblings, even our enemies and maybe even your unbelieving spouse. He is saying that He will not let the guilty go unpunished. He will punish them with an everlasting punishment. Now, if you still do not understand where I am getting that concept from, turn to the book of Revelation. If you read chapters 19 and 20, you will see that in the end Satan and his angels are thrown into the lake of fire and all of the sinners (disbelievers) with him. And the Bible says their suffering will go on day and night forever. They will forever be tormented in the lake of fire because the fire does not consume them. So it is an everlasting torment. Paste that picture into your knower!

Now, the question is, knowing what is true, will you choose to operate (live) in the image and likeness of Jesus? He came to earth to "seek and to save that which was lost" (Luke 19:10). So will you show the same character traits of God our Father and obey Jesus, our Master? Will you have compassion for the guilty? Will you demonstrate (by your actions) your lovingkindness and compassion for the guilty?

What am I talking about? What am I asking of you? We know that God has proclaimed and declared His everlasting punishment on those who do not believe.

Therefore the question is, are you willing to give of yourself, to stop thinking about yourself and start thinking about those on their way to hell, just like God thought about you?

You see, you do not sit here in this study with this book because you brought yourself here. God brought you here. So now, when you look out at the people who are rejecting Jesus, are you going to observe or judge them with a negative attitude? "I can't see why they are so averse to God and His church." Or, are you going to say, they were born dead and born blind. They do not know and they cannot see the light of the Gospel of Jesus Christ. They have no light in them. Therefore, because of my love (God's love in me), I will have compassion on them just like Jesus Had compassion on me.

Therefore, I will go to them and proclaim the good news of Jesus Christ. And when they do not want to hear it, I am going to patiently and compassionately persist and pray. I do not care how they rebuke me. I am going to think about their need, what is best for them in eternity. I will allow my feelings to be hurt (but not my person). I will allow myself to be ostracized or criticized. And I will pray continuously and fervently to save them from the wrath of God that is sure to come upon those who do not believe. That is what Jesus did and continues to do. He was ostracized. He was criticized. He was reviled. He was brutalized. He was even murdered for His efforts to show compassion, grace and lovingkindness for the benefit the guilty.

> "This is My commandment, that you love one another, just as I have loved you. Greater love has no one than this, that one lay down his life for his friends. You are

My friends if you do what I command you" (John 15:12-14).

So again, the question is, Are you going to walk in love, in compassion, and show favor to those who are perishing? And, no matter what they say to you, are you going to forgive them? Are you going to forgive their transgression and sin against you and bless them with your testimony, your witness and your prayers?

Any Questions? Please document your thoughts and prayers now.

For God is Love!

Love is integral to God's nature. Love is also integral to the culture of the Kingdom of God. Therefore, let us take a good look at our 1 John passage:

> Beloved, let us love one another, for love is from God; and everyone who loves is born of God and knows God. 8The one who does not love does not know God, for God is love. 9By this the love of God was manifested in us, that God has sent His only begotten Son into the world so that we might live through Him. 10In this is love, not that we loved God, but that He loved us and sent His Son to be the propitiation for our sins. 11Beloved, if God so loved us, we also ought to love one another (1 John 4:7-11).

This is an important point we want always to keep in mind—God is love! If He is love, He cannot help but pour out His love. If you are born again, you are born again to His likeness. And His likeness is love. His image is compassion. His image is forgiveness. His image is graciousness. His image is lovingkindness. His image is righteousness.

What does the Bible mean when it says righteousness? It is saying everything that God says and does is morally and ethically right. Therefore, you should operate in what God says is right. God's truth is righteousness.

You see, we were born in a lie. Satan has deceived all of us all of our lives. He has done such a great job of deceiving us that we think the lie is the truth. That is why when we read certain concepts in the Bible, we say the Bible cannot mean what it appears to be saying. It must mean something else because that cannot be its meaning. That does not make sense. Have you ever thought that? That is your flesh talking to you because Satan has deceived us all throughout these millennia.

Revisit verses 9-10 above. That is how God demonstrated His love for us. And the following verses tell us about demonstrating our love.

> "Beloved, if God so loved us, we also ought to love one another [do what is in the best interest of the other person]. 12No one has seen God at any time; if we love one another, God abides in us, and His love is perfected in us" (1 John 4:11-12).

You see, God could have developed a plan where He alone went out to save everyone chosen to be saved; where we had no opportunity to participate with Him. But that is not what He did. He designed a plan where He would take it upon Himself alone to save some and

He would invite us to participate with Him to save others. Because we are His children (if we believe), we ought to love what He loves, want what He wants, and do what He does.

Everything in the culture of the Kingdom of God is based in love. Take a look at 1 John 5:1-5:

> Whoever believes that Jesus is the Christ is born of God; and whoever loves the Father loves the child born of Him. 2By this we know that we love the children of God, when we love God and observe His commandments. 3For this is the love of God, that we keep His commandments; and His commandments are not burdensome. 4For whatever is born of God overcomes the world; and this is the victory that has overcome the world—our faith. 5And who is the one who overcomes the world, but he who believes that Jesus is the Son of God?

In John chapter 14, the Scriptures tell us that if we love God, we will keep His commandments. It goes on to say, "He who has My commandments and keeps them, he it is who loves Me" (John 14:21-23). Recall our definition of agape love—acts in the best interest of the other person. This is God's kind of love. Not in my interest alone, not in what is pleasing to me, not in what makes me happy, not in what I can get, but also in what I can give to others, how I might help others in their need. God has poured out His love on us so that we can in turn pour out that love on those who are perishing. We are not talking about this warm, fuzzy feeling kind of love. We are speaking of acts in the best interest of the other person. God has poured out His love. He has sacrificed His Son, offered you salvation and wooed you until you accepted it in demonstration of His love toward you. He wants you in turn to pour out that love on all those who are perishing. Demonstrate your love by spreading the good news of His compassion, grace, love and forgiveness made available to all humankind. And should they choose Jesus, you and your church are obligated to nurture them to maturity such that they too might be able to produce new disciples for Jesus Christ.

Four Basic Questions

When all is said and done, our prayer is, this adventurous journey (in the end) has inspired you to search your heart for the answers to four basic yet critical questions: "What is the church doing?" That is, what has the church been doing in the not so distant past through today? What is the church's focus and activities today? The second question we are asking is, "What should the church be doing according to the Scriptures?" Our third question, "Are the answers to these two questions the same?" If the answers to the first two questions are substantially the same, then we say let us go forward even more aggressively. But if these two pictures are different, then we must make a decision about the direction we (individually and collectively as the church) will go from this point forward? Lest we risk being a rebellious generation as Israel was during the Creator's visit to the earth.

Indeed, if your answers to the first two questions are not the same, then, seek God's advice for this question:

"What are you going to do about it in your own life and in your particular church family?"

Please try to keep the perspective of these questions in mind as we proceed to the end of our adventurous exploration of the Holy Scriptures.

Any questions? Please document them and your final comments in your notes.

Let us pray: Heavenly Father, You have asked that we would demonstrate our love toward our fellow humans, especially toward those who are perishing, especially those who are born in sin and shaped in iniquity and have not accepted the grace, the favor that Your Son offers to us. O' God, we know that You want us to join in the work that You are doing. And we know Your work in this age is seeking and saving that which You lost. So we pray, Father, that You would put in us a passion to do Your work. Put in us compassion for those who are perishing. Put in us a spirit of love that we would demonstrate Your love, the same love that You poured out on us. Empower us to demonstrate that love toward those who are perishing, toward those who are of our own household, toward those in our own extended families, toward those who are next door to us, in our neighborhoods, on our jobs and wherever we may go.

O' God, train us to do the deeds that You have shown us, that we may walk in the Spirit of Your Son, in His image, according to His likeness. We confess to You, Father, that we are unable to do it in our own efforts, in our own power. So we ask that Your power that resides in us through Your Holy Spirit would take charge of us. We give You the freedom to do what You will in us.

Help us, Father, when we fail to relinquish power to Him so that He would indeed have full dominance, all authority to take charge of us and help us succeed at that which You have commanded us to do. Let it begin right here where we are, then take us forth into the world, bringing life, changing individuals, changing households, changing communities, changing cities and changing even the whole world. This is our fervent prayer in the name of Your Son, Jesus, who died on a cross to save us all from eternal damnation. In His name we pray, amen.

17

MINISTRY OF RECONCILIATION

Scripture: Romans 8:1-18, Ephesians 4:11-16

Prayer: Heavenly Father, we thank You for Your goodness. We thank You for Your mercy. We thank You for revealing Yourself to us. We thank You for the provision of salvation which You have provided to us so undeservedly. We thank You for sending Your Son to be the propitiation for our sins and those of the whole world. And not only that, Father, (if we believe Your Son) You have given us Your Holy Spirit so we are sealed in Him, protected until the day of Your Son's return and the revealing of Himself as He truly is. O' Father, we have confidence that when He returns, we will indeed be like Him for we will see Him as He truly is.

And Father, we ask that You would bless us with Your presence here today. Make Yourself known in us, through us, and to us. Cause us indeed to feel Your presence today so that our heart may be rejuvenated.

We thank You, Father, for the millions who have chosen to study this book series. We thank You, Father, as well for those who have yet to choose. For we know You will cause the many to read and implement these lessons in due time as more disciples do their work. We pray that the deep treasures of Your Word would be revealed to all motivating them to spread Your good news. And we shall rejoice in Your presence forevermore. In Jesus name we pray, amen.

~

Well, today is the day. Now is the time. Therefore, I am going to let you talk to me today. I am going to try to do very little talking. Instead I would like to ask you to look back over these last few days, weeks or months and ask yourself, why did this man, Arlington McRae, write this book? Why has he spent all this time talking about people being born dead and the nature of humankind versus the character and nature of God? Why has he encouraged us to study the Bible every day?

Perhaps you have not heard other people talk about these things, at least not in the depth and from the perspective presented here. So, how has this presentation impacted you? Please take a moment now to jot down your response.

I also encourage you to post your thoughts about this series (and about Jesus Christ) on whatever site or location you used to purchase this book. Additionally, please post your thoughts and recommendations on all your social media sites. Brag about your new understanding and insight. Help us start an online conversation and a worldwide movement. Help us keep the many out of hell!

I thank you for choosing to purchase this book and for your diligence in reading it through to the end. My prayer is that you have in some way found this journey exciting, encouraging, uplifting and deeply insightful. May your life be blessed for all you are doing to expand the kingdom of our Lord, Jesus Christ.

Give Your Impression

So, we want to begin our discussion for this session by asking you this question: What impact has these sixteen sessions had on you, if any?

> "It has shown me a new way to listen to and interpret the Bible. It showed me a new way of listening to the messages that are given to me from the pulpit. It has given me a new way to approach people in the world and how to relate to them. Anyway, when I talk to them, I have a new way of talking to them now, just speaking to them in everyday conversation. It shows me a new way of talking to them because I did not have a way at first. But you have given me a way. I am learning the true and the right way in what to tell them about the Bible and about Jesus. It has changed my life a lot. I'm going to say it has made me a better person. And I appreciate that and I hate for this to end."

Wonderful! Any one else?

> "These past weeks have impacted me in that I have learned how to understand God's Word better when I read the Bible. And the reason why I say that is

because from the beginning when you were asking what is death, and when you took us through where Adam and Eve had eaten the fruit, the very verse where it says in Genesis the very day you eat you will surely die, I really understand now. I do not have to dig off in there and make it be something else. It is just what it says. And that has really helped me. I have read the Bible a lot. That is what I was doing, reading and not understanding. It helps me to understand now. Read what it says and that is what it means. It is just that simple. I got a better understanding. It keeps me focused on keeping Jesus out front. It keeps me reminded to try to do like Jesus, to try to live better."

Thank you both for your heartfelt response.

Please write your response in your notes now. Be as explicit as possible.

Thank you.

The Central Question

I contend that the central question in the Bible, from the beginning and throughout all the pages of the Bible, is a very simple one. And this same question is the New Testament basis for salvation. That question is simply this: Do you believe God? Or, do you believe Jesus, God's Son, who is also God in human form? It is really that simple. How do we obtain salvation? Believe God. Believe Jesus. What was the critical question confronting Adam and Eve? Will you believe God or will you believe the serpent?

Whom will you believe? Have you made a decision to believe Jesus Christ? Don't wait until it is too late!

The program of God is rooted in faith, evidenced in one's belief and trust in the messages of God's prophets and the Word of God's Son.

The Scriptures tell us,

> ...if you confess with your mouth Jesus as Lord, and believe in your heart that God raised Him from the dead, you shall be saved; 10for with the heart man believes, resulting in righteousness, and with the mouth he confesses, resulting in salvation (Romans 10:9-10).

Those who will not make it into God's rest are those who choose to disbelieve (reject) Jesus Christ. The central question today is, do you believe Jesus? Therefore, when we read God's Word, no matter how it may appear, we must choose to believe that which God has revealed to us. For,

> God is not a man, that He should lie, Nor a son of man, that He should repent; Has He said, and will He not do it? Or has He spoken, and will He not make it good (Numbers 23:19)?

You may not understand it, you may have questions, but accept it as true anyway. And then try to validate it with other Scriptures. Remember, the Bible explains the Bible. It may not make sense to you at the moment. So accept it as true. Then follow up that acceptance with fervent prayers for confirmation and understanding (Matthew 7:7-8). Continue to look for confirmation in the Scriptures as we have demonstrated to you. I know that God is able to provide the insight to make it clear so that it will make sense to you.

I know that Yahweh is a logical God and He is true. Therefore, His revelation is also logical and true when we study to see it through His eyes. And when you see it through God's eyes, it will be completely logical to you. When you study deeper and deeper with prayer and meditation, you will come away with the conviction that everything God says is completely logical when seen through His eyes.

Another thing, my saying that God is a logical God may not resonate well with you. Even so, God is still a logical God! You do not have to fully understand His revelation to believe it. But you do need to understand it to fully embrace it. Be aware that Satan will use your doubts against you to confuse you and mislead you. So ask Jesus to give you the understanding and clarity that will remove all doubt. Amen!

Any questions? Please make your notes now.

Ministry of Reconciliation

So this volume has had an impact on you. The next question I have for you is, based on what you have learned and your ruminations on what God has revealed to you, what should be the focus of your life going forward? And what should be the mission of your church in light of what you now know?

> What should the church be doing in light of what you have learned throughout this volume?

"Showing people salvation; trying to bring in lost souls. We should go out, not sit and wait for people to come to church. Go out!"

Is there anyone else?

"From what we have learned, I think the church should be teaching us more about Jesus where we can learn to evangelize and teach someone else about Jesus. To me we would get stronger if we had this kind of teaching all the time where the church members will be able to teach somebody else, if we constantly get this. We may not have it right now. But if we were constantly receiving this kind of teaching, we would get stronger where we could do this for somebody else. Teaching somebody else about Jesus is what it is really about. Learn more of the Word and learn how to live the way God wants us to live. I think that is what we should be teaching."

All right. In light of what she just said, I want you to think about the woman at the well in John chapter 4.

This is the story where Jesus meets the Samaritan woman at the well just outside the city called Sychar. We believe it was about midday. All the disciples had gone into the city to get food. And Jesus asked the woman to give Him a drink of water. And the woman said, how is it that You being a Jew ask me for a drink? Jesus told her, if you knew who it was asking you for water, you would have asked Him and He would have given you living water springing up to eternal life. You don't have anything to dip with, she said. How then do You give me this living water?

So you remember that story, right? If not, please pause now to read it in <u>John chapter 4</u>.

Now, based on the content, she spent just a few minutes with Jesus. If she had a Bible, it would have been only the old Testament. So how much did she learn about Jesus in those few minutes?

Her response to Him was, I perceive You must be a prophet. You people say it is in Jerusalem where we ought to worship. Jesus tells her the day is coming and now is that true worshippers will worship God in Spirit and in truth. So it is not worshipping in Jerusalem or in these mountains.

I just want to make sure you have sufficient understanding of the content of that story before my main point.

Now, after those few minutes with Jesus, the woman left her water pot and went into the city and told everyone about the Jesus she knew. Then she brought out of that city all the people to meet the Jesus she knew. How would you describe what she did?

> How would we label her actions?
>
> We would label that "witnessing or evangelizing".
>
> How much did she know to evangelize?
>
> "She didn't know much."
>
> "She had faith. She was confident."
>
> "I guess Jesus gave her something to tell them."

So, what is my point? *You do not have to have great knowledge to be a witness. You just have to know Jesus. And then go tell the people about the Jesus you know.*

We are commanded to be His witnesses to testify of what we know from our own personal experiences and our knowledge of His Word. Of course we must continuously study to show ourselves approved, a worker rightly dividing the Word of God (2 Timothy 2:15). But no matter how little you know, most likely you know much more than the unbelievers do. And if you do not, ask them to teach you. Then pray and listen very carefully. Ask questions so you can see what they see through their eyes. Perhaps Jesus will provide you a pathway to their heart.

Finally, let them know you are going to pray often asking our Savior to reveal the truth to them so they do not end up in hell. Let them know also that you are going to ask Jesus, when death is near, to give them an opportunity to surrender their soul to Christ in those final moments. Encourage them to call on the name of Jesus in their final minutes. If they cannot say anything else, tell them to say, "Jesus! Save me!".

You see, here in the United States especially, we are bent on having knowledge. And what we do is get knowledge so we can get knowledge, so we can get more knowledge. So we can get even more knowledge. But then, we do little in our own lives to apply the knowledge we already have. So what good is more knowledge if you are not going to put it to work (practice it) in your own life?

It reminds me of the parable of the talents where the master gave his servants talents (money) before he went on a trip. When he came back, the one who had been given five had doubled his. The one who was given two had doubled his. But the one who had been given one talent had done nothing with his one. And his master called him worthless. And the master took away what he had and gave it to the one who had ten (Matthew 25:14-30).

That story is talking about us. We have received knowledge. And we know Jesus personally (if we believe). Others do not! That is all we need to become an effective witness, producing fruit for God's kingdom.

Having applied knowledge is the way you become all that Jesus wants you to be. For your obedience must be based on your knowledge of God's Word. In light of that, it would be nice to have the theologians' depth of knowledge especially if we want to become master debaters. Many who disbelieve have great knowledge too. But many of those with such knowledge only use it to debate for debate's sake and to show off their biblical prowess . But here was my shocker! Many debating disbelievers are not actually seeking God! They simply enjoy making you sweat. But do not let that bother you. Instead, see it as an invitation to prayer. Pray fervently, therefore, that Jesus would keep them out of hell. Keep in mind always that true evangelism (and disciple-making) is more about your prayer life (1 Corinthians 2:12-14) than your knowledge. Pray fervently, therefore, for disbelievers to become strong committed believers who will mature to making other true disciples.

When you introduce Jesus to someone and they ask you questions you cannot answer, be comfortable telling them honestly you do not know. Ask them to share their thoughts on the matter as you pray silently. And if the Spirit leads you, respond appropriately to accomplish your objective such as asking them even more probing questions. Should they criticize you, be gracious and offer to get the answer for them, if you believe they are sincere in seeking true knowledge for the right purpose.

Take the little that you have and use it effectively so that when Jesus comes, He will say what? I am so proud of what you have done with the little you had. You have taken My little and turned it into two or three or ten or one hundred believing souls. Therefore, I am going to bless you to be over much.

Here is the thing we should keep in mind: The little that you know, no matter how little it is, was sufficient to convert you to a Bible believing Jesus disciple, a true convert (if indeed you are a believer). It was enough to draw you to Jesus. And look at you now! You are out here working to keep other people out of hell! Praise God!

Remember the Samaritan woman at the well. She used the little knowledge and experience she had with Jesus to save an entire city. Through faith and prayer, certainly you can accomplish much just as the Samaritan woman did at the well!

> Am I making sense to you?

> "Yes."

> OK then. On one hand, sister H says we should be getting out of the church and we should be telling the

people about Jesus. And I think sister Q essentially is saying, if I had more knowledge, I would tell more people about Jesus. And we seem to be on the path toward saying the church needs to do more to actually prepare its members to spread the gospel daily as they go through life.

Therefore, I have a challenge for you. Will you take it upon yourself then, from this day forward, to spread the gospel? Because you are the church. Or do you feel like you still do not have what you need to spread the good news that Jesus died for your sins? Then He got up from His grave and is now offering salvation to all who choose to believe Him (Romans 10:8-11)?

"Like you said, you do not need a whole lot to become a witness. You just need what you've got. You just need to know Jesus."

Matthew 28 says, as you are going through life, make disciples wherever you go. In Acts 1:8, "You will receive power after that the Holy Spirit comes upon you and you will be My *witnesses* in Jerusalem, in Judea, in Samaria, and in the utter most parts of the world."

Note the word, "witnesses". That is one thing I encourage you to keep in mind always. Be a witness wherever you go! What is a witness? A witness testifies to what she or he has seen, what she or he has heard and what she or he knows—this is what Jesus has done in my life; this is what I have seen Jesus do in the life of others; and this is what I have learned from my personal study of the Bible.

Your job is not to prove how much Bible you actually know. If the person actually needs it, refer them to your pastor or knowledgeable colleague or a well established commentary, if necessary.

When you are talking about your own experiences in this way, you are talking about what you know deep down in your heart, because you have actually experienced it. And your passion for what you know deep down in your heart will shine through and impact people and be more meaningful to them because you are speaking with conviction.

If you simply tell them what the Bible says and you are not confident in it yourself, they are not going to be convicted. But if you tell them of your own personal encounters with Christ Jesus, backed up with the Word you know, it will be persuasive enough to impact them. They will hear you saying, you had better listen to me before it is too late for you! Don't let me look over the great chasm, as Abraham and Lazarus did, and see you in torment, for eternity (Luke 16:19-31). Let them know, waiting until after death is not an option! Instant death may be their fate. It is imperative that they surrender their soul to Jesus while still in their body! Waiting until after death is too late!

Our children and other family members are perishing right before our eyes because we who know Jesus are not witnessing to them through our words and our deeds. The reality of Jesus is not a foregone conclusion in our everyday conversations and actions. We do not lift Him up the way He should be lifted up. And by that I simply mean giving Him credit where credit is due. Such as, "Let me tell you what Jesus did for me this week!" Instead of saying this is what happened to me; or let me show you what I got, say, "Do you know Jesus loves me?" "Let me show you what Jesus did for me." "Let me tell you what God showed me in His Word. You have got to see this!" "You are going to be amazed."

Think about it. You could simply take Genesis 2:16-17 and talk to people about that and its effect on the human race. Think about the impact that would have on folk's lives. Most people who have read the Bible say one of three things in regards this passage. They did not die when they ate. Or, they died later as in chapter 5. Or, they died spiritually. And when we say they died spiritually we act like it is not a big deal. They just died spiritually. We just go right on pass it. But when you know the truth about us human beings, you know that the essence of who we are is spirit. And if my spirit dies or is dead, I am in big trouble. I am dead! Dead! Truly dead!!

> So if the church's primary focus should be spreading the gospel, how do we get you and the other people in your church to do that and do it diligently, persistently, effectively and on purpose?

> "We must exhort them to go out and talk to people. And we get the people to come in to the church. When you are out in the street, talk to people about the Bible. Some will turn their back on you and not listen to you. But we keep going. We keep talking about God, about Jesus. People have turned their back on me many times. But I keep on talking to them and talking to different people. Sometime when sitting out on my porch, I talk to the people about the Bible. And some of them turn their back on me. But I pray for them."

One of the things I believe you should leave with anyone that does not want to hear you, that I think will be very meaningful to them, and maybe even save their life, is this: tell them, I am going to pray for you. I am going to ask Jesus to give you a few minutes just before you die. When death is eminent, I am asking God to give you the opportunity to call on the name of Jesus. So when that happens, you make sure you call on the name, JESUS. And get them to promise you that they will at least do that. For the Bible says, 'AND IT SHALL BE, THAT EVERYONE WHO CALLS ON THE NAME OF THE LORD WILL BE SAVED' (Acts 2:21).

Are you hearing me? God will answer that prayer! Based on what I have experienced in my own life, I know God has answered that prayer for me.

Putting It Into Practice

One of the things I asked you to do in a previous chapter was to read the entire book of 1 John and Philippians 2:1-16. As you read the book of 1 John, did it have more meaning to you as a result of your study of this volume? Maybe a better question would be, as you read it, could you see any influence from having the knowledge and insight you have gained thus far? Or, did you even bother to read it?

If you did not make time to read it, allow me to encourage you. Please read the book of 1 John and Philippians 2:1-16. I am asking you to read the entire book of 1 John at least once per day for the next week. You should be able to read it in less than thirty minutes. As you read it, look for a couple of things. Firstly, do you see in that book where John is referencing or alluding to the fact that people are born dead, that people are dead or death? Is he also alluding to life? Secondly, note if 1 John gives you a very good picture of what you, I and the church ought to be doing, what our focus ought to be. I want you to look for that. And the same holds true for Philippians 2:1-16.

Now, do you want to ask me any questions?

"How should we go out; what should we do?"

I believe you should be taking every opportunity, in your normal interaction with others, to at least try to interject Jesus into the conversation, as appropriate. Do not be intimidating or pushy. Know your objective! If they respond favorably, try to take it deeper.

Here is a simple thing you could do when you encounter a complete stranger: Once you have established your presence by way of a good morning, how are you today, etc.? When they respond appropriately after a brief conversation, then you could say, "May I ask you a question?" Then say something like, "Are you by any chance a student of the Bible?" Or, "Do you have your business straight with Jesus?" Or, "What are you doing about Jesus Christ?" Use either one or all of these questions though not back to back. Pray beforehand for the Holy Spirit to give you an appropriate reaction to their response.

Through the aid of the Holy Spirit, preplan your response according to how you anticipate their reaction to your questions. For example, you could use this series as one of your tools. Your question could be, "Are you a student of the Bible?" No matter their answer, tell them about this book series and its impact on your own understanding of the Bible. Tell them about your relationship with Jesus Christ. Maybe it needs improvement or perhaps you are simply overjoyed just thinking about it. Relax and be authentic in your response. No matter their initial response, encourage them to read the books in this series. Let them know how you have been impacted.

In further answer to your question, I believe that you should pray every morning for God to give you opportunity to witness to someone. Also ask that He would give you the grace, the strength, the heart, compassion and the words to witness effectively. Pray every morning and every evening. If you pray in the morning and Jesus gives you opportunity, as soon as you recognize that opportunity, pray right then—Jesus help me! Thank You Jesus.

One of the things I can tell you from my own experiences is people will call me. And as soon as they start telling me the issue they are calling about, the first thing I try to remember to say silently is, "Jesus help me". I am afraid to give them what I think. But it is a joy to tell them what Jesus and the Scriptures say and to hear their reaction.

In the evening when you return home and you are relaxing on the couch, perhaps you will recall that Jesus gave you opportunity to witness for Him. When you do, give Jesus thanks for that opportunity. Then review with Him how you handled it. If you see something in there that you did not do well, ask Him how you should have handled it. And ask Him to help you tomorrow when the next opportunity is presented to you. If you practice this daily, you will increase in confidence and be amazed at what you will experience in your own life.

So please! Keep a daily journal of your spiritual encounters so you can brag on your Jesus in your church and amongst your friends. Share your experiences with your friends and coworkers in order to encourage them to walk as you walk, pray as you pray, witness as you witness. Your reward in heaven and on the earth will be great!

In this regard, we tend to focus a lot on getting people to come to church. Do not make that your primary goal. Getting people to come to church should be a goal but not your immediate primary goal. So invite them at the appropriate time, when it feels right. However, if they show interest in coming to your church, do not discourage them. Invite them!

Your primary goal should be to introduce them to the Jesus you know. Once they get acquainted with Jesus, then invite them to church. But do not pressure them. If you will spend your time and energy in prayer, Jesus will encourage them to come to church. Your job is to sow the seed. Jesus is responsible for making it grow to producing fruit for His kingdom.

Keep this in mind as well: many people have an aversion to church due to bad experiences with church people and pastors. And who can blame them? The devil's people also go to church. So when you encounter such people, acknowledge their feelings and show your compassion and empathy for them. But keep the focus on Jesus Christ, our Deliverer.

Therefore, **you**, the disciple of Jesus Christ, start where you are. Say what you already know. (But continue to study diligently to increase what you know.) And use what you already have to the glory of Jesus Christ and to the expansion of His Kingdom.

Any questions or comments? Make your notes now.

Church Mission

In my closing remarks, I would like to encourage the church via the words of Ephesians chapter 4. Let us look at it for a few minutes to see what it says regarding the work and mission of the church:

> And He gave some as apostles, and some as prophets, and some as evangelists, and some as pastors and teachers, 12for the equipping of the saints for the work of service, to the building up of the body of Christ; 13until we all attain to the unity of the faith, and of the knowledge of the Son of God, to a mature man [or woman], to the measure of the stature which belongs to the fullness of Christ. 14As a result, we are no longer to be children, tossed here and there by waves, and carried about by every wind of doctrine, by the trickery of men, by craftiness in deceitful scheming; 15but speaking the truth in love, we are to grow up in all aspects into Him, who is the head, even Christ, 16from whom the whole body, being fitted and held together by that which every joint supplies, according to the proper working of each individual part, causes the growth of the body for the building up of itself in love (Ephesians 4:11-16).

Jesus gave gifts to the church—apostles, prophets, evangelists, pastors and teachers. For what purpose? To equip (teach, train and supply what is needed) the saints. Who are the saints? Everyone who has chosen to believe and trust Jesus is a saint.

Often in our church culture, we tend to think it is the work of the pastors and church staff to do the work of God in bringing people to Christ. We just come to church to worship God, pay our tithes and offerings and go home. There is a staff to take care of the other things.

But, that is not what this passage says God's people should be doing. It says the work of the pastors and teachers, the work of the evangelists, the work of prophets, the work of apostles is to equip you, the saints. Then you, the saints, are to go out and do the work. Do what work? The work of service. To what purpose? Let us see what it says, "to the building up of the body of Christ." What that simply means is bringing in new converts, mending, restoring and preparing them for the work of citizens and ambassadors of the Kingdom of Jesus Christ. This includes comforting, teaching, discipling, maturing and loving them. The work of service also includes performing any other aspect of the ministry of reconciliation so that the church will flourish, be efficacious and grow.

This is war! Satan is holding future kingdom citizens hostage! As soldiers in the army of our Lord, Jesus Christ, it is our duty to rescue them out of Satan's hand.

I want you to have a picture of this. Just imagine with me for a moment. Imagine, if in every church, every person whether sitting in the pews or not, every day, as they are going about their normal routine, is witnessing to people. They are talking about what Jesus is doing in their own lives. They are giving God the credit and praise He is due. Just imagine that for a moment. Every saint in every church every day as they are going about their daily routine, is casually witnessing (talking about the Jesus they know, etc.) to people in their routine conversations.

So what do I mean by going about? Sure, you could go door to door. But you could accomplish as much if not more when you encounter people as you go through your normal daily routine. Just think what would happen when you encounter people every day or even five percent of the people you encounter, (when circumstances permit) if you would take the opportunity to tell them something about Jesus. Something as simple as "Jesus loves me! And He loves you too." Or you could ask for permission to say grace for the entire table when you are out to lunch at work. Should someone refuse permission, simply bow your head and pray silently for the entire table and especially for the disbelievers. Take advantage of the opportunity to pray in a group setting.

Picture an army of saints (from every church) including Jesus (not "God" but "Jesus") in their normal conversations or acknowledging Him in some way every day. What would be the impact? It would be truly amazing. Simply amazing! Crazy really.

If this approach is untenable, then simply pray throughout the day for lost souls to be saved and for divine favor in that environment.

OK. Let us look at this passage a little further and our journey will be compete. Verse 13,

> "until we all attain to the unity of the faith and of the knowledge of the Son of God, to a mature man [or woman], to the measure of the stature which belongs to the fullness of Christ."

I contend that this verse is encouraging us to strive as diligently as possible to conform to the image and likeness of God in human flesh.

This is a picture of what the church really ought to be doing—equipping the saints for the work of service, to the building up of the body of Christ to a mature man [or woman], to the stature, which belongs to Jesus Christ. So what is the end result? What are we really trying to do as the church of Jesus Christ?

We are trying to create knowledgeable people who are striving to walk in love and in obedience as Jesus did. That is what we should be doing. That should be our focus with our primary goal being saving everyone from eternity in hell. The pastors cannot do it alone. It is enough if they can train you to know what you should be doing and exhorting you to actually make it a daily priority, as you are going through life.

Here is something that will encourage you. At least once per month, I believe we should have a brief time in our church services (or in Bible study) for people to report on what Jesus has done that week or the prior weeks in their witnessing (evangelizing) and disciple-making activities. Reports such as this:

"I would just like to share with you what happened to me three days ago. I asked God to show me somebody to witness to on Thursday. And this person came up to me, right! We talked a bit about miscellaneous matters. Then I said something about Jesus. And they started telling me about all sorts of issues and how life is so full of problems. So I listened to them intently. Then I simply spoke the words that came to me. Yeah, I spoke the words Jesus placed on my heart. And their whole countenance changed. I saw God move in their life. Their face revealed it all. They thanked me profusely. I was so excited!"

So why do we want to have that? You see, if I can tell you and others how Jesus moved so mightily in my own life as I witnessed last week, then that will encourage you to pray likewise this week with the expectation that He will also move powerfully in your life. That will help build others up and give them enthusiasm for Christ's ministry of reconciliation. And their enthusiasm will encourage you and me to do even more.

The signs of the approaching end of this age are all around us. They are indicating to us that the time of Jesus' return is drawing near—the beginning of birth pangs. These signs should also inform us that the need for the church to work diligently and on mission is even more critical than at anytime in the history of Christianity. Satan has built a wall of resistance around unbelievers to keep them contained inside his domain of darkness. Our job is to rescue them using spiritual weapons.

Please keep in mind always that God's standing general order (from the beginning) is *OBEDIENCE*!

The following illustrations provide a framework for getting your church on mission and keeping it there.

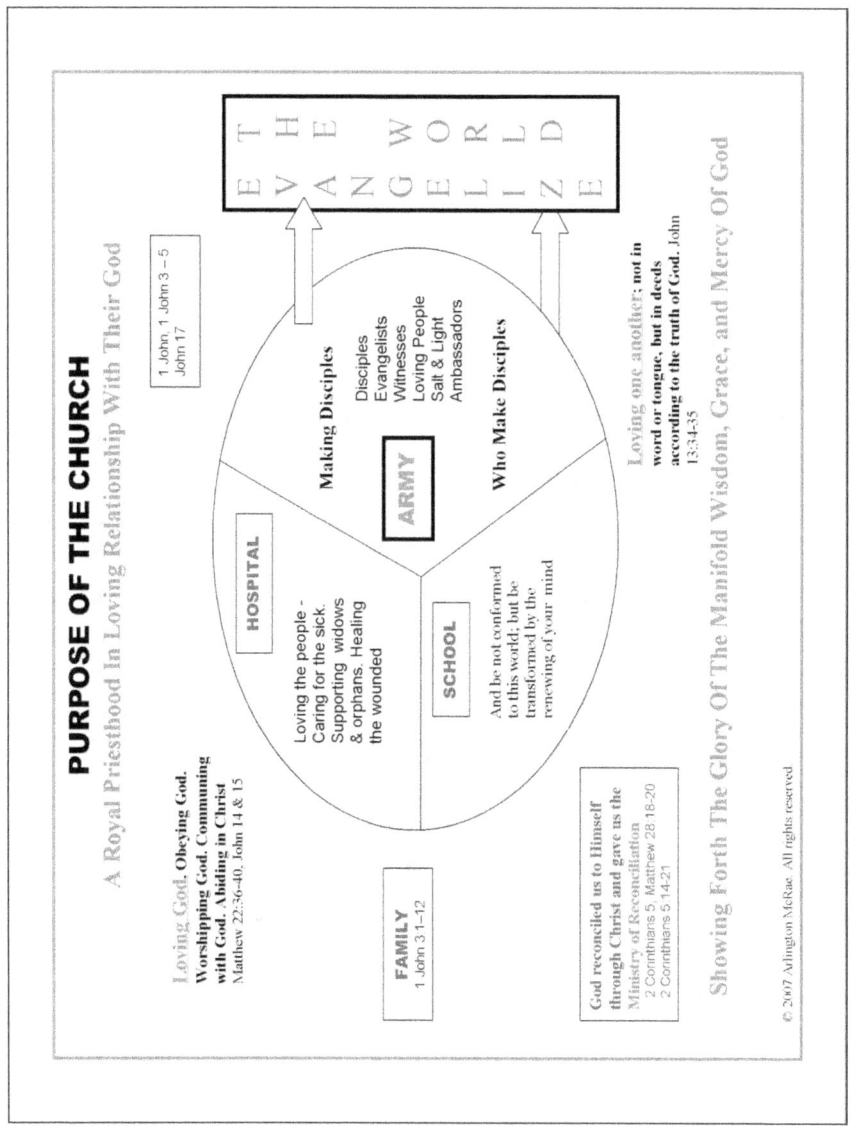

Church Purpose

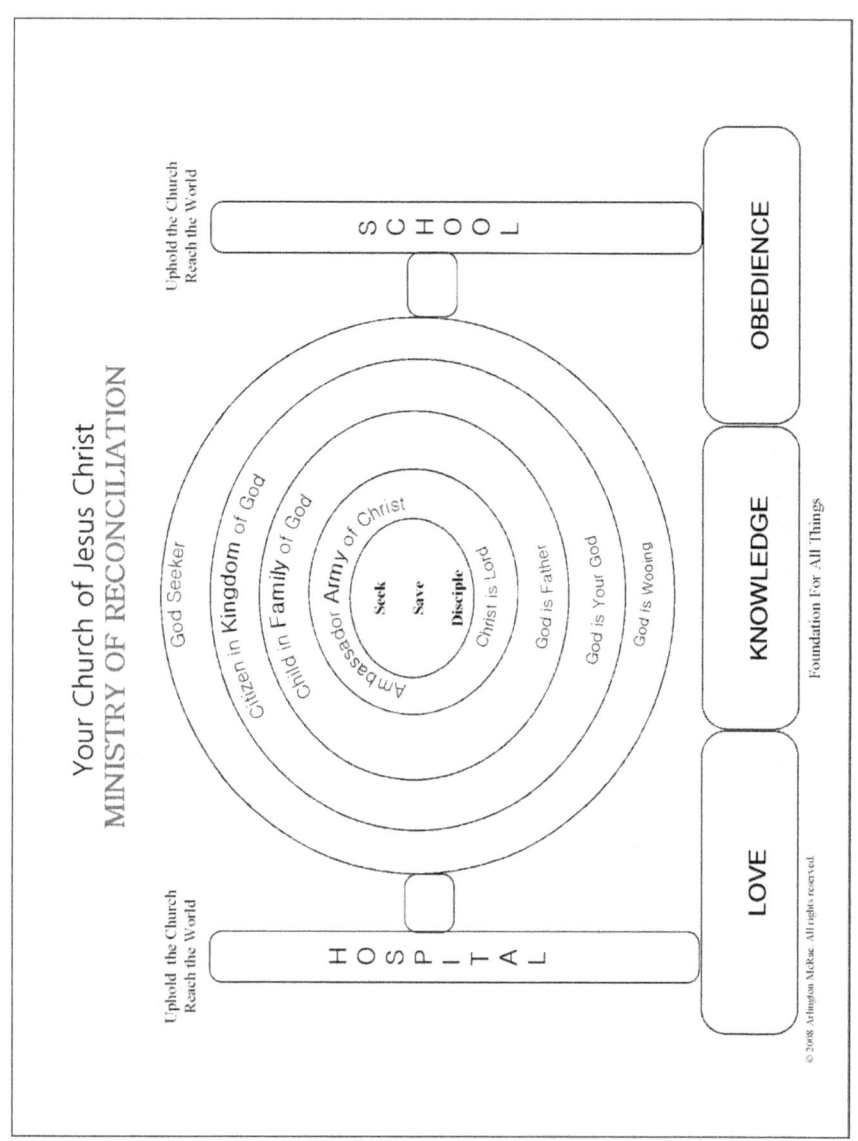

Ministry of Reconciliation

Your Church of Jesus Christ
Phases in Disciple-Making Process

WORLD

God SEEKERS: Citizens of the domain of darkness. Sons of disobedience. Children of wrath; dead in their trespasses and sins; blind and without hope; being drawn to the light. Romans 1:18-32, John 6:41-47, Ephesians 2:1-10,

KINGDOM
Matthew 1 - 28

KINGDOM citizen. Babe in Christ. Learning who God is and what He is truly like. Seeing who you really are compared to who God wants you to be. Learning to appreciate what Christ has done for the hopeless. Learning the core values of the Kingdom and to make them your own - the basis for your thoughts and actions. Philippians 2:11-21, 3:17-21, Colossians 1:13-23

Growing in Righteousness

FAMILY
Matthew 22::34-40, John, Philippians, 1 John

FAMILY member of the household of God. A child of God experiencing relationship transformation. Getting to truly know others the way they really are. Becoming known the way you really are rather than the way you seek to be known. Coming to realize who you truly are in Christ. Experiencing the love of God and of His Christ. Learning to display Christ's love in and through interaction with others. Romans 12:1-2. 1 John 4:7-21, Philippians 2::1-15. Romans 8:1-39.

Living the Great Commandment

ARMY
Luke 19:10, Matthew 28:18-20, 2 Corinthians 5:18-21

Soldier in Christ's ARMY of Ambassadors. The Army of the willing, the obedient; who loves what God loves; and grieves what God grieves. Is merciful as God is merciful. Who sacrifices for others the way Christ sacrificed for us. Working for Christ the way Christ worked for the Father. Presenting Christ's amnesty Gospel to all. On a mission to Seek, to Save, to Disciple through Christ's Ministry of Reconciliation. Colossians 1:28-29, Ephesian 4:11-16.

Working the Great Commission

© Copyright 2008 Arlington McRae. All rights reserved

Phases in Disciple-Making Process

See also the book, Simple Church by Thom S. Rainer & Eric Geiger.

Any final questions or comments? Please document them and your final thoughts on the impact and value of this volume.

Now It's Your Turn

Well, have you been enlightened? Are you encouraged? Has this journey been exciting or what? I truly hope you are indeed excited and encouraged. I pray you will never be the same. I trust that the seed has been planted deep within you and that God will cause it to germinate, grow, flourish and produce much fruit for the kingdom of His beloved Son.

One of the things that I asked of you from the beginning was to make copious notes. I asked you to make notes so that you would have them to refer to and share at a moment's notice when needed presently and in the future. Please review them frequently. I pray that you will diligently use your notes to teach others, many, many others.

Now is the time for you to become the teacher and spiritual activist, a true disciple who makes other true disciples. You will not recall everything. So review this book again. And if you will start talking about it, God will bring it back to your remembrance. Do not be afraid of looking bad or making mistakes in your witnessing. Everybody does, even the great theologians and the greatest minds. Trust God! Pray without ceasing asking God to give you wisdom, favor, courage, strength and boldness. I truly believe He will for He has certainly done so in my own life.

Now What?

I, therefore, the prisoner [servant] of the Lord, entreat you to walk in a manner worthy of the calling with which you have been called, 2with all humility and gentleness, with patience, showing forbearance to one another in love, 3being diligent to preserve the unity of the Spirit in the bond of peace. 4There is one body and one Spirit, just as also you were called in one hope of your calling; 5one Lord, one faith, one baptism, 6one God and Father of all who is over all and through all and in all (Ephesians 4:1-6).

Now all these things are from God, who reconciled us to Himself through Christ, and gave us the ministry of reconciliation, 19namely, that God was in Christ reconciling the world to Himself, not counting their trespasses against them, and He has committed to us the word of reconciliation. 20 Therefore, we are ambassadors for Christ, as though God were entreating through us; we beg you on behalf of Christ, be reconciled to God. 21He made Him who knew no sin to be sin on our behalf, that we might become the righteousness of God in Him (2 Corinthians 5:18-21).

Rejoice in the Lord always; again I will say, rejoice! 5Let your gentle spirit be known to all men. The Lord is near. 6Be anxious for nothing, but in everything by prayer and supplication with thanksgiving let your requests be made known to God. 7And the peace of God, which surpasses all comprehension, shall guard your hearts and your minds in Christ Jesus (Philippians 4:4-7). Amen.

Sow God's Seed

God provides seed to the sower. Therefore as you go through life, sow God's Word in the confidence that His Spirit is with you. Not only is His Spirit and power with you but His Spirit and His power is also in those who believe (John 14:16-17). Therefore, do not ignore the power within you that raised Jesus from the dead. Embrace Him. Abide in Him (John 15:4-8). Expect the Spirit's power to work mightily and faithfully in you as it did in brother Paul, the apostle to the Gentiles, who wrote half of the New Testament. He was just a human like you and me. And Jesus is no respecter of persons.

When possible, consume God's Word daily (as often as you consume food) even hours every day, accompanied by prayer, meditation and communion with Jesus Christ.

Stay in prayer. Pray without ceasing, always remembering the wisdom of those who have gone before us:

> No prayer, no power. Little prayer, little power. Much prayer, much power!!

Finally, please listen to and share the message, The Other Side of Death (or click here: jcembassy.wordpress.com) by yours truly, especially if you have yet to surrender your life to Jesus. Share it with your family, friends and even strangers who do not know Jesus. By right-clicking near the play button on wordpress.com, you will be offered an opportunity to download the video (it is actually a mp3 audio) file. Whatever the source, you may freely distribute this file as long as it is done without charge. Make it a point to share this audio message (or link) frequently, as well as God's Plan of Salvation on the Bible.org website, especially with all those who have yet to surrender their lives to Jesus Christ, our Lord and our Savior! Join me in this effort to keep the many out of hell for all eternity.

The love and compassion, mercy and grace, faithfulness and power of our Lord, Jesus Christ, be with you all now, henceforth and for evermore. Amen.

Let us pray: Heavenly Father, You have been so very good to us. You have shown us a new way. You have given us a new perspective and a new context. You have touched our hearts deeply. We thank You. We thank You, Father, that we will no longer be what we once were, for You have given us new insights into your Word and a fresh vision for Your church, those whom You have called out of this dark evil world.

Your Word tells us to look out over the fields and see that the fields are white for harvest. We see the people longing for You and searching for You in all the wrong places. And we commit ourselves to go out into the harvest to reclaim that which You have lost. And we go, Father, in the confidence that Your Spirit is within us. We go with confidence that Your Spirit gives us power, that Your Spirit will bring back to our remembrance all that You have taught us, and that we are able to proclaim the good news with boldness, with conviction, with passion, but also with compassion in love.

We see the people as they are, living in darkness, without Christ in their lives, deceived by the devil, lost, separated from their loving and compassionate Father. And just as You and Your Son are working to reclaim them, so we join You in Your work. Be with us. Walk with us. Talk with us. Guide us. Comfort us. Encourage us. Give us strength. Give us power and give us boldness that together we may bring hundreds of millions of lost souls from around the globe into the kingdom of Your Son. Bless us and our works that we would glorify Your name in the earth.

I have sown and I am sowing the seed You have given to me. Others are receiving that seed and sowing it as well. I beseech You therefore, Father, to provide seed to the sower. Provide the sunshine and rain that will cause it to sprout up and grow to maturity producing much fruit in every household, village, community, town, city, state (province) and nation.

In the awesome and the mighty name of Jesus, the Christ, we pray, amen, amen and amen!

TARES EXPLAINED

Then He [Jesus] left the multitudes, and went into the house. And His disciples came to Him, saying, "Explain to us the parable of the ᵃtares of the field." 37And He answered and said, "The one who sows the good seed is the Son of Man, 38and the field is the world; and as for the good seed, these are the sons of the kingdom; and the tares are the sons of the evil one; 39and the enemy who sowed them is the devil, and the harvest is the end of the age; and the reapers are angels.

40"Therefore just as the tares are gathered up and burned with fire, so shall it be at the end of the age. 41"The Son of Man will send forth His angels, and they will gather out of His kingdom all stumbling blocks, and those who commit lawlessness, 42and will cast them into the furnace of fire; in that place there shall be weeping and gnashing of teeth. 43"Then THE RIGHTEOUS WILL SHINE FORTH AS THE SUN in the kingdom of their Father.

He who has ears, let him hear. [36 ᵃOr, darnel, a weed resembling wheat" (Matthew 13:36-43).

FINAL PRAYER

Heavenly Father, we are truly thankful that You have sent Your children and Your lost sheep this book to learn of You and to learn the true nature of all humankind. I have planted the seed that You gave me to plant. Now Father, we ask You to cause that seed to take root, grow, prosper and produce much fruit. Cause it to spread to all the nations of the earth, to the heart and soul of all Your peoples, to every man, woman, boy and girl. Cause it to continue to produce great fruit for centuries after I am gone so that hell might be made smaller and the kingdom of Your Son would become much larger. Hear our prayer, O' Lord, and answer us according to the greatness of Your love and Your compassion for us. In Jesus name we pray, amen. Thank You Jesus!

SUGGESTED RESOURCES

NASB Study Bible by Zondervan Publishing House

NET Bible with Full Notes by Thomas Nelson

NKJV Study Bible by Thomas Nelson

The Bible Knowledge Commentary: Old & New Testament, 2 Volumes by John F. Walvoord & Roy B. Zuck)

BE Series Commentary (50 Volumes) by Warren Wiersbe

Various books by Dr. Tony Evans

The Purpose Driven Church by Rick Warren

Simple Church by Thom S. Rainer & Eric Geiger

Bible.org

Biblehub.com

Blueletterbible.org

BULK PURCHASES

Bulk purchases are available at a discounted price plus taxes and shipping.

Please contact us for details via email at embassyonepub@icloud.com.

ABOUT THE AUTHOR

Arlington McRae is an emerging award-winning author of Bible study guides. This is the second volume in his anointed new series, *BIBLE THREADS: Keys to Understanding the Bible*.

Since 2000, after receiving a visitation from the Lord and since Jesus Christ spoke audibly to him saying, "Feed My Sheep," he has fully committed his life, his body, his mind, his ambition, his work and his devotion to Jesus Christ and His ministry of reconciliation.

He is an ordained minister and an outstanding teacher/lecturer who devotes his life to encouraging others to learn of his Jesus from first-hand knowledge —the Bible.

Arlington and his wife, Pauline, have been married for over fifty years. During that time, Jesus has blessed them with two wonderful sons (both deceased). They are also blessed to cherish two granddaughters, five grandsons, and two greatgrandsons.

He is a retired CPA and entrepreneur who holds a Master of Arts in Biblical Studies (MABS) from Dallas Theological Seminary and a Bachelor of Arts (BA) from Howard University.

ALSO BY ARLINGTON MCRAE

Currently Available

The Bible For Beginners And The Rest of Us, available in digital and print wherever books are sold. If not available in your local library, please request that they order it for you.

Future Volumes

A Hostile Environment

The Bible in 3D

Why Do You HATE Me?

www.ingramcontent.com/pod-product-compliance
Lightning Source LLC
Chambersburg PA
CBHW070125080526
44586CB00015B/1564